BUR

AND SHAKESPEARE'S STAGE

By

Charlotte Carmichael Stopes HON. F.R.S.L

Diplomée Edin. University.

Author of
"Shakespeare's Warwickshire Contemporaries"; "William Hunnis
and the Revels of the Chapel Royal"; "Shakespeare's
Family," etc.; and Editor of "Shakespeare's
Sonnets" (King's Classics)

University Press of the Pacific
Honolulu, Hawaii

Burbage and Shakespeares's Stage

by
Charlotte Carmichael Stopes

ISBN: 1-4102-2092-3

Reprinted from the 1913 edition

University Press of the Pacific
Honolulu, Hawaii
http://www.universitypressofthepacific.com

In order to make original editions of historical works available to scholars at an economical price, this facsimile of the original edition of 1913 is reproduced from the best available copy and has been digitally enhanced to improve legibility, but the text remains unaltered to retain historical authenticity.

PREFACE

THE Lives of the Burbages ought to have been written long since by others. For many years I have desired to do this work, and published instalments in "The Fortnightly" and the "Athenæum," 1909, but the decision of the Shakespeare League to raise a Memorial to them in Shoreditch, determined me to do so at once, in order to help that Memorial Scheme. Therefore the collection, arrangement and publication of my materials, have at the last been rather more hurried than I would have liked, and some details may have been left in a state of comparative incompleteness which more leisure would have remedied. I would have liked to have said something of the lives of other contemporaries, such as Edward Alleyn, "who was Esquire made," and Ben Jonson, who criticized and praised Shakespeare; and to have aired some of my theories regarding the dramatic history of the time. But I did not wish, by presenting too many interesting people in the background, to distract my readers' attention from the central figures, or to divert their thoughts from the facts presented, to any discussion of my views.

I may now, however, make some trifling suggestions regarding the facts on which I have so long dwelt. It may be noticed, by those who read my Note 28, the list of "the performances for 80 years of the Burbage Company," that there is a gap during which they do not perform at court, i.e., between 1563 and 1572. This may have arisen from lack of business qualities in the manager. It is quite possible that Burbage was only an ordinary member of the Company at its commencement, and that the first manager, after failing so long to attract the favour of the Master of the Revels, was superseded by him about 1570. (At least it is a fact that the Company came into renewed importance from the time Burbage's name became associated with it.) I know that this is only an hypothesis.

I put forward with a stronger faith, another suggestion, that Burbage did not remain in the company till his first Master died, but left it between 1582–4. I am not clear whether the date of the transference coincided with the *first* performance of Lord Hunsdon's Company at court, or whether it took place in the following year when all the companies were " harrowed." I have shown that Richard Burbage began his work in 1583. The following year James acknowledged as his Master, Lord Hunsdon, who shortly afterwards became Lord Chamberlain, and after that there is no uncertainty as to the company with which he was concerned, though the Lord Chamberlain's and the Lord Admiral's sometimes played together. I believe also that Shakespeare joined the Lord Chamberlain's company at the beginning of his career, and never changed his " fellows."

An interesting suggestion also rises through the Subsidy Rolls. They show that by 1595 at least, Shakespeare was occupying a more important house and was rated higher than either of the Burbages. Does this suggest that he had at some time his family with him in London, before his son Hamnet's health failed ?

I must here explain, that writing of Burbage, I was forced to look at the words and actions of the *Authorities* of the time, Lay and Clerical, as they must have appeared to *him*, as a series of hindrances and complexities retarding the completion of his *Idea*. But, looking at the actions of the objectors to the Stage, from their own standpoint, I can see them justified. There is no doubt that in relation to the cosmic scheme of the Lord Mayor and others the players *were* the apparent cause, direct or indirect, of many of the evils then censured. The hitch came in the fact that this cosmic scheme was unbalanced, that, in their war against effects, they confused causes. They wanted to prevent the spread of the plague, and they prevented the people assembling together, instead of making the people, their streets, and dwellings, clean and wholesome. They aimed at making good workmen, and clean money in those days, and they thought they attained their object best by an unbroken *grind*, relieved only by heavy meals and heavy slumbers. Amusement seemed to them a distraction from the main duty of life, the recuperating value of relaxation they had not learned; they fought even against the games we consider healthful.[1] The very stringency of trade rules threw many men out of occupation, and the unemployed naturally sought assemblies so as to be occupied as well as to be amused. The preachers had a similar view in religious matters, that it was difficult to combine seriousness with enjoyment of life. But it was not revealed to their Authorities, that to the " unruly people " they tried to coerce, the Theatres were the great civilizing influences of the day. They were the Clubs, the Lecture Halls, the Concerts, the Social and Religious Guilds, the University Chairs of History, Poetry and Rhetoric. The players' audiences of the time could feel and respond to what they heard at the Theatres. They co-operated in a way of which modern audiences know nothing. They were prepared (as strings are prepared by a violinist) to be played on to the themes of the elemental passions of humanity. For the " unruly multitudes " that the Lord Mayors repressed, was "Henry V" written, with its patriotic fervours, its reverent attitude to the Unseen, its self-forgetfulness in brave work ; and they were moulded to nobler things through its teachings. The Theatres were the only avenue through which the bulk of the people became sharers in the influences of the *Renaissance*, and out of *the despised art* arose the vivifying breath of what can neither be defined nor described, but can only be named as the *Spirit of the Sixteenth Century*.

They obeyed the impulses of healthy evolution when they pressed in crowds to the plays. To many who could neither

[1] Stow regrets the passing of the people's games by his time.

read nor write were they a mine of wealth ; to many who could write, but could not invent, were they a treasure house of memoranda. As Marston says in his " Scourge of Villainy,"

> "Now I have him that nere of oughte did speake,
> But when of playes or plaiers he did treate,
> Hath made a commonplace book out of playes."

And among players' *poets* who made their power for good, there was none who better served his day and generation, in raising their moral tone, their mental status and their æsthetic sense than Burbage's " deserving man," *William Shakespeare !*

In claiming for James Burbage the building of the first stone, as well as the first wooden Theatre, of course I meant it to be the designing and alteration rather than building, for the " great stone walls," as well as the chambers, were part of his Blackfriars purchase. But in the rectangular hall of the Blackfriars, covered and lighted, he created new conditions, invented new arrangements and developments, and made new access to the stage, impossible before. (No gallants had sat on the stage, in Theatre or Globe.) It may be asked why I have made no reference to the earlier Blackfriars of twenty years before ? Partly because that was conducted on an entirely different system, it was not like Burbage's, meant for a high-class *public* theatre, but chiefly because the discovery of its existence was not mine. It was very unlucky for me that when, in 1905, I asked leave from Mr. More Molyneux to go down and inspect his papers at Loseley, I received for answer, from a friend of the family, that the owner was abroad, and the papers had gone to the care of the *Hist. Man. Comm.*, and would not be available for some time, but that he had taken voluminous notes, and would be glad to assist me in any way he could. I replied that I wanted to know if there was anything about William Hunnis, Master of the Children of the Chapel ; of the Earls of Southampton (more than Kempe had given), and of the general history of the Drama. He said there was nothing about Hunnis, but much about the other two. I then said I should *wait* till I could have access.

rather than trouble him. There is always something to do in research work. Shortly after I heard that Professor Feuillerat was at work on these papers. Being certain they would be treated well in his hands, I thought I could still wait a little. But when I heard that he had found Hunnis after all, and in connexion with the earlier Blackfriars Theatre, I blew him up for not sooner publishing his discovery that I might have completed my Hunnis book, even by borrowed matter duly acknowledged. The other facts I wanted from these papers I have since secured for myself.

When I began work long since, I wanted to get a more thorough knowledge of Shakespeare than I had. To do so I felt I must know about the predecessors who moulded his conditions, and the successors who were affected by him, as well as the contemporaries among which he moved.

So I measured out a very liberal century to work in, from the accession of Henry VIII in 1509, to 1640. After bringing out the second edition of my " Bacon Shakespeare Question answered " in 1889, which was chiefly based on printed books, I devoted myself altogether to manuscript work. During 1890 I worked at the Guildhall Records, and took out everything concerning Players and Poets of the time, which material I have frequently used since in my papers. My special " find " was that concerning William Hunnis, which gave a clue to so much more. I turned aside from my main work to write about him, because he was the designer of the main Kenilworth " devices " ; which I believe stimulated young Shakespeare's imagination, and because " of his life very little was known." But I never gave up my search after traces of Shakespeare, in every possible department open to me. When I was going consecutively through the Coram Rege Rolls of James I (the most *uncomfortable* of records to read), Dr. Wallace plunged into the middle of my work, in 1905. I met him on the twenty-eighth of October of that year, the day on which he brought out his first paper about Shakespeare's wishing the title deeds of his Blackfriars purchase. He told me he was doing the Children of the Chapel

under Nathaniel Giles, I told him that I had done " the children "
under William Hunnis, his immediate predecessor, and that my
book was in the press.   I found he was not then in touch with
the London Shakespeareans (he thought that Dr. Furnivall was
dead by that time).   So I invited him to tea to meet our Chief,
and asked the Secretary of the Shakespeare League to send him
invitations to our meetings, especially to our excursion to Hampton Court, under the guidance of Mr. Ernest Law. The date
is important, for a few months after Dr. Furnivall told me that
Dr. Wallace had, from the uncalendared papers of the Court of
Requests, found some Shakespearean things. I asked Dr. Furnivall if he knew how he had been allowed to get these out, when
I had asked for them three or four times, and had been told to
wait until they were classified.   Dr. Furnivall confessed he
had forgotten that I had not yet had them, and had himself
signed Dr. Wallace's application for permission to search them.
As he was not a resident in London, they agreed to let him have
them out.   I naturally therefore insisted on having them also,
though I knew there was no chance of me, single-handed, and
handicapped by other duties, catching up two devoted workers
with a three months' start.   But I could *see the things for myself*,
which is after all the genuine object of research study.   Believing they had begun with the reign of James I, I began with
that of Elizabeth, until I found the things I wanted, then I
turned and completed the reign of James I before I completed
that of Elizabeth.   After doing the *whole* of these, I did a part
of Charles I before I returned to my normal path, with a good
many extra notes in hand.   Even where references were not
taken, I found this series of papers exceptionally interesting
and very easy work, as compared to some others.

In regard to " authorities " I have placed at the end of this
book I must explain my methods. I always *insert* the double date
at the beginning of the years. Everybody may be aware that
the year began on the twenty-fifth of March in those days,
but nobody can be quite sure whether a writer is dating in old
or new style. There can be no mistake when *both* are given,

On the other hand, as there was a limit to space I always cut off the *flourishes* of the regnal years, which I reduce to bare fact, as " 2 Eliz.," etc. I also always cut out repeated references to " his heirs, assigns, executors and administrators," and similar repetitions unnecessary to modern understandings, and I write money statements in modern terms. Space would make it impossible to give all the originals *in extenso ;* and in regard to Giles Alleyn's cases, it would become monotonous to do so, for the whole story of " the lease " is repeated *every time.* So I have had to cut that out as much as possible. I fear I have repeated too much. Sometimes therefore I give a shortened paper, at other times only an abstract, according to the degree of interest. I generally leave the old spelling ; but if a scrivener has spelt " him " three times normally and three times as " hym," in the same page, and my printer insists on uniformity, I am not sure that I should correct either as a printer's error, because I am writing a biography of *Burbage,* not of the *clerks* whose idiosyncrasies are shown frequently by their *preference for a variety* in spelling even in the course of the same article. It is the desire of exactitude in *facts* which fills my mind. When I find these important, even to details, or when I wish to preserve them for my own use, I give them *in extenso,* as for instance the pleading before the Lord Chamberlain in 1635. It took me a very long time to find this, nobody could locate it for me, it never having been asked for. Since I found it, the references have been changed three times, now I think they are permanent, and so give them. That is printed, among his copies, verbatim by Halliwell-Phillipps (except for the table), but it was too interesting to me not to include my own transcript. I do not repeat his other copies of the easily accessible correspondence between the Privy Council and the Lord Mayor about the limitation of the Theatres in 1600–1601, as they do not concern Burbage. I must give some explanation of the peculiar methods of this writer, to whom all Shakespeareans owe so much for his indefatigable labours. With all his virtues, he had two faults. He did not, or very rarely did, give his references, and when he did so, he more rarely gave them fully. He told Dr. Furnivall this was intentionally done, " If I give references, they quote them, if I give none, they have to quote me," knowing as he did, the predatory instincts of lazy *writers*. He goes even further. He seems at times to try to mystify his readers as to his sources of information. For instance, in his valuable note on " The Theatre and the Curtain," he speaks of " a suit instituted many years afterwards," of " a deposition taken in 1602," and alludes, in seven or eight disconnected and scattered phrases to the same case, as if they were different originals, though I have found they are all drawn from " Earl of Rutland *v.* Alleyn," Exchequer proceedings, see my note 14, p. 185. Neither does he give all the important facts in full, even of the papers he hints at. For instance, he seems to have heard of, rather than seen, the Star Chamber Case, see my Note 21, p. 220, for he only gives the earlier and least interesting part of it under the indefinite title, " Complaint. Alleyn *v.* Burbage, 44 Eliz," whereas the remainder of paper is much more interesting and gives a key to all Alleyn's litigation. I know that, at least in later life, he employed others to do his research work, and that they did not always proffer further information than he asked.

He copies faithfully the Indenture of purchase by which James Burbage secured the Blackfriars ; but gives no reference. When I hunted, and found it for myself among the Loseley papers, I found he had omitted the signature which interested me, " James Burbadge," and does not mention the Seal used, a very perfect " Griffin." He must have used the enrolment only (Close Rolls, 1540, m. 28).

I have not dwelt on the papers found by Mr. Greenstreet and worked out so fully by Mr. Fleay in his " History of the Drama," as full references are given.

I have made no use [1] of the work of Dr. Wallace, preferring

---

[1] A friend has pointed out to me that Dr. Wallace published in " The Times " this year, the little incident about Burbage and Rice in Munday's device, see my p. 108. I have had that by me since 1890,

to give readers references to his own papers, except in one case, where I give the original reference, seeing it had not been yet published.

Mr. T. F. Oudish's work on "The Early London Theatres" is known to every one. It is however more topographical than biographical.

Mr. E. K. Chambers and I seem to have been working independently at the same time on the same papers, as may be proved by our publications. But the things new and old that I have collected, are only brought together to make concrete the vision of the Burbages in the midst of their work, and the suggestion of the College in which Shakespeare learnt some of his law. I am aware there are many imperfections. I know that I am a bad proof-reader, and I have no help; my mind is so filled with *things in themselves*, I sometimes omit to note the fringes of the " garments that we see them by."

I must not forget to thank the Officials of the Record Office and the British Museum for their unfailing courtesy and frequent help ; Dr. Reginald Sharpe, late keeper of the Guildhall Records, for similar kindness, and the Rev. E. R. Ford, Vicar of St. Leonard's, for giving me access to the Register of the Parish, selections from which close my text (see p. 139). I regret the delay in publication, but that did not arise from my slackness, but from some hitch at the printers.

CHARLOTTE CARMICHAEL STOPES.

HAMPSTEAD,
    15th *June*, 1913.

I have frequently used it in my Lectures, some of which were reported last year. On the eighth of March of this year I asked leave to go to Guildhall to check it, but was told on the tenth that Dr. and Mrs. Wallace were working there (and there was no convenient room for more than two), but a checked copy was sent. This I enclosed with my book to the printer the following day, and Dr. Wallace's communication did not appear until the twenty-eighth of March, so my conscience does not trouble me much for not having acknowledged it in the text.

CONTENTS

CHAP.   PAGE

  I   JAMES BURBAGE 1

 II   JAMES BURBAGE'S SONS. 67

III   WHAS WAS LEFT OF THE BURBAGES . . . 124

AUTHORITIES

NOTE.

    I   ELIZABETH'S PROCLAMATION. 1559 145

   II   THE DANGER OF CONVENTICLES 145

  III   THE LORD MAYOR'S ORDERS 1574 146

  IV   MIDDLESEX SESSIONS ROLLS 149

   V   CONCERNING PLAYERS 153

  VI   BURBAGE v. BRAYNES 154

 VII   BRAYNES v. BURBAGE, AND MYLES v. BISHOP . . 159

VIII   PECKHAM v. ALLEYN 166

  IX   BURBAGE'S PURCHASE OF BLACKFRIARS . . . 170

   X   PETITIONS OF INHABITANTS OF BLACKFRIARS . . 174

  XI   THE ROSE AND SWAN 177

 XII   MERES ON SHAKESPEARE 183

XIII   BURBAGE v. AMES 184

XIV   EARL OF RUTLAND v. ALLEYN AND BURBAGE . . 185

NOTE.		PAGE
XV	Subsidy Rolls.	194
XVI	Site of the Globe .	196
XVII	Augustine Phillipps Examined.	197
XVIII	Alleyn v. Peter Street .	198
XIX	Burbage v. Alleyn.	200
XX	Alleyn v. Burbage, Coram Rege Roll	217
XXI	Alleyn v. Burbage, Star Chamber	220
XXII	Player's Patents .	228
XXIII	The Actors in Shakespeare's Plays .	229
XXIV	The Complaint of Young Players	230
XXV	Privy Council Register .	240
XXVI	Censorship of Plays	242
XXVII	Burbageana .	243
XXVIII	Performances of Burbage's Company	246

Burbage

and Shakespeare's Stage

Burbage, and Shakespeare's Stage

CHAPTER I

JAMES BURBAGE

THE story of James Burbage is a wonderful record, not only for the work he did, but for its results. His life is well worthy of being enrolled among the treasured biographies of his time. Through his courageous struggle against unceasing difficulties he became the founder of the modern British Stage, the teacher as well as father of its greatest actor, and the discoverer of its greatest Dramatist. It was he who gave Shakespeare the chance to make the best of the life he had not willingly chosen,[1] and he was able to do this because he himself always tried to do the best possible to him under his circumstances. He impressed himself upon his times without their fully being conscious of it. Our eyes are more able to measure his position than were his contemporaries, stirred as they were to fever-heat by polemic storms that now leave us calm.

It is trying to find dullness in preliminary matter before we reach the story. But it must not be forgotten that it is out of broken chips one creates a mosaic, and it is from the petals of Detail that one distils the Idea of a Life, and the conception " of the form and fashion of the time."

In attempting to make a pen and ink sketch of it, I must ask my readers, as Shakespeare asked his audience in " Henry V " to " piece out my imperfections with your thoughts . . .

---

[1] " O, for my sake do you with Fortune chide . . .
That did not better for my life provide."—Sonnet cxi.

and when I speak of *Burbage,* think you see him " in the stress and strain of the life he lived, always buffeted with difficulties above his fellows, never acknowledging or accepting defeat, and always forging ahead as pioneer in the path he had designed for himself.

We all know somewhat of the world into which he stepped, a world in the convulsions of a great upheaval, plunged into the melting-pot of Fate, with no certainty as to the mould into which its future would be cast.   It had been stirred to its depths by mighty religious influences spreading from Germany and Switzerland.   Its perceptions had been stimulated by the Italian renaissance, which travelled to us through France. A demand for knowledge of the new learning came from all classes, a supply of translations attempted to answer the demand.   As a new world had been given to them out of the haze of the West, which widened their horizon, and stimulated their faculties of wonder and imagination, so a new world had been unrolled to them by the miracles of the printer's shop. Its conservative and reproductive powers made books cheap. The people began to buy them, to read, discuss and understand them, in a way hardly understood by modern readers.   Everything seemed new and fresh and interesting in the third quarter of the sixteenth century.   The political despotism of the Tudors had not yet produced rebellion.   The dissolution of the monasteries and the confiscation of their property, one outcome of these influences, had resulted in social, educational, and economic changes, as well as further religious developments.   Whatever may have been the faults of some of their inmates, the convents had remained, in general, the centres of education, the guardians of literature, science, art, and empiric knowledge, the dispensers of hospitality, medical treatment and charity. Though a future was assured the better-class priests willing to conform at home, or brave enough to make a career for themselves abroad, their suppression flung on the world numbers of helpless and inferior monks and servitors, whose so-called " pensions " were too irregularly paid to be any security against want. Armies of old mendicants, formerly their pen-sioners, some of them harmless and only helpless, others the "sturdy beggars" of later statutes, became deteriorated through the disappearance of their regular reckonings of work and provision at the Abbeys. Driven along with those *on the hunting ground of the road* were many "poor scholars," many younger sons of the minor gentry even, whose family estates had been seized for recusancy ; apprentices from various trades whose apprenticeships had been broken from an awakening to independence of thought and action, under the harsh rules a severe master had power to impose ; wounded soldiers for whose support there was no proper provision ; cozeners, thieves, highwaymen at war with society. Short shrift were allowed the latter, the gallows at once for them (*when they were caught*), for human life was then of less value than the means of supporting it. From all these classes arose groups of men who earned a precarious livelihood by satisfying the *tastes* of the people. To these also had come a modification of the renaissance, a spirit from the outer world had stirred among the dry bones.

Men hungered to have their imaginations stirred by romance, wonder, harmony after conflict ; they absorbed and repeated the old legends and romances ; they ran after translations, they were interested in *humanity* in all its aspects. Music was already a national possession, Church music, chamber music, folk music, dance music.

There was no art in England, that is to say in its limited sense of painting pictures or chiselling statues. There was not a sculptor in all England above the level of a tomb-maker ; there was hardly a native painter before Hilliard, and he became a painter after being a carver of jewellery. If men wanted their portraits painted they sent for foreign artists ; if they wanted landscape pictures, they had to content themselves with natural scenery, or landscape gardens as the background for architecture, a form of art which throve in the country. Though the printers had introduced some woodcuts into a few of their books, they seemed to be rather decorations than illustrations. There was not a picture gallery to be seen. For the encouragement of pictorial art and scientific research, men had to wait till the coming of the Stuarts ; for the overflowing of these into all national industry, we have had to wait till our own times.

But our ancestors had already begun to develop a native form of mixed art, in the beginnings of the drama which gave them something to stimulate their art-instincts. The Church had for a long time represented to the unlearned multitude the Bible Stories in a concrete form, to hold the hearer's attention. The people wanted to share in the art, so the Miracle Plays of the Church evolved into the Mystery Plays of the Trades-Guilds, performed on their Saints' Day, Foundation Day ; on Midsummer's Eve they had pageants in their processions, at Christmas they had various shows amid mirth and misrule.

In the Courts there had been morality plays and allegories, as well as religious plays. Bands of interlude players, as well as musicians, were kept by the sovereigns ; and the gentlemen and children of the Chapel Royal had special presentations of their own, having the charm of song to add to their other attractions. There were masques, prepared for royal disport, in which royalties themselves occasionally joined. The Renaissance may be credited for introducing more mirth and humour into Court plays, translations of foreign romances were moulded into interludes ; satirical skits and topical allusions spiced even solemn subjects. The gentlemen of the Inns of Court and the scholars of the Universities performed dramas from classical sources on great occasions.

The great noblemen who were forced to live in their far-away castles through official duties, to lighten their absence from Court had similar amusements provided for them by their own household servants and their own chapel boys. The people themselves provided companies for the minor nobles and gentry, companies which were never salaried, being paid only by their performances, but who generally managed to persuade some nobleman to allow them to wear his livery, to be called by his name, to perform for him when he wanted them, but when he did not want them to let them wander over the country, finding from their own audiences their own means of support. Such companies sometimes visited the metropolis, heard far off of the doings of courts, and while they were *on the road* home were too glad of the chance to show " the latest play from London" in provincial towns to bailiffs and aldermen and their friends, in their guild halls or inn-yards, or in lowlier districts even on the village green, where payment would be poor and uncertain. To the rustics they gave joy of a kind they knew not how to produce for themselves, until by repeated "views," some of them even desired to imi-tate.

The love of changing one's attire, and pretending to be some-body else, is a natural instinct of humanity, beginning even in early life. Thus the love not only of seeing plays but of acting them, pervaded all ranks of society. To the companies of players *on the road* resorted many classes, the poor scholars, able to *make* or to translate a skeleton plot ; the old monks who once had acted in their monastery, and who could still be eloquent, and knew how to dress and advise ; the old sol-diers, ready to teach fencing or display their skill with the sword in martial parts ; ancient minstrels, by this time discredited in their art, but knowing how to draw music from unlikely instru-ments and to add a varied attraction to a play. From all these elements rose the people's companies, who created a national drama of the people's own. Fragments of romances translated or home-grown, legends, stories, traditions, as of Robin Hood and Maid Marian ; all were rendered concrete to the imagination, pictured to the eye, by the players in hall or hovel. In the limbo of forgotten things are scores of their skeleton plots of comedies and tragedies, made ready to be filled up by the actor's wit, of which we can only assume the exist-ence by later allusions. We have none of their " play-books " preserved, but we have an illustrative example in Bottom's play in "Midsummer's Night's Dream" based clumsily upon a classic story.

Round such players would gather at country fairs palmists and sorcerers to tell fortunes, jugglers and acrobats to display dexterity ; bear-wards to awake a fascinating terror, rivals or *jackals* to the mummers' fraternity. The efforts of sovereigns and officials had long been spent in attempting to clear the road of all these. Henry VIII and Edward VI had done something. Mary had attempted to reform " printers, prechars, players." In 1556 all justices of the peace and other officers were commanded not to allow wandering players and musicians to go about, " for that kind of lazy people frequently in their songs and acting shew forth various heresies and seditions." And a special mandate was given them to seek for the disseminators of " false rumours " everywhere. (St. Pap., Dom. Ser., Mary, viii. 50.) On May 16th, 1559, a Royal Proclamation restricted plays. (See Note I.)

Into this world James Burbage stepped. I have not yet found the date of his birth, probably about 1535 ; I do not know where he was born. Some have suggested Warwickshire on the strength of the fact that a John Burbage was Bailiff of Stratford-on-Avon in 1555. There were Burbages, however, also in Leicestershire (whose wills are yet to be read) ; there were some in Somerset, some in Hertfordshire, some in London, the latter evidently in later years acquainted with James Burbage. We know nothing of his childhood, though we may infer that he had been taught to read and write then (he might have been a choir boy). But we do know something of his youth. He succeeded to no estate, he went to no university, he was apprenticed to a *joiner* by trade, and must have persevered through his apprenticeship and taken up his freedom, as he was often in later years called a " Joiner." When or how the spell of the player's life lured him away from the safe beaten tracks of his trade I know not, nor how and when he worked himself into the better class of actors who wore the livery, retained nominally as " the servants " of some great lord. We do not know where and how he found his "Master," but as when he does appear it was as the chief of Sir Robert Dudley's (then the Earl of Leicester's) players, it may reasonably be inferred it was about the beginning of Elizabeth's reign. Sir Robert Dudley wrote to the Earl of Shrewsbury in June, 1559, requesting that his servants might be allowed to play in Yorkshire, as other Lords Lieutenants of other shires had allowed them to do in their districts, and certified them to be "honest men, and shall play none other matters than such as are tolerable and convenient" ("Lodge's Illustrations," i. 307). We may be sure that the critical and magnificent Sir Robert Dudley would not have been satisfied with second-rate "servants." His acceptance argues not only James Burbage's honesty and prudence, but his handsome appearance, charming manners, tact and ready wit.

Players were not welcome to the Church of the time. The Bishop of London, writing of them in 1563, describes them as "an idle sort of people, who have been infamous in all good communities."

We hear nothing definite about them until after the Pope sent his ill-advised Bull against Elizabeth to England in 1569, and the consequent rising in the north. After the comparatively placid ten years at the beginning of Elizabeth's reign, this was a call to action, definite and decisive on both sides. Religion became henceforth inseparably associated with politics. Some of the old faith resisted, and all were suspected and carefully repressed, punishments were decreed for disobedience to order, in money if they had any, in person if they had none. Old laws not openly dealing with the question were made indirectly able to do so, former repressive laws were enforced with increased severity. New laws were drafted. The Pope became indirectly the exciting cause of unexpected domestic legislation, of new official efforts to *clear the roads*. Because it was seen that besides giving an opportunity of reforming the habits of those who lived on the road, more stringent than any previous efforts had been, it might also help the authorities in spreading their

net over " suspects," priests and men in sympathy with, and
acting in obedience to an alien political Power, through faith
in his religious authority.   Those who had slipped on a lord's
livery over their own old coats, had to make their position more
assured.   By Burbage's forethought at the end of 1571 he
secured a licence from the Lord Mayor of London, " Item this
day licence is geven to my Lord of Leicester's men to play
within this Cittie such matters as are allowed of to be played, at
convenient howers and tymes, so that it be not at the time of
Devyne Service."   Jovis, 6th Die Decembris, 1571.   (Guildhall
MSS., Repertory 17, 239ᵇ).

In the following month, 29th January, 1571-2, " a license
was granted to the Lord Abergavenny's players *during my
Lord Maior's pleasure.*"   I have noted no other actors who took
this step then.   The players of Sir Robert Dudley (afterwards
the Earl of Leicester) had meanwhile played frequently at Court
for the " solace " of the Queen, and were known in other great
cities ; for instance, the Gloucester Records have, 1569-70,
" In rewarde to the Erle of Leyseter's players playing before
Mr. Mayor, 13/4."

" 1571.   Also given to the Erle of Leyseters plaiers for playing before Mr. Maior 30th April 13/4.   Spente on them at the
taverne, 3/8."

On 3rd January, 1571-2 there had been issued a proclamation
against retainers, ordaining that Lords should not " retain "
more men than they actually used as " servants," domestic or
otherwise ; and those who did so after this notice, beyond the
20th of February next were to be visited with the Queen's displeasure.   14 Eliz.   (See Brit. Mus. Proclamations, G. 6463.)
This was specially directed in appearance against players.   It
brings James Burbage definitely into view at last, for some
time in January or in the first twenty days of February, he,
and his fellows, wrote an undated letter to his master peti-
tioning for a closer relation in domestic service.   This must
be printed here in full :—

" *To the Rt. Hon. Earle of Leicester, their good Lord and Master.*
" Maye yt please your honor to understand that forasmuch
as there is a certaine Proclamacion out for the revivinge of a
Statute as touching Retayners, as your Lordshippe knoweth
better than we can enforme you thereof, We therefore, your
humble servaunts and daylye orators, your players, for avoyd-
ing all inconvenients that maye growe by reason of the saide
Statute, are bold to trouble your Lordshippe with this our
suite, humblie desiringe your honor that (as you have always
been our good Lord and Master) you will now vouchsaffe to
reteyne us at this present as your houshold servants and daylie
wayters, not that we meane to crave any further stipend or
benefite at your Lordshippe's hands, but our Lyveries as we
have had, and also your Honor's Licence to certifye that we
are your Household Servauntes, when we shall have occasion
to traveyl amongst our frendes, as we do usuallye once a yere,
and as other noblemen's players do, and have done in tyme
past, wherebie we maye enjoye our facultie in your Lordshippe's
name as we have done heretofore. Thus beyinge bound and
readye to be always at your Lordshippes commandmente
we committe your Honour to the tuition of the Almightie.

> Long may your Lordshipe live in peace
> A pere of noblest peres
> In helth welth and prosperitie
> Redoubling Nestor's yeres.

Your Lordshippes servaunts
Most bounden
JAMES BURBAGE
JOHN PERKINNE
JOHN LANEHAM
WILLIAM JOHNSON
ROBERT WILSON
THOMAS CLARKE
(Docketed Your L. Players) "
(No date.)

Copied by Rev. J. E. Jackson, Hon. Canon of Bristol, from the Marquis of Bath's papers at Longleat, and printed in "Notes and Queries," 3rd Ser. xi, May 4, 1867.

The proclamation was intended to help officials to force into the open many questionable characters, among whom are not named, but fully intended, all Jesuits and messengers from Rome. That "proclamation" would send more dismissed men *on to the roads*, whence a statute was being prepared to clear them, one that has been carefully studied by all social workers, and by all dramatic scholars. It also was intended to check religious and political spies and messengers. The Act of 14 Eliz. C. 5, 1572, generally spoken of as the Act for punishing rogues and vagabonds, and for relief of the poor. Previous statutes are repealed. Any one over 14, convicted of being a rogue or vagabond, was to be grievously whipped, and pierced in his right ear, "unless some honest person shall take him into his service." If he depart from such service he is to be treated as a felon and sent to jail. "For the full expressing what . . . persons shall be intended . . . to be Roges, Vagabounds and Sturdy Beggars . . . all idle persones using subtyll crafty and unlawful games or playes, and some of them fayning themselves to have knowledge in phisnomye, Palmestrye, or other abused Scyences, whereby they beare the people in hand they can tell their destinyes, Deathes and Fortunes, and such other like fantastical imaginations . . . and all Fencers, Bearewards, Comon Players in Enterludes and Minstrels, not belonging to any Baron of this realme or any other honorable personage of greater degree; all Juglers, Pedlers, Tynkers, and Pctye Chapmen, who shall wander abroade and have not licence of two justices of the peace at leaste, whereof one to be of the Quorum, wher and in what shier they shall happen to wander."

No one was to harbour them or give them lodging. This Act was to continue in force for seven years, and to the end of the Parliament next ensuing.

This, it may be seen, besides many other things, was an Act against the exercise of "imagination." It would no doubt be a great benefit to the bonâ-fide travellers of the time, a benefit even to the rogues and vagabonds themselves, for some of them would bestir themselves to get " suited " ; some of the poor would be provided for, and the competition for the survivors *on the road* would become less. It would give the better class an opportunity of rehabilitating themselves, it would make them more careful in their behaviour. Especially it would benefit those players, servants to noblemen, who were exempted, and clear out of their way rivals doubtless very often troublesome.

But the statute, while decreasing the number of real " Rogues and Vagabonds," would increase the number of players, who were careful to seek a great lord's protection from the scourge of vagabondage. Players were protected by the very statute that seemed to be directed against them. Danger made them more circumspect. Such companies had an ambition which tended to their improvement. They naturally desired to excel each other. But they also wanted to excel themselves, not only to please their own " masters," but also the Master of the Revels, that they might become worthy to be invited to play before their Sovereign, in competition with her own salaried servants. How they did this, how they succeeded in ousting and superseding, for a time at least, Court performers, is a part of the general history of the Stage.

The treatment of players by municipal bodies was very uncertain, depending upon the tastes and creeds of the mayors and corporations of the time. To a certain extent this was true also of London, but the balance was generally set against them in the Common Council and in their favour in the Privy Council. The lords encouraged their companies, as a means of winning favour from the Queen by some brilliant dramatic success. After the statute there were more performances than ever in the Metropolis. The corporation would have preferred it if they could have classed *all* common players as vagabonds, it would have simplified matters so much for them. They did what they could to preserve the powers that remained to them.

On the 2nd March, 1573–4, the servants of the Earl of Sussex asked a licence to be allowed to play in the city, as they needed a place for rehearsals there, being summoned to play before the Queen. The Lord Mayor refused his permission. Sussex was Leicester's greatest rival then, high in the Queen's favour, and it is more than probable that Burbage would again address his master and remind him that the next sufferers would be *his* servants. On the 22nd March the Privy Council wrote to ask the Lord Mayor why he restrained players so, and received no satisfactory answer.

Determined that his servants should not have to submit to such a restriction, within two months Leicester had got through all its stages the first " Royal Patent " ever granted to players. It is an item in general stage history. It not only raised the *craft* of the vagabond into the profession of an artist, but through its verbal construction it gave the Earl of Leicester's " servants " power (on paper) to act independently of the commonalty, and to defy all repressive authorities. It is hardly to be wondered at that no other nobleman of the time seems to have had the will, or the power, to secure a similar patent for his " servants." Perhaps even Leicester saw that he had gone too far. The Patent does not seem to have been much used, except perhaps in the country. The copy in Rymer's " Fœdera " omits all reference to the Lord Mayor of London. Indeed, it was a practical infringement of civic rights, and helped to precipitate a crisis.

This is too important a document in the history of Burbage's Life, to be relegated altogether to the chapter on " Authorities."

On 7th May, 1574, the Royal Patent [1] addressed to all mayors, bailiffs, and officials, warned them to permit " to James Burbage, John Perkyn, John Laneham, William Johnson, Robert Wylson and others, servants to our trustie and well-beloved Cousin and Counsellor, the Earl of Leicester, to

---

[1] See Ayscough's " Cat. of Sloane MS.," 4,625, f. 198. The original Privy Seal is in the Chapter House at Westminster.

use, exercise and occupie the art and facultie of playing Comedies, Tragedies, Interludes, Stage Plaies and such other, like as
they have already used and studied, or hereafter shall use and
study, as well for the recreacion of our loving subjects as for our
solace and pleasure when we shall think good to see them . . .
together with their musick . . . as well within our city of
London and the Liberties of the same, as also within the liberties and freedoms of any other cytyes, towns, boroughes, etc.,
whatsoever throughout our realm of England, willing and
commanding you and every of you, as ye tender our pleasure, to
permit and suffer them therein, without any your letts hindrance or molestation, any act, statute, proclamation, or
commandment heretofore made, or hereafter to be made to the
contrary notwithstanding.   Provided that the same . . . be
allowed by our Master of the Revels and that they be not published or shewen in the time of Common Prayer, or in the time
of great and common plague in our said City of London."

On 22nd July, 1574, the Privy Council granted a licence [1] to
them to go to London and to be favourably used there, and a
letter was written to the Lord Mayor to that effect.

The battle between the Common Council and the Privy
Council raged all the more hotly after Leicester's servants
were "patented." The corporation were naturally exasperated
and did not tender the "Queen's pleasure" in regard to players.

They had some reasons, which must be respected.   On the
6th December, 17 Eliz. 1574, they explained these in a preamble to their " Order." [2] They considered the inordinate
haunting of plays prejudicial to peace, to industry, to health,
to morality, and to religion.   They believed that it increased
poverty, the temptations to robbery, and the risk of accidents
and death by the falling of scaffolds. (This latter phrase is
noteworthy because the great Paris-Garden accident had not
happened by that time.) They determined therefore that *no
player* should perform without the *Lord Mayor's licence* and

---

[1] Privy Council Register.   [2] Lansd. MS. xx. 10.

that they should give large shares of their profits to the poor. This was not to extend to plays in private houses.

Either through submission to these orders or without, Burbage's Company managed to have rehearsals that month and to perform before the Queen twenty days later, on St. Stephen's Day. They also opened the year of 1574-5 by playing at Court on New Year's Day.

A good deal of confusion has been caused among writers on this period, through the Lansdowne MSS. xx. 10, 11, 12, 13 having been, by some official hand in the past, dated " 1575." Now these " Orders " are dated " 6th Dec., 17 Eliz." Consequently, they clearly should have been entered as 1574. The others are undated, but may be dated roughly by careful study. The petition of Her Majesties poor players must have been later as they were not appointed until 1583. The letter of the Lord Mayor, and the answer to the " player's articles," must have been somewhat later still.

Two documents are missing from the series. The player's " articles," and the second municipal " Order," both referred to in those that have been preserved. The " articles " seem to have been entirely lost, though their purport may be gleaned from the reply preserved, which is evidently in 1584. But the second " Order" which strayed, probably because it had been *printed*, has been preserved elsewhere. This comes into a totally different category from the others.

I notice that Mr. E. K. Chambers says that Mr. Ordish, and consequently many others, are incorrect in stating that " the Lord Mayor expelled all players from the city in 1575." Perhaps the language is too strong and misleading, as applied to *players* instead of plays. But its correctness depends on finding with certainty the *date* of this " Order," which is not at all certain as it stands. Mr. Chambers refers it to a time near to the Player's " Petition." Several facts tell against that opinion. In the first place the "Order " is printed in a municipal publication, called " Orders for the Relief of the Poor," and for setting rogues and idle persons to work, printed by Hugh Singleton, undated, where it is slipped quietly into article number 62. In the answer to the player's petition, the Lord Mayor says he encloses "*two* acts of Common Council," the first was made in " 17 Eliz., tempore Hawes," " *Afterwards*, when these Orders were not observed," " in an act of Common Council for relefe of the poore, *which I send you here printed*," in article 62 it is enacted " there are no interludes allowed in London." These words show this is the Order referred to. " *Since that time*, and namely upon the ruine at Paris Garden sute was made to my Lordes to banishe playes wholly in the *places adjoyning*." Now Paris Garden disaster took place on 13th January, 1582–3 and the " Order " must have been made at least before that date. It is not referred to in " Remembrancia," which *begins* in 1580.

We may therefore look into the Order itself, and we find there is no allusion to the Paris Garden disaster or even to the earthquake of 1580, and the causes given for inhibition are the danger of infection of plague, immorality, withdrawal from Church Service, waste of time and money.

There is no allusion to " disturbances," no suggestions of the existence of " the Theatre " and " the Curtain," and therefore I think it is most naturally dated at the end of 1575, or the beginning of 1576, that is in the time of the Lord Mayor who succeeded " Hawes." The Corporation felt that their Orders of 1574 had been too long to be read or attended to ; now they formulated an Order, short and definite, which, once read, could not be forgotten. Its importance to the subject in hand makes it worth printing in extenso here, all the more so as there is some difficulty experienced by students in finding it, not being classified in relation to Players or the Stage.

" *Order for relief of the Poor*

Containing
" Orders for setting Rogues and idle persons to work," Hugh Singleton, (undated) B. M. 796, e. 37.
" Section 62. Forasmuch as the playing of Enterludes and

the resort to the same are very dangerous for the infection of the plague, whereby infinite burdens and losses to the cittie may increase, and are very hurtfull in corruption of youth with incontinence and lewdnesse, and also great wasting both of the time and thrift of many poore people, and great provoking of the wrath of God, the ground of all plagues, great withdrawing of the people from publique prayer, and from the service of God ; and daily cryed out against by the grave and earnest admonitions of the preachers of the Word of God : Therefore be it ordered that all such Enterludes in publique places, and the resort to the same, shall wholly be prohibited as ungodly, and humble sute be made to the Lords that lyke prohibition be in places near unto the Cittie."

It was necessary to complete the discussion of the date of this Order, and the facts gleaned from the Lansdowne MS. xx., as it is very important in Burbage's life, whether it was drawn up in 1575 or 1576, or at a much later date.   I am in favour of accepting the earlier date.

The Earl of Leicester's servants the players were certain to have been employed during the summer of 1575 at Kenilworth, where their master received the Queen with the most magnificent festivities known in our history.   Doubtless they worked at part of the great device of Master William Hunnis there called " The Lady of the Lake," [1] and were in readiness to perform that other unfortunate device of the Goddesses by George Gascoigne [2] which was three times postponed because of the weather, and never came to hearing.   The wonderful time is best described in a letter by Robert Laneham, [3] keeper of the Council Chamber door, probably a brother of John Laneham, one of Leicester's player-servants, and " fellow " of Burbage.

It is not too much to believe it possible that the eldest son of Master John Shakespeare, late Bailiff of Stratford-on-Avon,

[1] See my " William Hunnis and the Revels of the Chapel Royal."
[2] " The Princely Pleasures of Kenilworth," by George Gascoigne.
[3] "Laneham's Letter," edited by Dr. Furnivall, New Shakespeare Society.

should have been present, as Leicester sought popularity and co-operation from neighbouring corporations. And there is much to support the belief in the possibility to be found in a careful study of " The Midsummer's Night's Dream," with these other authorities.

One can well imagine Laneham and Shakespeare spoke of the same scene, Laneham in the fresh enthusiasm of a late experience, describing Arion on the Dolphin's back and the delectable music " in the evening of the day resounding from the calm waters " . . . " the hole armony conveyed in tyme tune and temper thus incomparably melodious " . . . " with what lyvely delighte this might pearse into the heerers harts, I pray ye imagine," and Shakespeare, feeling through the lapse of years the first great stimulant of his youthful imagination, the music on the waters. It was Oberon himself who spake

> Once I sat upon a promontory . . .
> And heard a Mearemaid on a Dolphin's back
> Uttering such dulcet and harmonious breath
> That the rude sea grewe civil at her song
> And certain starres shot madly from their spheres
> To heare the sea-maid's music."—(M.N.D. II. 2).

And July *is* a time for shooting stars to start.

When they had once more returned to the City after the notable " Progress," they again played before the Queen at Court on Innocents' Day, 1575, and again on the Sunday before Shrove-tide, following. For the first time they were fully described in their Warrants for payment as " Burbage and his company, Servants to the Earl of Leicester," as may be seen in the " Privy Council Register," and the " Declared Accounts of the Treasurer of the Chamber." But they could not hope to live on a Christmas Box even twice a year, and the Kenilworth festivities were not events to be expected every year.

James Burbage must have been making up his mind by this time that he needed some more regular sphere of work. If the second Order of Common Council was drawn up at this period, it might act as the illuminating cause of decision ; if it was not,

C

then he must have had some prevision of its approaching publication. We do not know anything of the places in which he had resided before this, but we know from the Registers of St. Leonard's, Shoreditch, that by this time he had shaken off the dust of London from his feet and removed from the unappreciating City to the Northern Liberty of Shoreditch just outside the walls of Finsbury Fields and the City's jurisdiction. We know he was a married man, married probably in the adjoining parish of Whitechapel to Ellen Brayne,[1] daughter of a deceased Mr. Brayne, and sister of John Brayne, citizen and grocer of London. They had had at least two sons by this time, Cuthbert and Richard, at dates not yet discovered, and had settled in Holywell Street early in 1576, probably a short time before that. There a daughter Alice was born to them on 11th March, 1575-6. It is interesting to note from the same Registers that many other players must have gone to live there about the same time ; musicians too, among them the Queen's musicians the distinguished brothers Bassano. It is not clear whether his exodus to the Northern Liberty had been planned for the purpose, or if the purpose took shape after he found himself there. But it is quite clear that the signs of the times spoke to him of his great *Idea* as clearly as did the Brazen Head " Time is ! " And he rose at once to the first call.

With all James Burbage's advantages he suffered from one disadvantage, common to many inventors and pioneers, the lack of money. Without that his great Idea could not become materialized.

He knew he would be forced to borrow at the high rate of interest then legal, and I think he began at first to borrow from John Hyde, citizen of London, who became so mysteriously connected with his enterprise in later years.

It is probable he also discussed his plans with others, especially with his wife's brother, John Braynes, but they do not seem to have come to an early agreement.

---

[1] I have just noted that *Brayne* is a name in Stratford-on-Avon about the same time as John Burbage, but I do not wish to build on this fact.

About a month after his daughter's birth, on 13th April, 1576, he signed and sealed his half of the Indenture of Lease he had secured of an extensive tract of land formerly part of the old Priory of Holywell, lying between the property then held by a long lease from the Crown by the Earl of Rutland, and the brick wall which bounded Finsbury Fields.[1] These fields were in reality the City's "Common" where children went forth to play, maidservants to dry linen ; men to practise archery apprentices to amuse themselves by the games of the time, and lovers to go a-courting. The old Priory grounds belonged to Master Giles Alleyn, who signed the other half of the Indenture and thereby came into the whole future life of James Burbage, and much of that of his sons. But at first it was all sunshine and plain sailing. Giles Alleyn signed the lease, knowing perfectly well the use to which that land was to be put, knowing also how much the Corporation would object to that use. But he also knew that James Burbage was a favoured "servant" of the powerful Earl, whom it was not quite prudent to ruffle just then. Besides, he had just secured for his company that magnificent brand-new "Royal Patent," which gave them such large liberty.

The agreement seemed very reasonable, indeed, on the face of it, liberal. The rent was to be only £14 a year, with £20 down by way of a fine. The owner would not give a longer lease than twenty-one years at first, but was willing that at the end of the first ten years it might be extended for another ten years, if both parties agreed. The conditions on the landlord's side were, that James Burbage before the end of that term of ten years should have expended on the rebuilding or restoration of some tenements on the property at least £200, and that he should pay the legal expenses of drawing up this second agreement.

It is more than probable that James Burbage was in possession of the property some time before the final Indenture was signed, as was the custom then. Indeed, his lease was reckoned

[1] See p. 33 .

from 25th March, quarter-day, and may have begun even earlier. Before he had secured the land he had planned what to do with it. As the lease shows, there were included cottages, barns, gardens, a well, sewers, a pond, and a piece of " void ground." There was also an inn on the estate, the *George Inn*, which comes into the history afterwards, and may be the very one that suggested Shakespeare's words about

> " St. George that swinged the Dragon and e'er since
>   Sits on his horse-back at mine hostess' door."

But the Mayor's Proclamations had forbidden players to play in the city, in inn-yards, he had also forbidden them to play in open spaces.   So James Burbage, while seeming to obey in every point to the *letter*, struck out a new form of *liberty* in the *spirit* by building a *house* for himself.   He was his own architect and builder and put into his building all his experience, tastes, desires and hopes.   His old inn-yards gave him suggestions as to enclosures and galleries, but he did not follow them in shape, making his building round ; the carefully prepared halls and chambers in royal and noble houses where he had been allowed to perform, gave him the recognition of the attractiveness of decoration, the ominous warnings of the Orders of 1574 made him see to it that his stages and galleries were made of seasoned wood, of solid proportions, soundly fixed.   He made his building also of wood (the material of which he knew most) supported by brick at the foundations.   Doubtless he secured some of the boards and pillars frequently sent prepared from the country to some of the river wharfs, as Peter Street afterwards spoke of doing, and I am certain he rushed it up in a very much shorter space of time than is generally estimated Men were not bound to work only eight hours a day then.   He was able to do so much himself, and he had many to encourage and help.   All the company, idle at that season, would be only too eager to help him, at least with the lighter jobs, to get the place ready the sooner for their plays.   I believe that he would be able to complete all that was necessary to do at first, within a month; and it would be sure to cost as little as possible.

But, careful as he was, he found it was costing more than he had anticipated, more than he had. It seemed fortunate for him at the time (though it turned out differently afterwards) that his fervours had infected his wife's brother, John Brayne, a comparatively rich man, who had a wife but no children, and who had always, therefore, spoken of the young Burbages as his heirs. He became willing to invest in Burbage's venture half the outlay, so that he also shared the profits.

Burbage called his building by a new name, The Theatre, a pioneer in that also, for its particular name became the general name of all its successors.

The building was its own advertisement. From the playgrounds of Finsbury Fields it could be watched as it rose, curiosity and eager anticipation would certainly fill many hearts there. As it approached completion, it could be seen even from the Bankside (where afterwards it was to be transported); when its flag flew, the Lords of the Privy Council at Whitehall might see that the play was about to begin.

When it was ready, probably in that very April, 1576, we may be sure that it would fill only too rapidly. Extra crowds would go from curiosity, willing to pay if only to see the house, even larger crowds of the impecunious people hoping for chance access, as they formerly had had occasionally in inn-yards, and always in " open spaces." But for the first time there was a *check at the door*, no admission to the house without payment, no waiting for a collection afterwards. Turmoils would be sure to ensue, the impecunious unwilling to leave, the fee-provided eager to pass through. When they struggled through, what did they see? They found themselves in an enclosed central space, which we now call " the pit," but without seats, and without a roof. When they looked above, they saw the sky and faced the elements. When they looked in front, they saw an open stage crossing one end of the circle, at the back of it were doors and curtains, above it a Player's House, which was to represent a balcony, a tower, a steeple, a bridge, a prison, or anything that required a higher level than the stage.   If they looked round they would see galleries, as they had been wont to see in inn-yards, but much more gorgeously draped than they; seats were there also, of varying degrees of comfort; from the ordinary gallery, to the " Lord's Rooms." And over all the galleries as over the stage was a thatched roof, with projecting eaves.   If the first comers had a suspicion of the probable coming of rain, they would probably make a rush for the galleries.   But here they would have to pay anew, according to the degree of the gallery.   If they could not, or would not pay further, they would stay where they were, on the ground floor, the first samples of those who were afterwards called " groundlings," somewhat protected from the wind, little protected from the rain, and not at all protected from their neighbours, amid crowds who surged in until all were wedged together beyond hope of comfort, the good-humoured ones cracking nuts, the ill-conditioned picking quarrels with each other.   It would seem so long to wait, however short it was, and when the drum beat and the gorgeously dressed actors entered, a sudden stillness would fall on the multitude eager to hear.

One would like to know what was Burbage's first play, performed at the Theatre ?   Was it the play he had performed before the Queen the Sunday before Shrove-tide, or was it an older one ?   Was it one of those he had helped to brighten at Bristol or Gloucester, or other places to which he had travelled ? Was it a play specially compiled for this great occasion of founding the British Stage, or was it, amid the hubbub of the disappointed men outside, merely for the occasion " feats of activity." [1] We know not, but we do know that it must have been some of these, and that its performance only whetted the appetite of the audience and sight-seers for more.   " The

[1] I only know the names of a few that belonged then to Leicester's Company, "Chariclea," " Predor and Lucia," "Mamillia," "Philemon and Philecia," " Panecia," and they might have been preparing the "History of the Collier " for the following Christmas at Court. (Dec. Acc., Treas. Chamb. and Off. Var. 1213.)

Theatre " leapt into fame and popularity at once. James Burbage's dreams of the possibilities of his Idea had come true. But immediately a cloud of troubles arose over his head, and dimmed his bright prospects of paying off his debts with speed. The first of his troubles was rivalry, the second was litigation, the third was the frequent recurrence of the plague, and the fourth the ever constant disturbances among those coming or going to " the Theatre " or surrounding it, that is, among those outside of his personal responsibility. We hear no story of disturbances *within* the theatre. James Burbage could manage them there himself. It was outside the Theatre that troubles arose.

His first rival was, like its name, a veiled one. We know nothing of its foundation, its owner, and little of its career. It " rose like an exhalation," and though often a threatened life, it managed to live longer than any other playhouse and escaped the litigation that nearly ruined James Burbage. The only good these old lawsuits ever did to any one, they have done to us—they have preserved the story of the pioneer who breasted the first difficulties, and made the path easy, and the fortunate founder of the Curtain is forgotten. Only one thing we do know of it is, that it stood very near " The Theatre," in the same Liberty, in the same Parish, on another part of the same old Holywell Priory ; on the grounds of the Prioress's wing indeed. And it is not a little curious that Maurice Long, citizen and Clothworker of London, who had bought for £60 " All that House, Tenement or Lodge called the Curteyne, and the parcel of ground close walled, called the Curteyn Close, etc." had sold it for £200 on the 23rd Aug., 14 Eliz. 1571 to Sir William Alleyn, then Lord Mayor of London. Whether the negative peace of the Curtain Theatre was due to the fact that it was built somehow on land belonging to Sir William Alleyn is not certain, but the question may be considered yet. (See Chancery Claus, 9 Eliz., f. 14, and the " Curtain Theatre," Shakespeare Society Transactions, 1844, p. 29.)

One can realize all the jealousy kindled against James Burbage in the hearts of less successful men, all their machinations and ruses ; all the righteous wrath of the preachers, all the efforts of the Corporation to check and minimize what to them seemed sources of danger to the common weal. We can realize them because some information concerning these can be found, scattered through old records.

The name of " The Theatre " first appears in the Privy Council Register, for a letter was written by the Privy Council to the Middlesex authorities on 1st August, 1577, instructing them, for fear of the plague, to " take order with such as use to play without the Liberties . . . as at the Theatre and such like, to forbear playing till after Michaelmas." It is hardly to be supposed they were allowed to play even then, because the plague continued, as we may learn from " A sermon preached at Pawles Crosse on Sunday, the thirde of November, 1577, in the time of the Plague," by an uncertain " T. W." This has been translated by some into Thomas White, by others into Thomas Wilcox. It was printed in 1578–9. A second copy is preserved in the British Museum, with a different title page affixed, dated 9th December, 1596, but at the end there is the same date as the above, " 1578." It is not however a dupli-cate, as stated in the B. M. Catalogue. *Sign. A* at least has been reprinted and much altered. It has been bound up by some previous owner with a sermon preached by T. White, and hence the usual ascription, which is however unsup-ported by any evidence. (See Harrison's " England," ed. Furnivall, 4th vol., p. 343.)

This sermon is very severe upon the sins of the people, which, the preacher thought, had brought down God's wrath on them in the Plague. " Look but uppon the Common Playes in London and see the multitude that flocketh to them, and followeth them ; beholde the sumptuous Theatre houses a continual monument of London's prodigalitie and folly. But I understand they are now forbidden, because of the Plague. I like the policye well, if it *holde still,* for a disease is but bodged or patched up that is not cured in the cause ; and the cause of the plague is sinne, if you looke to it well; and the cause of sinne are plays; therefore the cause of plagues are playes." The preacher supported this logical inference and went on, " Wherefore if thou be a father thou losest thy child, if thou be a maister, thou losest thy servaunt ; and if thou be what thou canst be, thou losest thyself that hauntest those schooles of vice, dennes of theeves, and Theatres of all lewdnesse ; and if it be not suppressed in time, it will make such a Tragedie, that all London may well mourne whyle it is London, for it is no playing-time." It is difficult to harmonize these severe charges with the accounts that have come down to us of Burbage's work. It is more than probable the preacher had never visited the Play-house, and formed his opinion from garbled accounts. One cause of the Corporation's practical objections was the bringing together of so many crowds, some of them recovering from, others sickening for the plague, and the enormously increased danger of the rapid spread of infection. But that danger, at least, would be common to assemblages in churches, or at St. Paul's Cross. Yet apparently the crowding was *not* so serious at the sermons as at the plays.

The month after T. W.'s sermon, on 2nd December, 1577, John Northbrook entered at Stationer's Hall, his " book against Dicing, Dauncing, Vain Plays or Enterludes." He too refers to " The Theatre " and adds the " Curtain." Youth asks him, " Doe you speake against those places which are made uppe and builded for such playes and enterludes as The Theatre and Curtaine is, and other such like places besides ? " Age replies, " Yea, truly, for I am persuaded that Satan hath not a more speedie way and fitter schoole . . . than those places and playes and theatres are." The Earl of Leicester's players played at Court that Christmas, showing that they and their plays were appreciated there.[1]

Again on 17th April, 1578, the Privy Council instructed the Middlesex authorities to restrain players till after Michaelmas because of the plague. (See Privy Council Register.)

[1] Pipe Office, Dec., Acc., Treas. Chamb. 541.

John Stockwood preached a sermon at St. Paul's that year, and is also severe upon the players. He printed his sermon the same year, and dedicated it to the Worshipful Company of Skinners. " A sermon preached at Paules Crosse on Bartholomew Day, being the 24th of August, 1578, by John Stockwood, Scholemaister of Tonbridge."

At page 23 he commences the charge : " More resorte to playes than to sermons." " Wyll not a filthye playe, with the blast of a Trumpette, sooner call thyther a thousand, than an hour's tolling of a Bell bring to the Sermon a hundred ? Nay, even here in the Citie, without it be at this place, and some other certaine ordinarie audience, where shall you finde a reasonable company ? Whereas if you resorte to the Theatre, the Curtayne, and other places of playes in the Citie, you shall on the Lorde's daye have those places, with many other that I can not reckon, as full as possibly they can throng."

Stockwood comes back to the Theatres on page 135, which he censures along with other " divelish inventions, as Lords of Misserule, Morris Dances, Maygames," etc. " What should I speake of beastly playes againste which out of this place every man crieth out ? Have we not houses of purpose built with great charges for the maintenance of them, and that without the Liberties, as who woulde say, ' there let them saye what they will saye, we wil play ! ' [1] I know not how I might with the godly learned especially more discommende the gorgeous Playing place erected in the Fieldes, than to terme it, as they please to have it called, a Theatre, that is, even after the manner of the old Theatre at Rome, a show place of al beastlie and filthy matters. . . . I will not here enter into the disputation whether it be utterly unlawfull to have any playes, but will onely joyne in this issue, whether in a Christian Common-wealth they be tolerable on the Lord's Day, when ye people should be exercised in hearing the word. . . . If playing in the Theatre or any other place in London, as there are by sixe that I know,

[1] This is one of the phrases which suggest that the Corporation Order had been passed by this time.

be any of the Lordes wayes . . . then, not only it may, but ought to be used . . . I speak not howe little pollicie it is to suffer so much mony to be so ill spente, which might be employed to better uses. For reckoning with the leaste, the gaine that is reaped of eighte ordinarie places in the Citie which I knowe, by playing but once a weeke (wheras many times they play twice and sometimes thrice) it amounteth to £2,000 by the yeare, the suffering of which waste must one daye be answered before God."

At page 147, he also inveighs against the " reding of filthie books " as the " Amadis of Gaul,"[1] the " great Pallace and the little Pallace of Pleasure, with a number moe of such filthie books."

Now it is true that the plays prepared for performance at that time were not always perfect in tone and taste ; nor were the novels on which they were based. But Burbage (as the Master of the Revels did) " chose the *best* that were to be had," and later notices show that his actors even were " free from scurrility."

The complaint of the *waste of time* is genuine. Far more people at the close of the sixteenth century attended the theatres in proportion to the population than now do. They had no other excitements, no newspapers, picture galleries, lectures, concerts, and few games that were not also disapproved of. And the plays were performed in the afternoons, that is, *in business hours*, so that, between the going to the Fields to hear a play, the waiting there, the play itself, and the return home, probably delayed by a supper at the inn, havoc would be played in the day's work, especially among the apprentices. We must not forget that the psychology of the time did not recognize the needs of relaxation to all, and of amusements for the young.

[1] Thomas Payne's translation of " Amadis of Gaul " published 1567. William Paynter's " Palace of Pleasure," published 1st vol. in 1566, 22nd volume in 1567. George Pettie's " A petite pallace of Pettie his pleasure " in 1576.

"All work and no play, makes Jack a dull boy," was a proverb not understood in its full bearing. So that many more amusements which seem to us quite innocent, were also anathematized by the voluntary Censors of the times, such as football and other games. The preachers certainly had an effect upon the Corporation, who always went officially to hear them at Paul's Cross.

This latter serœon, printed also in 1578, gives us some interesting points of information. The defiant phrase, attributed to the Theatre out in the Fields, "as who would say there, let them saye what they will saye, we will playe," is curiously illustrative of Burbage's attitude to those who sought to hinder him. The fact that Stockwood knew *at that date*, of six or eight playing places *in the city* shows that other companies of players, supported by the populace, had ignored municipal orders, as later correspondence proves. It also gives some notion of the estimate formed by the outside world of the players' earnings. Of course the sum of £2,000 a year must have included the whole of the six or eight companies, and even that, for the time, was probably a sum much above the reality. The deductions for expenses, and for seasons of "sickness," as the plague was then generally called, were probably not made at all, and the best days reckoned as an "average day."

Such sermons could not have had a beneficial effect, either on Burbage's business or himself.

In this year 1578 another and entirely unexpected trouble touched him, which did not entirely leave him all his life. H s brother-in-law, probably under the influence of his wife, began to refuse to contribute to the expenses, though he still expected a share in the profits of the common concern. Of course, the whole of his original share had been spent in the building, as well as James Burbage's, and working expenses were necessary. So bitter had the discussion on the subject become that they had to seek arbitrators, who found in favour of Burbage, and caused Braynes to be bound to him in a bond of £200, that he would pay his share of the expenses, or forieit **the bond,** which was to be increased under some condition which I have not been able to clear. Possibly Braynes at first, stimulated by the decision, obeyed the finding of the arbitrators, having hope in the repaying powers of the concern, but evidently it was not for long.

In spite of the sermons [1] the Earl of Leicester's players had a licence to play in the City, on 24th December, 1578, because they were going to perform before the Queen on St. Stephen's Day. This they did, but on the Shrove Tuesday following they were paid in full for coming, though a play, by her Majesty's command, was supplied by others. This would rather seem to have arisen from a Royal tiff with Leicester than from any attempt to pacify the preachers. Promptness, gorgeousness and success could not be attained without money.

For some mysterious reason Burbage, that year, on 17th September, 1579, mortgaged the "Theatre" to one John Hyde, grocer. It is probable that he found the heavy rates of interest too much for him, through such long continuance of plague, and the withdrawal of Braynes' contributions to expenses, or it may have been to protect the building from the claims of Braynes and other creditors, trusting to the one in preference to whom he owed most.

Of course Burbage remained ostensible owner and manager, and it is probable that the mortgage at the time was kept private, except to those concerned and their attorneys. But it was a step which caused much misunderstanding afterwards, and gave a handle to his enemies against him for years.

Against the dangers of debt and public and private interference, Burbage still bravely fought, and the cessation of the plague gave him new courage. But the very return of liberty excited the people to more eager desire for the amusement they had so much appreciated, and from which they had been

---

[1] "Newes from the North," 1579, says, "The Theaters, Courtaines . . . where the time is so shamefully misspent, namely the Sabaoth days unto the great dishonour of God, and the corruption and utter destruction of youth."

so long restrained.   Greater crowds than ever hurried through the fields to Holywell, and disturbances arose.   His popularity was made the grounds for a summons to appear before the Middlesex authorities, as " John Braynes, yeoman, of Shoreditch, and James Burbage, yeoman, of the same parish, to come before the Middlesex Assizes at Clerkenwell Sessions on 21st February 22 Eliz., 1579–80." [1]   The charge formulated against them was curiously worded, " for bringing together *unlawful* assemblies to hear and to see certain *colloquies* or *interludes* called playes or interludes, exercised and practised by the same John Braynes and James Burbage, and divers other persons unknown, at a certain place called the Theatre at Holywell in the county of Middlesex, by reason of which great affrays, assaults, tumults, and quasi-insurrections and divers other enormities . . . were perpetrated to the danger of the lives of divers good subjects . . . against the form of the Statute," etc.   This was found preserved among the Middlesex County Records of the reign of James I by Mr. Cordy Jeaffreson, and translated by him out of the original crabbed legal Latin into English.   This teaches us many things. It shows that John Braynes though entered in no list of the Earl of Leicester's players, or any other company, was performing at least on this occasion.   It hardly supports Mr. Jeaffreson's contention that he must have been the *chief* player, and the proprietor of the Theatre.   Braynes might very well have been placed first as being the elder man, apparently the richer of the two, and a freeman of the proud Company of the Mystery of Grocers, or the two might have agreed to put Braynes forward as the chief, so as to bear the examination with more innocent demeanour, while Burbage was looking after his plays, his house, his rehearsals and his audience. Braynes was a business man, quite able to face an attorney and a magistrate, but he was certain to play second fiddle at the Theatre.   No record of any decision is preserved.   It is probable that they were bound over to keep the peace, and dismissed,

---

[1] Middlesex County Records, vol. ii, xlvii, by Mr. Cordy Jeaffreson.

but there would certainly be some expenses, and a good many
extra " gratifications." One would like to know what was
the " Statute " referred to. Was it the municipal Order ?

God's " admonition " was the earthquake on 6th April, 1580.
Enemies read into it tokens of God's wrath against the Theatre.
Ballads were written, and good advice given [1]—

> " Comme from the Plaie,
> The House will fall so people saye,
> The earth quakes, lett us hast awaye."

Munday says only, " At the play-houses, the people ran forth
supprised with great astonishment," but Stubbes says that
many were " sore crushed and bruised," possibly from a panic
at the exit. But we have no record of any damage done at the
Theatre beyond a " crack." Burbage the Joiner had done good
work in its building, and not a stage or gallery fell, not even a
chimney-pot in Burbage's house in Holpwell Street, though
many chimneys fell in more respectable places.[2] The only
chimney that fell in Shoreditch was in Alderman Osborne's
house.

Immediately after the earthquake there were new troubles.
From the " Remembrancia " in Sir Nicholas Woodroffe's time
we learn that the Lord Mayor on 12th April, 1580, complained
to the Privy Council, and then stopped proceedings when he
heard that " the Lords " had already taken action. " Where
it happened on Sunday last that some great disorder was committed at the Theatre, I sent for the Undersheriff . . . and
for the Players to have appeared before me, the rather because
these playes doe make assemblies of citizens and of their
families, of whom I have control " ; but hearing that the
Lords were considering the matter he " surceased to proceed," only he thought it his duty to remind them " that the
players of playes which are used at the Theatre and other such
places . . . are a *very superfluous sort of men*, and of such

---

[1] See Halliwell Phillipps' Outlines, note, " The Theatre and Curtain "
[2] Stowe's " Chronicles," p. 686.

facultie as the lawes have disallowed, and their exercise of those playes is a great hindrance of the service of God, who hath with His mightie hande so lately admonished us of our earnest repentance." The end of this complaint is not preserved here.

There were many Gossons in Shoreditch, and it is to be supposed the scourge of the players was a native. He had been a player and had written plays himself in his youth. He tells us himself that one of them, " Catiline's Conspiracy," had been performed at the Theatre. But he had learned to see the evils associated with playing-houses then. On 22nd July, 1579, had been licensed his " Schoole of Abuse," a pleasant invective against Poets, Pipers, Players, Jesters and such like Caterpillars of the Commonwealth," and it would be in every man's hands early in 1580. It had a personal interest in being dedicated to Sir Philip Sidney, without permission asked or accorded, and it was soon publicly known that Sir Philip had been displeased [1] with the dedication. Gosson also wrote in 1580 a " second and third blast of retreat from plays and Theatres," and [2]

> " A ringing retreat couragiously sounded
> Wherein plays and players are fitly confounded."

Thomas Lodge answered him effectively in his defence of " Poetry, Music and Stage plays," but his pamphlet was suppressed by authority. It is to be believed that Sir Philip Sidney himself meant a dignified reply in his " Apologie for Poetry." Thomas Lodge returned to the defence later, in his " Alarum against Usurers," dedicated to Sir Philip Sidney himself, while Gosson tried a dedication to Walsingham, Sir

[1] Spenser writing to Gabriel Harvey, 16th Oct., 1579, says that Gosson " was for his labour scorned " as far as so gentle a spirit could show scorn.

[2] Stat. Reg., 18th Oct., 1580. Lycensed unto Henrie Denham under the Warden's hands a seconde and a thirde blaste of retrait from playes and Theaters vi^d ; " 10th Nov., 1580, Allowed a ringing retraite couragiouslie sounded wherein Plaies and Players are fytly confounded to Edward White iv^d."

Philip's father-in-law. "The Play of Playes" was acted by Lord Leicester's players at the Court and at the Theatre against Gosson's attacks. The paper war went on for some years.

Five weeks after the earthquake, the plague recommenced, and doubtless it was again read as a sign of the wrath of God against the playhouse. On 13th May, 1580, an order of the Privy Council was issued to forbid all plays in and about the city till Michaelmas next.

Poor Burbage, five months' forced "unemployment" with his rent, the interest of his loans running on, his creditors clamouring, his company worrying him for advances, and his housekeeper asking him for daily bread. His was the fate of Tantalus, for the golden stream was ever at his lips. If only he could be let alone to *supply* the eager *demand* of the people, his outlay would return to him an income sufficient to pay all his debts and be a free man. Minor battles he might fight, but a Privy Council Interdict and a threatening plague were too much even for a stage manager of his calibre.

It is possible he went on tour. But he played at Court that Christmas as usual. A new and entirely unexpected set of troubles commenced for James Burbage in 1581, through, though not by his landlord. To understand this, as it has been mentioned by no historian of the Stage (see p. 52), we must go back to the past history of Holywell Priory. The Priory had been granted to Henry Webbe, gentleman porter of the Tower, who had only one daughter and heir, Susan. Sir Edmund Peckham had arranged with him for a marriage between his son George, afterwards Sir George Peckham, and Susan. Webbe settled the Priory upon his daughter and her heirs, failing whom upon George and his heirs. But there were certain conditions, that George should marry her willingly, and should do so before a certain date. Having arranged everything, 28th February, 6 Ed. VI., as he thought safely, Webbe died, and George Peckham married Susan. In a very few months they sold the Priory to Christopher Bumpstead, citizen of London, for £533 6s. 8d., and there

D

was a fine levied in the Court of Common Pleas, in Michaelmas
Term, 2 and 3 Philip and Mary. Susan died December 1555,
leaving her son Edmund, one day old. Bumpstead sold the
place very shortly after for £600 to Christopher and Giles Alleyn.
When his father Christopher died, it came to Giles Alleyn as
survivor, and he had held it ever since. But in 1581 Edmund
Peckham, having grown to manhood, claimed it, saying that his
father Sir George had very unwillingly married Susan Webbe,
that he did not marry her at the date agreed on, and therefore
that the Priory ought to come to Susan and *her heirs*. His father
George Peckham had sold it without her will or signature ;
and she died shortly after, leaving him, Edmund, her heir, one
day old. He therefore, when he had come to his majority, had
considered the question and now claimed the property. He
had found a jury to agree with him, not understanding the
case, and his emissaries were prowling about, in James Burbage's leasehold, trying to effect an " entrance," and gave him
no end of trouble and unnecessary irritation. This is fully
described afterwards in the Court of Wards and Liveries, for
Edmund Peckham having died, his son George, a minor, became
a Royal Ward, and the claim was revived again for his benefit,
with further discomfort and loss to Burbage. This is pointed
out still later in the litigation between Giles Alleyn and Cuthbert about the Theatre (see Note XIX). In 1581 Tilney had
a licence to take up men artificers, etc., for the Queen's
service ; and another to make players and play-writers come
before him to recite their plays and have them reformed.

On 10th July, 1581, the Privy Council wrote[1] to the Lord
Mayor, to allow no plays or interludes in the City or liberties,
till the end of September, unless the plague had disappeared.
To this he gladly assented, and on 13th July, 1581,[2] ordered
every alderman of the city to see that no plays or interludes
were shown in their wards.

On 14th November[3] the same year the Common Council

[1] Privy Council Register of date.   [2] Repertory 20, f. 152.
[3] Journal 21, f. 151b.

resolved that if any should presume to allow plays he should be sent to prison.

The Lords of the Privy Council wrote, on the 18th of that month,[1] to the Lord Mayor, that as the sickness had ceased they required him forthwith to suffer the players to perform and to use such plays as were ready in their usual places as they were wont to do.

But the Lord Mayor paid no attention to this. He was not going to countermand his own orders. Indeed, he proclaimed a new restraint on his own account. But he was justified by a return of the plague, and so the Lords of the Council held their peace. Mr. E. K. Chambers seems to think that Hugh Singleton's printed " Order " comes in here, because on 11th April, 1582, the Lords of the Council wrote the Lord Mayor about the plague : " We have therefore thought good to pray your Lordship to revoke your late inhibition against their playing on holidays." [1] But the wording of that inhibition has no relation to the terms in Hugh Singleton's order.

The falling of a stage at the Beare-baiting at Paris Garden on 13th January, 1582–3, when several were killed and many injured, had a great effect on people's minds, and it was taken as another testimony of God's wrath against sight-seers. Though James Burbage did not erect that frail woodwork, and his own galleries stood firm, and though his plays gave much more humane and intelligent spectacles than bear-baiting he suffered for it all the same, as we may see later. The murmurings against the plays in the Liberties increased.

In March 1582–3, the Queen, through Walsingham, took a step fraught with serious consequences to many players. In order to keep more control over them, and to keep pace with her nobles, she resolved to have her own Royal Company of Players. She had been accustomed through her officers to take up singing children for her chapels. But she also had a right to take up any workman or artificer she had need of. Exercising that right, she *took up*, or selected, twelve men from

[1] Privy Council Register of date.

the various companies then in existence to be her own servants, and grooms of the Royal Chamber.   We do not know the names of the whole of them who were chosen, but we know that Richard Tarleton and Robert Wilson were among them.[1]

Of these Howes, in continuation of Stowe, writes (naming Robert Wilson, " Thomas "), 1583, p. 697 : " Thomas Wilson for quick delicate extemporall wit, and Richard Tarleton, for a wondrous pleasant extemporall wit, he was the wonder of his time."   Richard Tarleton does not seem ever to have belonged to Burbage's company, though he lived and died in Shoreditch. The Curtain was his sphere when he played in that neighbourhood.   He made his will in 1588, and mentions William Johnson his fellow.

James Burbage does not seem to have been " selected." He must have been getting on in years by this time, and had probably gone somewhat out of the " form and fashion of the time."   Besides, he was the only player of the time who had a play-house of his own to tie him.

We know that John Laneham continued Leicester's man for a time, for he was the leader of Leicester's reformed Company who followed their lord abroad to the Low Countries.

This politic move of Walsingham led to far-reaching re-arrangements.   I hardly fall in with all Mr. Fleay's kaleidoscopic changes of " companies," at least for Burbage's men. The Lord Mayor's letter of the following year gives a better account of it, as changes of individual members of companies. To this date I refer the association of James Burbage with Lord Hunsdon, which continued till the end of his life.

One of the changes of this year has never been noted by any

[1] Mr. Hunter finds a list in the Early Lay Subsidies, 1588, which he gives in his " Collections," p. 354.   Richard Tarleton, John Laneham, William Johnson, John Towne, John Adams, John Garland, John Dutton, John Singer, Lyonell Cooke, and Davy Duboys. Add. MSS. 24,497, p. 59.   From orig. in Excheq. Lay Sub., 69/97.   This suggests that they were salaried servants, successors of the old Royal Interlude Players.   Richard Tarleton had by this time offended the Queen by a satire on Sir Walter Raleigh, and he died that year.

writer on the Stage. *Richard Burbage,* James's second son, began his career as an actor that year, as his brother Cuthbert said of him later, he had had " 35 years paines." (See Lord Chamberlain's accounts, L. v, 94, 95.) After 1583, therefore, we may begin to look for Richard as a performer.

He might have been a chorister in some church or chapel, he may have acted among the " Earl of Leicester's boys." But we are sure that James Burbage poured into him all his experience and skill, and made him the pride of his life. We know the date of his beginning from Cuthbert Burbage's pleadings in 1635, which have been too much neglected in the history of the Stage. He began early, it is certain, to fill up some of the vacancies made in the various companies. He most likely followed Robert Wilson in his career, as the description of him and his acting reads more like Wilson's than any other's. Richard was evidently handsome, charming in manners and talented ; it is nearly certain that in his early days he would be cast for the women's parts. But he rose almost at once to the chief parts, in Tarleton's " Deadly Sins " even to doubled chief parts,[1] and a long career of glory raised not only his own and his father's name, but that of his whole company and his whole profession through him.

James Burbage had evidently given his sons the best education he could give them. Cuthbert, the elder, seemed to have been trained as a lawyer and business manager. His name appears in no records as an *actor*, he may not have been fitted for the profession. But as proprietor and business manager his interest would be sure occasionally to induce him to be a sort of under-study, stop-gap, a " servitor " or an odd man in a crowd when he was needed. He was the son of the provident and worldly business side of James Burbage, as Richard was evidently the son of his ideal side, inheriting his good looks, charm and inspiration.

[1] See the Dulwich MSS. xix. for a " Platt of the second part of the Seven Deadly Sins of Tarlton." Richard there plays both " King Gorboduc " and " Tereus."

The "Anatomie of Abuses" by Philip Stubbes, 1st May, 1583, was dedicated to the Rt. Hon. Philip Earl of Arundel.   In the preface he says he does not dislike all plays, as they might give a good example.   But in the book itself he describes plays as " invented by the Devil, practised by the Heathen Gentiles, and dedicat to their false gods."   The matter of both tragedy and comedy is sin.   " Theatres and Curtains are Venus Pallaces.   I beseech all players and founders of plaies and enterludes, to leave off that cursed kind of life, and give themselves to honest exercise."

In spite of the Royal appointment, the Corporation in 1583 made a determined attempt " to thrust the players out of the city, and to pull down all playhouses and dicing-houses in the liberties."   (D. N. B.)   The Lord Mayor writing to Walsingham on 3rd May of that year for powers to destroy the theatres mentions among the dangers from stage plays at *The Theatre* " the peril of ruins from so weak a building."   But no reference then or afterwards suggests that any accident had at any time befallen any part of James Burbage's good work.

The troubles came to a head in the following year, and the story thereof gives a reason for believing that James Burbage had chosen him another master [1] by this time.   It is too interesting and illustrative to miss, and I give Mr. Fleetwood's " Report of Sundry Broiles in Whitsontide, 18th June, 1584 " (Lansd. MS. 41 art. 13).   " Upon Sondaye my Lord sent two Aldermen to the Queen's court for the suppressing and pulling down the Theatre and Curtain.   All the Lords agreed thereto saving my Lord Chamberlen,[2] and Mr. Vice Chamberlen, but we obteyned a letter to suppress them all, and upon the same night I sent for the Queen's Players, and my Lord of Arundell his Players, and they all willinglie obeyed the Lord's letters.

---

[1] I have sometimes wondered if James Burbage had in any way become affected by the Earl of Leicester's destruction of Edward Arden, of Park Hall, Warwickshire, in 1583.

[2] The office of Lord Chamberlain, both in patent and performance changed frequently about this period.

" The chiefest of Her Highness' Players advised me to send for the owner of the Theatre, who was a stubborn fellow, and to bind hym. I dyd so, he sent me word that he was my Lord of Hunsdon's man, and that he would not come to me, but he wold in the morning ride to my Lord. Then I sent the Undersheriff for him, and he brought hym to me, and on his coming he scoutted me out very lustie, and in the end, I showed hym my Lord his master's hand, and then he was more quiet, but he die for it, he wold not be bound. And then I mynding to send hym to prison, he made sute that he might be bownde to appear in the Oier and determiner, the which is tomorrow, where he said that he was sure the Court would not bynd him, being a Counsellor's man. And so I have graunted his request, and where he shal be sure to be bownd or else to do worse " (ff. 35, 36).

So he must again have appeared at least a second time in Court. We do not know the conclusion of this case.

Again, however, Burbage's " whole state of man " must have been racked by fears and anxieties. Never before had *all* the Lords gone against him and his house, but times were changed. Nevertheless he must have had some faint hope lingering in his breast, that something would turn up to save him. Wherever or however that help came we know not, but the Theatre was not then destroyed. And now we must consider the Landsdowne MSS.[1] misdated as 1575. Do they fit in here, in the late autumn of 1584 ?

Lansd. xx, 12.

" *To the Right honorable the Lordes of her Matie's Privie Counsell.*

" In most humble manner beseche your Lordships your dutifull and daylie Orators the Queenes Maties poor Players.

" Whereas the tyme of our service draweth verie neere, so that of necessitie wee must needes have exercise to enable us the better for the same, and also for our better helpe and relief in

[1] See p. 14.

our poore lyvinge, the season of the yere beynge past to playe att anye of the houses without the cittye of London, as in our articles annexed to this our supplication maye more att large appeere unto your Lordships.   Our most humble peticion ys that yt maye please your Lordships to vowchsaffe the readinge of these few Articles and in tender consideracion of the matters therein mentioned, contayninge the verie staye and good state of our lyvinge to graunt unto us the confirmacion of the same or of as manye or as much of them as shalbe to yor honors good lykinge.   And therewith all your Lordships favorable letters unto the Lord Mayor London to permitt us to exercise within the cittye according to the articles, and also that the said letters maye contayne some order to the Justices of Middlesex as in the same ys mentioned, wherbie as wee shall cease the continewoll troublinge of yor Lordships for your often letteres in the premisses, So shall wee daylie be bownden to praye for the prosperous preservation of your Lordships in honor helthe and happiness long to continew.

> " Your Lordships most humblie bownden and
> daylie Orators,
> " her Majesties poor Players."

Their articles are lost, but the Mayor's reply gives a suggestion of them.

Lans. MS. xx, 11.

" It may please your good Lordship—

" The orders in London whereunto the players referr them are misconceaved, and may appeare by the two acts of Common Counsell which I send you with note directing to the place.

" The first of these actes of Common Counsell was made in the Maioraltie of Hawes, 17 Regine, and sheweth a maner how plays were to be tolerated and used, althoughe it were rather wished, that they were wholly discontinued for the causes appearing in the preamble, which is for that reason somewhat the longer.   Where the players reporte the order to be that they shold not play till after service time, the boke is otherwise, for it is that they shal not onely not play in service time, but also shal not receive any in service tyme to the same : for though they did forbeare beginning to play till service were done, yet all the time of service they did take in people, which was the great mischefe in withdrawing the people from the service.

" *Afterwards* when these orders were not observed, and the lewd matters of playes encreased, and in the haunt unto them, were found many dangers, bothe for religion, state, honestie of manners, unthriftinesse of the poore, and danger of infection, etc., and the preachers daily cryeing against the Lord Maior and his brethren, in an act of Common Counsel for relefe of the poore which I send yowe printed, in the article 62 the last leafe, is enacted, as there appeareth by which there are no enterludes allowed in London in open spectacle, but in private houses onely, at marriages or such like, which may suffise, and sute is apoynted to be made that they may be likewise banished in places adjoyning.

" *Since that time* and namely upon the ruins at Paris Garden sute was made to my Lords to banishe playes wholly in the places nere London, according to the said lawe, letters were obtained from my Lords to banish them on the Sabbath day."

(This is *evidently part of No.* 13, *following.*)
Lans. MS. xx, 13.

(Answer, evidently incomplete, seems to follow No. 11.)

" Now touching their petition and articles, where they pretend that they must have exercise to enable them in their service before her Majestie.

" It is to be noted that it is not convenient that they present before her Majestie such playes as have been before commonly played in open stages before all the basest assemblages in London and Middlesex, and therefore sufficient for their exercise and more comely for the place that (as it is permitted by the sayd lawes of Common Counsell) they make their exercise of playing only in private houses.

" Also it lyeth within the dutiefull care of her Majestie's

Royal person, that they be not suffered, from playeing in the throng of a multitude, and of some infected, to presse so nere to the presence of her majestie.

" Where they pretend the mater of Stay of their lyving :

" It hath not been used nor thought meete heretofore, that players have, or shold make their lyving on the art of playeing, but men for their lyvinge using other honest and lawfull artes, or reteyned in honest services have by companies learned some enterludes for some encrease to their profit by other mens pleasures in vacant time of recreation.

" Where in the first article they require the Lord Maiors order to continewe for the tymes of playeing on hollydaies : They misreport the order, for all those former orders of toleracion are expired by the last printed act of Comon Counsell, allso if the toleration were not expired they do cautelously omitt the prohibition to receive any auditorye before common prayer be ended, And it may be noted how uncomely it is for youths to come streight from prayer to playes, from God's service to the devells.

" The second article, If in winter the dark do carry inconveniance and the short time of day after evening prayer do leave them no leysure, and fowlnesse of season do hinder the passage into the fields to playes : The remedie is ill conceyved to bring them into London, but the true remedie is to leave off that unnecessarie expense of time wherunto God himself geveth so many impediments,

" To the Third,

" To play in plagetime is to encrease the plage by infection : to play out of plage time is to draw the plage by offendinge of God upon occasion of such playes.

" But touching the permission of playes uppon the fewness of those that dye in any weke : yt may please you to remember one special thing. In the report of the plage we report only those that dye and we make no report of those that recover and cary infection about them either in their sores running or in their garments, which sort are the most dangerous. Now my Lord when the number of those that dye groweth fewest, the number of those that goe abroad with sores is greatest, the violence of the disease to kill being abated. And therefore while any plage is, though the number of them reported that dye be smaller, the number infected is so great that playes are not to be permitted.

" Also in our reporte none are noted as dying of the plage except they have tokens, but many dye of the plage that have no tokens and sometimes fraude of the serchers may deceive. Therefore it is not reason to reduce their toleration to any number reported to dye of the plage. But it is an uncharitable demand against the safetie of the Queen's subjects, and by consequens of her persone, for the gaine of a few whoe, if they were not her majestie's servants, shold by their profession be rogues, to esteme fifty a weeke so small a number as to be the cause of tolerating the adventure of infection.

" If your Lordships shal think reasonable to permit them, in respecte of the fewnesse of suche as dye, this were a better way. The ordinary deaths in London when there is no plage is between forty and fiftie, and commonly under 40 as the bookes do shew. The residue or more in plage-time is to be thought to be the plage. Now it may be enough if it be permitted that when the whole death of all diseases in London shal by 2 or 3 wekes together be under 50 a weke, they may play (observatis alioque observandis) during such time of death under 50 a week.

" Where they require that only her Majestie's servaunts be permitted to play. It is lesse evell than to grant moe. But therein if your Lordships will so allow them : it may please you to know that the last year when the toleration was of the Quene's players only, all the places of playing were filled with men calling themselves the Queen's players. Your Lordshipps may do well in your letters or warrant for their tolleration to expresse the number of the Queene's players and particularly all their names.

The Remedies.

" That they hold them content with playing in private houses, at weddings, etc., without public assemblie.   If some be thought good to be tolerated ; that then they be restrained to the orders in the act of Comon Counsell tempore Hawes.

" That they play not openly till the whole deaths in London have been by 20 daies under 50 a weeke, nor longer than it shal so continue.   That no playes be on the Sabbath.

" That no playeing be on Holy daies but after evening prayer, nor any received into the auditorye till after evening prayer.

" That no playeing be in the dark, nor continue any such time but as any of the auditorie may returne to their dwellings in London before sonne set or at least before it be dark.

" That the Quenes players only be tolerated and of them their number and certaine names to be notified in your Lordships letters to the Lord Maior and to the Justices of Middlesex and Surrey.   And those few players not to divide themselves into several companies.   That for breaking any of these orders their toleration cease."

A very different list of performances before the Queen was drawn up that Christmas.   No servants of the Earl of Leicester, or of Lord Hunsdon's, except as individuals perhaps.   " A pastorall of Phillyda and Choryn presented and enacted before her Majestie by her Highness Servauntes on St. Stephens daie at night at Greenwich, whereon was ymployed — yardes of Buffyn for Shepherd's coates 30 ells of sarcenet for fower matadeyne sutes one greate curteyne and scarfes for the nymphes one mountayne and one great cloth of canvas and vi peeces of buccram.

" The History of Agamemnon and Ulisses presented and enacted before her maiestie by the Earle of Oxenford his boyes on St. John's daie at night at Greenwich.   Dyvers feates of Actyvetie were shewed and presented before her Maiestie on Newe Yeres daie at night at Grenewiche by Symons and his

fellows. . . . The History of Felix and Philiomena shewed
and enacted before her Highness by her Maiesties servauntes
on the Sondaie next after Newe Yeares daye at nighte at
Grenewich, wherein was employed one battlement and one
house of Canvas.

" An Invention called Five playes in one presented and enacted before her Maiestie on Twelfe daie at nighte in the Hall
at Greenewich by her Highness servants . . . An invention of
three playes in one prepared to have ben showed before her
highnes on Shrove Sondaye at night and to have been enacted
by her Maiesties servaunts at Somerset House. But the
Queen came not abroad that night. . . . An antick play and
a comodye shewed presented and enacted before her Highnes
on Shrove tewsdaie at night at Somerset Place by her
maiestie's servants."

How the players, especially those of Burbage, got out of the
imbroglio, and continued to perform in companies, is not
clear. The appointment of Lord Hunsdon to be Lord Chamberlain shortly after probably helped.

The position was hard enough for players, but it was much
harder for play-house proprietors ; 1585 would be among the
" lean years " which ate up James Burbage's earnings. And
just then his brother-in-law got into trouble too, and gave him
his share of it.

I found a little undated case in the Uncalendared Court of
Requests of this year, not important, except as showing that
John Braynes had by this time had some losses.

" John Braynes Citizen and Grocer of London complained
against Roger Ward citizen and stationer of London." It
seems that Christopher Ames of Stepney had agreed with Roger
Ward to buy certain goods of him for £15, entering into a bond
to pay £30 if it were not paid by a certain time. But Ward
would not take the bond of Ames alone, and associated Braynes
with it, and as Ames had not paid, the creditor naturally sued
Braynes. The conclusion of the proceedings is not preserved
but Braynes would be sure to lose such a case.

The year 1586 was fraught with matters of weighty import to James Burbage. In spite of all the disturbances, threats and excitement about the destruction of the " Theatre," he was planning to extend its existence. It was the year during which he might get the lease of the Theatre grounds extended, if so be it he had observed the conditions. One may be very certain that James Burbage had been provident enough to do so, as well as he knew how. Before April he had had the new lease drawn up at his own expense, as agreed to, as a lease for twenty-one years from that date, all other conditions remaining the same. There was to be a free seat in the gallery for Giles Alleyn and his family in the Theatre whenever he chose to come to the play, *should he come in time*. Untempted by that attraction and forgetful of his promise, the owner of Holywell Priory refused to sign that lease. He refused to believe that the £200 had really been spent upon the upkeep and restoration of the tenements on the estate, and insisted that the new lease was different from the old one. Burbage said that he could prove that the £200 had been spent on the property, and that the only difference between the two leases lay in the fact that the scrivener had naturally not inserted a clause for the extension of lease at the end of ten years. Nothing would satisfy the irascible landlord ; he insisted on drawing up a new lease himself now, and when he presented his there *were* changes. He evidently had exaggerated ideas of the net profits realized at the Theatre, and he wanted to raise the rent from £14 to £24 a year, and to make the condition that if he did add ten years to the lease, then the use of the Theatre for playing purposes should be restricted to five more years. During the remaining five years Burbage might retain it, and use it for any other purpose he pleased. It was evident that a theatre owner could not and would not sign such a lease. He might have paid more rent, for the advantage of remaining, but to pay more rent and not be allowed to use his building as *a Theatre* for the last five years, was prohibitive. Alleyn would not sign the one, nor Burbage the other, and the year fixed for extension drifted on to its completion, and neither lease was signed. We know that conferences continued upon the subject during the whole period of the original lease and beyond it, till the *grand finale* in 1598. The details of the later litigation prove that.

On 11th May the Privy Council sent a letter to Lord Mayor to restrain plays for fear of the plague. (See Register.)

Another important set of troubles developed a new phase this year. It is evident that John Braynes had not always remained, as he had begun, the perfect partner and brother-in-law. He had not contributed to the expenses of the Theatre, in spite of the original agreement, and the 1578 arbitration, and thereby had legally forfeited £200 and his share of expenses. Burbage seems to have contented himself by growling at him, and by taking more and more absolute control of the concern. Bad feeling seems to have been engendered on both sides, fostered by the reproaches of Mrs. Braynes. Then John Braynes died. It is well to remember the married women's inheritance laws of the time. When a married man died, if there were children the property was divided into thirds, one for the wife, one for the children, one for the dead. If there were no children it went in halves. If there were no will, the widow inherited the one half, and the other half went to the nearest heir of the husband's family. Had there been no will, therefore, as there were no children, half the property would naturally have devolved on the widow, and the other half on Mrs. Ellen Burbage and her children. But there seems at a period before the investment in the theatre to have been some form of old will, in which it is said Mrs. Braynes was left heir, and she wanted either the half of the Theatre, the half of the profits, or the £500 she claimed that her husband had put into it. Burbage, on the other hand, said Braynes had lost that share through not keeping to his agreements ; that the old will did not deal with this investment, and that John Braynes had always promised that his sister's children should be his heirs, had indeed re-affirmed it solemnly on his death-bed.[1] Some

[1] This was then held legal, as a nuncupative will, if attested by witnesses afterwards.

sort of agreement might have been come to among the relatives had they been left to themselves, but unfortunately there were several other complexities. At some time since the arbitration, either at the time when James Burbage had mortgaged the Theatre, or before the time of the suit with Roger Ward, John Braynes had executed a deed of gift of all his goods and chattels to Robert Myles, goldsmith, to one Tomson and also to one Gardiner.

It evidently was not a genuine sale, as Braynes seems to have received no return for it. It was apparently a trust, or a ruse to protect the goods and chattels for the use of Braynes and his wife, from landlords, partners, arbitrators and creditors. But such plans do not always perfectly succeed. The trustees were quiet enough during John Braynes' life, but as soon as he had died, as executors they attempted to secure not only the other goods and chattels left at home, or in other investments, but they wanted to secure the share of the Theatre too. And Margaret Braynes learned to her surprise that they wanted to secure these things for themselves and not for her. Death made further complexities, for John Gardiner, one of the executors, dying, his administrator, Robert Gardiner, laid claim to his brother's interest. Margaret Braynes had to go to law with her husband's executors at the first while they and she were worrying James Burbage by cross-suits, and trying to get him shut up in prison to force him, rather than let the whole of his business go in his absence from its control, to pay up. So he had at last to go to law himself. He could not, if he would, give up the half, or his venture would be wholly ruined.

John Hyde sat tight on it, fortunately for the family. From the Book of Chancery Decrees and Orders we can glean something of the amount of litigation which waged round Burbage's devoted head. But it tells so little. Margaret Braynes had had her suit against Robert Myles filed in 1586, and by Easter, 1587,[1] " a week is granted him to make answer or an

[1] Chancery Proceedings D. & O., 1586, A. Book, 384, Braynes v. Myles—6th May, 29 Eliz. (see Note VII).

attachment will be granted." After a second complaint she seems to have given that up, or agreed with Myles. Burbage was a more promising prey. The worry galled him, and he opened a cross-suit himself. Halliwell-Phillipps, and all the writers who follow him, say that his first action was in 1590. It was certainly before that. He had never seen the earlier suit of Burbage v. Braynes, nor followed its various stages through Chancery. The record is very much injured, and the complete date is uncertain.[1] I believe it is 1588, as the only number visible is 8. The plaintiffs are James Burbage, Ellen his wife, and Cuthbert, Richard, Alice, and Ellen their children, *versus* Margaret Braynes. It is this complaint which explains fully how he had taken the land from Gyles Alleyn, his brother-in-law had agreed to go shares with him in The Theatre and " The George Inn " ; and how Braynes had forfeited a bond of £200 through not obeying the arbitration of July 12, 1578, about the conveyances to Myles and Gardiner. He bitterly complains that Robert Myles " enters the Theatre, and troubles your orator and his tenants," and that Robert Gardiner the administrator of John Gardiner, who died in 1587, " goes about to sue the said James Burbage in two several bonds, and by reason of the multiplicity of their conveyances they joyn together to imprison your said orator to enforce him to yield to their request." They will not pay the forfeited bond, their action is costly and leads to his impoverishment. He prays relief. Their answer is, of course, that his is an untrue and insufficient bill. His reply was that theirs was an insufficient demurrer. This is the case referred to in the [2] Decrees and Orders, Book A, f. 454, 22nd February, 1588–9. It was referred to Mr. Dr. Carew, and if he thought it insufficient a subpœna to be awarded against the defendant.

Margaret Braynes, Myles and Gardiner had meanwhile brought a cross-suit against the Burbages, and in that, on 21st May, 1590,[3] the Court was informed that the defendants had

---

[1] Chancery Proceedings, Series II, 222/85
[2] Ch. Proc. Dec. and Orders, A. Book, 454, 22nd Feb. 1588–9.
[3] Ibid. 610, 1590.

put in an insufficient demurrer, and it is also referred to Mr. Dr. Carew for consideration.   This came up again [1] next Trinity Term, and on 4th November Mrs. Braynes appeals again [2] through Mr. Scott for the moietie of the Theatre and other tenements, as she and her husband had been at very great charges for the building thereof, to the sum of £500, and did for a time enjoy the moietie.   It is ordered that if the defendants (that is now the Burbages) do not show good cause, sequestration of the moietie shall be granted.   On 13th November 1590,[3] Mr. Sergeant Harrys for Burbage, prayed consideration of a former order made in his behalf in the suit of Burbage v. Braynes.   Sequestration was stayed.   This seemed to promise peace : but on 20th January, 1590–1,[4] Robert Myles made oath that the Burbages had broken an order made in court on November 13th ; therefore an attachment was awarded for contempt of court.   On 30th January [5] Cuthbert Burbage made his appearance in person to save his bond to the Sheriff of London, and nothing further was done on that count at the time.   On 23rd March,[6] it was stated in court that the Burbages had been examined upon interrogations and that these had been committed to the consideration of Mr. Dr. Cæsar.

On 24th April, 1591,[7] Burbage continued his suit against Mrs. Braynes, she having put in an insufficient demurrer, and consideration was referred to Mr. Dr. Carew.   On June 15th,[8] as nothing material had been advanced on her side, Burbage asked for a subpœna against her and Myles.

On 20th July [9] Margaret appeared to follow her own case against Cuthbert and James Burbage ; they also appeared, but the Master in Charge could not attend.   On 12th October,

---

[1] Ch. Proc. Dec. and Orders, A. Book, 15, 1590.
[2] Ibid. 109, 1590.   [3] Ibid. 145, 1590.
[4] Ibid. 270, 1590–1.   [5] Ibid. 317, 1590–1.
[6] Ibid. 456, 1590–1.   [7] Ibid. 493, 1591.
[8] Ibid. f 720, 1591.   [9] Ibid. 818, 1591.

1591,[1] it was decided that no advantage should be given until it was found whether Burbage had or had not committed contempt of court ; and on 13th November [2] this question was heard again.   It had been referred to Mr. Dr. Stanhope and Mr. Dr. Legg, who had heard counsel on both sides, but they declared they could not proceed to examine the parties before they examined John Hyde of London, grocer, Ralph Myles of London, soapmaker, Nicholas Bishop and John Allen, upon the contempt pretended.

The need of considering these witnesses arose through Burbage's having in 1579 mortgaged the Theatre to John Hyde, who, after holding the mortgage for ten years had released it in 1589 to Cuthbert Burbage, not to James.   Whether this happened because Cuthbert had paid off the loans, or whether it had been arranged so for further protection of James, does not clearly appear.   At some date, following his brother-in-law's lead, James had transferred all his property to his sons (a King Lear who was not made to repent the deed).   Probably in an attempt at pacification, the " George Inn " had been leased to Robert Myles ; and Myles had let the stables and some of the rooms to his son Ralph,[3] and his follower, Nicholas Bishop, for a soap factory.

The plague caused a lull in the Chancery proceedings, but they started again.   Latterly Margaret Braynes either tired or died, and her name disappears from the Chancery proceedings. But Robert Myles continued *versus* Burbage, and Burbage *versus* Myles, and the litigation went on till he died.

Delay was the next best thing for him to winning his case. But only think of the wear and tear of the proceedings, the money, time, strength and brain-power, spent in litigation, and the hindrance to Burbage's full success.   I thought it was wiser to finish talking about this case, because it would have been a source of constant interruption to writer and reader alike

---

[1] Ch. Proc. Dec. and Orders, A. Book, 16, 1591.
[2] Ibid. 151, 1591.
[3] Chancery Proceedings, 2nd Series, 245–85, Myles *v.* Bishop.

(as it was to Burbage) if it had been allowed constantly to crop up in pages devoted to other details.

On 23rd November, 1588, the Corporation moved the Privy Council to suppress plays and interludes within the City and the Liberties (Repertory 21, f. 203b). " The Theatre " came back to its builder in 1589, through his son Cuthbert. Meanwhile Burbage had other troubles. It may be remembered (see p. 34) that in 1581 Edmund Peckham had brought a suit against Giles Alleyn for the possession of Holywell. He had found a jury to agree with him, and had shortly after died, leaving his son George a minor. On 9th June, 1589,[1] Richard Kingsmill, Attorney-General to the Court of Wards and Liveries, sued in that court an *information* of what he took to be the situation on behalf of George Peckham, a minor and a Royal Ward, and also on behalf of the Queen as guardian, and Chief Lord. Again there were emissaries from Court, trying to effect an entrance on the premises occupied by James Burbage, which must seriously have annoyed him and troubled him at times, and are indeed mentioned as one of the causes of non-payment of rent, and the absence of things to distrain, complained of by Giles Alleyn.

There were constantly minor interferences and inhibitions and checks, but in that same year of 1589 their troubles entered on a new phase. Some of the players having interfered in the Martin Marprelate controversy, Burghley authorized Tilney, Master of the Revels, to command all players and playmakers to appear before him, and hand in the play-books they had in readiness, in order that anything tending to immorality or sedition should be reformed.

This would involve a considerable amount of trouble, and some expense ; the " reforming of plays " at first would probably be to the humiliation of the poet, and the confusion of the player. But it would have a good effect upon the future of the drama, for it would force poets and managers alike to be

[1] Pleadings, Court of Wards and Liveries. See Note VIII.

careful as to what was written and what was performed. It also gave some check to the impromptu and audacious sallies of the players themselves, who often brought authors into trouble. It is comforting to know from later authorities that Richard Burbage was " never scurrilous."

It may be asked, why I am so long in introducing Shake-speare.? The answer is, we have no stage record of him up to this date. Whatever great thing Shakespeare was, he was *not* a *pioneer*. He waited until a stage was made ready for him on which to act, and until crowding suggestions from previous plays would stimulate his receptive imagination.

We know but little of him from other sources. I absolutely refuse to believe any of the so-called " traditions " which have come down to us (for none of them can be proved to have been recorded in times even nearly contemporary), especially about the cause of his leaving Stratford-on-Avon and coming to London. That he should have fled for fear of a whipping, is, on the face of it, too absurd to be even discussed by those who know the customs of the period.

That he fled to escape the normal consequences of stealing Sir Thomas Lucy's deer, I have dealt with in " The Fort-nightly," February, 1903, showing that Sir Thomas Lucy had no park then to steal deer from, etc. He came to London because he had been bred to no trade, his father having ex-pected him to become a little farmer on his mother's inherit-ance of Asbies. When that was seized by his uncle Edmund Lambert, he did not know what to do with himself. But as he had a family to keep, he must do something, and he came to London with hopes of something turning up for him, perhaps even at court. There had been two Shakespeares there before him, Roger and Thomas, the one in Mary's reign, the other in Elizabeth's.[1] If he did consciously bend his steps towards that bourne he fulfilled his desire before he died, though not in the way he planned.

His father and mother and he had found John Lambert even

[1] See my paper, "Shakespeare of the Court," "Athenæum," 12th March, 1910.

harder to deal with than his father Edmund.   They had showed
him how and why he should restore Asbies to them on their
paying the mortgage, and failing that, why it should be treated
as an ordinary and honourable sale, in which the purchase-money
paid was much below the value of the property bought.   They
asked £20 more for it, and John Lambert had seemed to them
to yield and then had ignored the arrangement.   My theory of
the cause of Shakespeare's advent in London at a particular
date is one which has never been suggested by any other.   It is
that he came up personally to press the lawsuit his father and
mother and he were bringing against John Lambert.   He was
the prospective heir, and nothing could be done without his
signature; they had had to wait till he came of age before even
discussing it.   But after the delays in Stratford and in London,
that suit came to the hearing, but not to the decision, in the
Queen's Bench in Mich. term 1589.   In the draft of that case
then, appears the first mention of " William Shakespeare " in
London.   Having come, he probably remained, dangling about
the law-courts in the intervals of seeking something to do.
He would probably live with his friend, Richard Field, and
read the precious volumes in his shop which leave their traces
in his plays, waiting, waiting, waiting.[1]   And when all his bright
hopes faded one after another, the Theatre, which he would
have been sure to have frequented as a solace and recreation,
would become the means of opening to him a way of earning his
daily bread, which, if humiliating to his pride,[2] yet came easily
to his intelligence, and was ready for his entrance.   If it be true,
as has been suggested by others, that James Burbage was a
Warwickshire man, that might have given a reason for the
Stratford man wishing to join him, or it may only have been
that Burbage was the best manager going.

Shakespeare was a little old to begin to learn the art of playing, and he would need to content himself at first with being an
apprentice or servitor while he learned, and to take very inferior

[1] See my " Shakespeare's Warwickshire Contemporaries," chap. i.
Richard Field.   [2] See Sonnet CXI.

parts. The good actors around him would soon inspire him, and once admitted his progress would be rapid. And again, having been prepared by his life's experience, and by that wonderful bookseller's shop in Blackfriars, he began to read the players' " books," to criticize them, to see their faults, and to *correct* them all, and to remake some altogether. And thus we may take it, Burbage had the high honour of discovering Shakespeare at the critical moment of his life, of securing him, of giving him his life's chance, and us the heritage of his genius. Probably he added to his kindness a temporary home in Holywell Street.

The first notice of Shakespeare is written by an enemy and is all the more valuable. It tells us a great deal in a few words. They are known to all scholars, but in case any one has forgotten, I give them here. Poor, dying, grumbling Robert Greene, brought out as his last words his " Groat's worth of wit," 1592. He was warning some of his fellow-scholars (among them Nash) not to waste more time in writing for the players, they were false, ungrateful, jealous, and now one of them was trying to ape the poets, and " thinks himself able to bumbast out a blank verse as well as the best of you.

" Young Juvenal, that biting satyrist, and those no less deserving than the other two. . . . Base-minded men all three [1] of you, if by my misery ye be not warned ; for unto none of you (like me) sought those burres to cleave, those Puppits (I meane) that speak from our mouthes, those anticks garnished in our colours. Is it strange that I, to whom they all have been beholding, shall (were ye in that case that I am now) be both at once of them forsaken ? Yes, trust them not ; for there is an upstart crow, beautified with our feathers, that with his *Tiger's heart Wrapt in a Player's hide*,[2] supposes he is as

[1] Marlowe, Lodge and Nash.

[2] " Oh, Tiger's heart wrapt in a Woman's hide," " King Henry VI," part 3. Probably Marlowe and Greene were part authors of the two parts of the Contention, and " the true tragedie," on which Henry VI was built.

well able to bumbast out a blanke verse as the best of you; and being an absolute Johannes Factotum, he is in his own conceit the only Shakescene in a countrie. Oh that I might entreate your rare wits to be employed in more profitable courses; and let these Apes imitate your past excellence, and never more acquaint them with your admired inventions. . . . Whilst you may, seeke you better maisters, for it is pittie men of such rare wits should be subject to the pleasures of such rude groomes."

This shows, to me at least, conclusively that Shakespeare was by this time a recognized actor, and that he, the first actor recorded to have done so, had before this time critically begun to improve upon their poets' plays.

He must have already become acquainted with the Earl of Southampton, through whose inspiration he was writing his first poem then, and, I believe, the earlier sonnets. It was the custom of the times for the young noblemen who sat in " The Lord's Rooms " at the Theatre, to be patronizingly friendly to the players. It must not be forgotten in the making of the man that the Theatre, maligned as it was by the Corporation then, was an academy of the fine arts to a certain degree, of elocution, language, dancing, deportment, manners, *jeux d'esprit*; that the painstaking rehearsals before the ageing James Burbage, would be supplemented by the critical censorship of the upper class audience, who would be too pleased to check a blunder or a gaucherie in the stories of a court, and who would delight in whispering the first rumours of a scandal about to come out, and thereby bring their protégés often into hot water for making fun of it on the stage in impromptu waggery. With such polishing, the susceptible inland-bred youth soon learned to speak and act as to the manner born, a fact which is witnessed to even by the poets of his time. He had the advantage, too, of acting with Richard Burbage, who had been trained as an actor from his youth, and had apparently been prepared by the " Divinity that shaped his ends," to be his mouthpiece in his later creations. It may also be taken as an advantage for Shakespeare that he came fresh from all the legal formalities of the land-transfers [1] among the members of his family, with the fortunes of his own lawsuit constantly running in his head, to a family where legal questions were of daily and absorbing interest. The Baconians scornfully ask us, where could Shakespeare learn his law? I answer, *Those who study Shakespeare's life faithfully and intelligently find no difficulty in answering that question.*

About this time a new rival playhouse started on Bankside, in the Rose, where Henslowe and Alleyn reigned. Just then, in 1592, their old enemy the plague came down on the people and the players, the plague, and inhibitions, and starvation threatened but for the manager's chest. Yet it was through the gloomy experiences of the plague year, that Shakespeare wrote the light and sunshiny poem of " Venus and Adonis," a classical translation, based on the new edition of " Ovid " which had lately been brought out by Vautrollier and Field, a poem by which he became enrolled as a Spenserian *poet*, a much higher thing to his contemporaries than a play-actor or even a play-maker. To the making of it what went? The readings in Field's shop (there were many poetic translations at the time)—there was Puttenham's Art of English Poesie, a book that gave rules for criticism on the method of the poet's art, reasons for the use of blank verse in the drama instead of the old " jigging lines "; there were other books and manuscripts awaiting him at Southampton house,[2] where an enthusiastic young noble had discovered something in the player and tried to urge him on to better things; and there was somebody behind the scenes, was it Lady Southampton, or her friend Sir William Harvey, who had urged Will to use his influence to get the Earl safely married to Burleigh's granddaughter, and out of the danger of Burleigh's displeasure. He had tried his

---

[1] See my " Shakespeare's Aunts and Snitterfield "—" **Athenaeum**," July 24, 1909.

[2] See my edition of the Sonnets, King's **Classics**, **Preface**. Chatto and Windus.

" pupil pen " in the early sonnets, speaking against his will for his patron's good, and now he wrote a poem to dedicate to that patron.   It illustrates his position, a heart too busy with other things to be moved by the pleadings of love, even of its Queen.

> " Describe Adonis and the counterfeit
> Is poorly imitated after you."

On 18th April, 1593, " Richard Field entered for his copie under the hands of the Archbishop of Canterbury and Master Warden Stirrup, a booke intituled Venus and Adonis v*d*."   The printing and publication would take some months, it is true, but it came out within the year.   The first heir of his invention took the literary world by storm, and surprised both the poet and his patron.   It raised the status of the poet among his fellow-players, and they heard of him at court.   What then ? He was still working, still writing, he was keeping his word about that " graver labour " he had promised to do for the honour of the young nobleman who had been so kind to him. Kinder than he had expected far, so when he wrote the dedication of his new poem in the following year, it was to no far off patron now, but to one who had made himself—

" Lord of my love."

Is this not an echo of the 26th Sonnet ; which well read as an accompanying private dedication ?

> " Lord of my love to whom in vassalage
> Thy merit hath my duty strongly knit,
> To thee I send this written embassage
> To witness duty, not to show my wit ! "

In the spring of 1594 the " Rape of Lucrece " was entered in the Stationer's Register ; it would likely be published ready for October when his friend attained his majority, and became free from the leading strings and match-makings of Lord Burleigh, free also, as soon as it might be arranged, from the trammels of the Queen's guardianship in money matters.   He could marry whom he pleased now, and when he pleased, or he could remain one of the Queen's bachelors like Fulke Greville, which he would have done awhile had he been wise.

Shakespeare's new poem is the reverse of the picture in the first. The theme is no longer chastity through indifference to temptation, but the fierce chastity which makes itself essential to the completeness of moral being.

In the same month as the completion of his " graver labour " is dated for us, his patron's mother, Mary Countess of Southampton, married Sir Thomas Henneage, Treasurer of the Privy Chamber, a trusted friend of the Queen, and a patron of poetry himself. It is quite probable they had a play at their marriage-feast, as the city " orders " imply it was usual to have. And if they had a play who so likely to write it as their son's protegé ; and what play was he so likely to write for the occasion as " The Midsummer's Night's Dream," a story laden with remembrances for all who had been at the Kenilworth festivities, as both bride and bridgroom had been, and probably many of their guest ? sThe wedding of Theseus and Hippolyta was a classic story harmonious enough to lead it off ; the love stories of Athens, if we knew more, we might find to have been associated with contemporary life ; the delicate compliment to Elizabeth (written before Shakespeare's heart had been embittered against her) showed the poet's tact. She was probably present. The Fairy scenes, the very coinage of Shakespeare's brain, were from Warwickshire, where Shakespeare knew their haunts, and the poet's romantic feeling had been called forth, like Laneham's, by the unforgettable charms of the Lady of the Lake at Kenilworth. The inimitable humours of Bottom the weaver, or the artisan performance, original to Shakespeare, was fitted into the frame, as a rustic desire to please the Queen, just as the Warwickshire men had tried to do in 1575. And here may I be allowed to romance a little. It is not at all improbable that this little play was grafted upon early memories of James Burbage, in some of his wanderings. But it came to performance in his later years, when he had probably retired from active service. Did he appear on this occasion ? Was it a little bit of good-humoured raillery, that Snug *the joiner*, in Bottom's play, was given the *Lion's part*, who had nothing to do now but *to roar ?*

Early in that year Fleetwood, the Recorder of London, had died. He was remembered by Wood in his " Athenæ Oxonienses " with praise ; also by an epigrammatist who said,

" He was the enemy of all poor players."

When Shakespeare did play at court that Christmas on the 26th and 28th December, the first recorded occasion in which his name is used at court,[1] in two plays, neither of which are named, was one of them " The Midsummer Night's Dream " ? I have shown fully elsewhere my reasons for believing that the other performed on 28th December, 1594, was the " Comedy of Errors " [2] *in the afternoon* at Greenwich, as that was the one performed by the " common players " at the Gray's Inn Revels that night, which was ever afterwards called " The night of Errors." It was considered the crowning disgrace of Gray's Inn until Bacon took away that disgrace a fortnight later, by presenting triumphantly his " Divers Plots and Devices." That was the first form of the Bacon-Shakespeare question, which may be studied with advantage still, as it gives a clear illustration of the distinctions between the authors. His fellow-students then preferred Bacon's " Divers Plots " ; we moderns prefer Shakespeare's " Errors " to Bacon's perfections ; and delight in realizing the pictures in Gray's Inn Hall on the two evenings.

James Burbage by this time had seen some of his conceptions realized, and his credit assured among the better sort, as well as his popularity among " the baser sort." There seems to have been about this time a temporary relaxation of Cor-

---

[1] " To William Kempe, William Shakespeare, and Richard Burbage, servants to the Lord Chamberlayne . . . for two several comedies shewed by them . . . on St. Stephen's daye and Innocent's Daye . . £20." at Greenwich, Dec. Acc., Treas. Cham., Pipe Office, 542, 2076.

[2] Shakespeare Jahrbuch, 1895. " The first official record of Shakespeare's name."

poration interference. He appears to have had a happy home, where all his family co-operated harmoniously with him. But trouble was never far away from him and there were jagged rocks ahead in the stream of his life.

There was still the unsigned extension of lease haunting him, and undefined possibilities of loss associated therewith. He had doubtless at times been handicapped by the proximity of his rival, " The Curtain " (unless he had managed, by some astute arrangement, to get some share in that for himself). But as I have said, there is no record of the business of " The Curtain," as it escaped all the lawsuits which might have told us somewhat. Before Burbage's mind must already have loomed large the consequences of an ejection order, and a forced removal. Where should he go ? In the Liberty of Bankside there was the Rose[1] in which Henslowe reigned ; and to which Edward Alleyn's attractions drew every one. Henslowe and his son-in-law had been as fortunate and their lives had been made as easy, as Burbage's had been made difficult for him. They were quite friendly where they were, but they might not be so friendly if he were to plant himself down by their side, and try to share their gains, as " The Curtain " had done to him. Besides, he heard the rumour that the rich Francis Langley, Alnager of Cloth, meant to build a playing-house on Bankside, which should eclipse in grandeur all that had hitherto been reared. He was rich enough to buy the land, to do without any interfering and hindering partners, he had influence beyond any that Burbage could command, and the founder of the Theatre doubtless made up his mind then, that though South-

---

[1] A property transfer on Bankside shows the site of a previous " Rose," whence the name was probably borrowed. John Payne lets the capital messuage and tenements called the Barge, the Bell and the Cocke, etc., " lying between the King's highway next the water of Thames on the north, against a tenement called the Rose on the other side, and a tenement sometimes the Lady Stratfords on the west side and against Maiden Lane on the south." 1st Aug., 24 Eliz. Eg. MSS., 2,623.

wark might support *two* theatres, there would be little chance for *a third*.   I have found a good deal of *new* matter concerning Francis Langley, which will be fitted into its place.   Mr. E. K. Chambers says " there is no proof the Swan was built before 1598."   But it must have been built by 1595.   The Lord Mayor wrote to the Lord Treasurer on 3rd November, 1594, that Francis Langley, one of the Alnagers for the sealing of cloth, intended to erect a new stage or theatre on Bankside, and praying that the same might be prevented on account of the evils likely to arise therefrom (" Remembrancia," ii. 73).

Nobody has noted that Langley went over to Shoreditch for a wife.   On 15th January, 1594–5, he married Hester Saule in St. Leonard's Church there, " with a Bp. Cant. Licence." Then he started building his theatre.   When he was at it, he was not going to be niggardly in the matter of size or of decorations.   That is the reason that John de Witt in a visit to London in 1596 describes the new theatre.[1]   He said there were four large and splendid playhouses in London, the Theatre and Curtain towards the north, the Rose and the Swan towards the south.   He estimated the latter as able to hold 3,000 spectators, and gives a sketch of it, which is a most valuable help towards understanding the stage of the time.   These notes had been long buried in the Library of Utrecht.   Dr. Gaedertz discovered them, published them, lent the MS. to Dr. Furnivall and the New Shakespeare Society, who printed a pamphlet and reproduced the drawing.[2]

Three thousand was a large estimate for one theatre in a relatively small-sized city such as London then was.

But we have many proofs that in the lesser London of the day, there was a much greater proportion of theatre-goers. When in later years new threats were made to pull down the Surrey theatres, the watermen of London brought in a petition for them, because they reckoned the chief part of their business arose from carrying theatre-goers over the water.   " The

[1] *The Times*, 11th May, 1888.
[2] New Shakespeare Society publications, Mr. H. B. Wheatley.

Swan " was not doomed to be very successful or long-living, in spite of its richness of adornment.

One little incident, hitherto unknown, hit Langley hard in 1597. He had arranged with the Earl of Pembroke's company to play for a year in his house, when an inhibition closed all the theatres because of the plague. When this was lifted, the players took out a new patent to play, but Langley did not take out a licence for his house, as he should have done. They reproached him for this and said that if he did not take out a licence for his house, they would have to go and play for Henslowe at the " Rose." He bid them " go," apparently in derision, they went and there they stayed and joined the Admiral's company under Henslowe's management. Hence a lawsuit, which gives the story (see Note XI).

The rising of the Swan seemed a signal to James Burbage to keep away from Bankside. So he turned his attention to a very different Liberty ; not one that held all the off-scourings of the city, as Bankside was said to do, nor one that had all the disadvantages of Holywell, but a real Royal Liberty, among aristocrats and well-to-do respectable people, many of them of the Court, Blackfriars. For this, originally built outside the walls, had been later enclosed within the walls of the city, yet was not of the city. After the dissolution it had become Crown lands. Though disposed of to tenants in chief, the Crown remained Chief Lord. Battles royal had been fought between the Court and the City over various rights in Blackfriars, and more were to be fought. But James Burbage imagined that he had reckoned all round, and preferred a better-class neighbourhood where, he thought, there would be less danger of those disturbances which had so often injured him. He would be nearer the Privy Council than the Common Council—nearer a cultured class, and nearer supervision of Royal authority, which he never shunned. So he decided to risk the chances and try his second venture in the Liberty of Blackfriars. He thought himself fortunate to be able to buy for £600 from Sir William More of Loseley, on February 4th, 1595–6,

a suite of rooms, which he saw might be modelled into another
style of theatre, more after the Court fashion, with safe roofs
over-head to protect from all weathers. It was to be independent of daylight, too, for it would be artificially lighted. He
hoped to draw an audience from the neighbourhood, who were
not forced to get home before dark. Into this work he put his
soul and his " invention." He wanted it ready before the Holywell lease should have completely run out, that he might be
able to transplant his company of brilliant players at once,
without a forced interval of unemployment, and with no
future fear of being turned out by a grasping landlord. His
property would necessitate a good deal of rebuilding to fit it for
his purpose, stone and lime for walls and pillars, and wood for
stage, benches and boxes. Decorations, too, must have been
new instead of being carried from the Theatre. He seems to
have made for himself a temporary home there, to have been
his own clerk of works, because there, according to Mr. Collier,
he lost a daughter Helen, buried at St. Annes, Blackfriars,
13th December, 1595.

An evil omen, as well as a heart-wound, he would take it.

But an even more evil omen was the death of his master, the
Lord Chamberlain, Henry Carey, Lord Hunsdon, on 23rd July,
1596. His son succeeded to the title, and to him James Bur-
bage transferred his company's allegiance. But the new Lord
Hunsdon was neither so cordial nor so powerful as his father,
and the Queen did not make him, at the time at least, Lord
Chamberlain. She put another man in his father's place, Lord
Cobham who was no friend to Lord Hunsdon's players. Lord
Cobham did not like the character given to ' Sir John Oldcastle,'
after changed to ' Falstaff.'

James Burbage's heart sank within him. Already the Corporation were making things very difficult for him. It was
easier to do so when his " master " was not a Court official.
The Earl of Essex, also a friend to players, was abroad.

Nash, the dramatist, wrote in 1596 :—

" The Players . . . are piteously persecuted by the Lord

Mayor and the Aldermen, and however in their old Lord's time they thought their estate settled it is now so uncertain they cannot build upon it " (Grosart's " Nash," I. lxi.).

He knew that Myles was meditating more mischief in the law-courts, that Giles Alleyn meant to trick him in Holywell, but it was a woman who led the unexpected attack at Blackfriars. The Dowager Lady Elizabeth Russell did not like the notion of the fashionable district of Blackfriars becoming contaminated by the evils she had heard surrounded the public theatres in the Liberties. She bestirred herself to collect signatures for a petition to the Privy Council against the plans of Burbage. She does not seem to have found very *many* of her own class to sign this, but she found, and persuaded somehow, the most important man, Lord Hunsdon, the " Master " of James Burbage and his company. He must have groaned in spirit when he heard that name. The other petitioners were chiefly insignificant men, except *one*, Richard Field, the printer, the publisher of " Venus and Adonis," and " Lucrece." His name in that list must have hit Shakespeare hard. It was " Et tu Brute," with him then. The petition is undated and many writers seemed to think it had no effect. But a later petition in 1618–9 to the Lord Mayor refers to it as having been presented in November, 1596, and as having been successful in staying the public theatre there and then.

Collier produces a forged counter petition of the players, which is preserved at the Record Office, though the dates it gives convict themselves of being impossible. Burbage knew, of course, nothing of *that*. Battered, bruised and beaten in the development of his second idea, James Burbage, the first builder of theatres in stone as he had been the first builder of theatres in wood, at last yielded to Fate. He had spent a life of incessant toil, constantly thwarted and handicapped in all his undertakings. But though less successful than he meant they should be, he had been enabled to do through them more for the British Stage than all the other actor-managers put together. He was not young then, his body was not equal in

F

bravery to his soul, and just a year after he had bought his Blackfriars property,[1] he lay down to rest.   He was buried at St. Leonard's, Shoreditch, probably in the churchyard, on 2nd February, 1596–7, just six weeks before the termination of the Holywell lease.

Oh ! Brave James Burbage !

[1] From a letter among the Loseley papers written by Lord Hunsdon, Lord Chamberlain, to Sir William More 9 Jan. 1595–6 we may see that he wished to purchase this for himself.   This must have caused some friction between him and his "servant."

CHAPTER II

JAMES BURBAGE'S SONS

CUTHBERT and Richard Burbage entered on a critical
year. The fame of Richard had been spreading, and
the dramas of their poet Shakespeare had redounded to their
credit, as well as to his own. The loss of their father was not
only a domestic affliction, it was the loss of the captain of their
ship on a stormy sea. They succeeded to his *Ideas*, and to
their results, but the constant difficulties and oppositions he
had endured seemed also entailed upon them. James Burbage left no will. Cuthbert, as we have seen, had become owner
of the Theatre in 1589. The Blackfriars James had bought
and altered for Richard, and had apparently given it to him
during life. It was of more value than the Theatre even in its
present peril. But apparently the brothers harmoniously
shared their business properties amicably and equally. They
allowed their mother Ellen to take out letters of administration, and apparently there was little to administer save the
furniture and goods at Holywell Street, as Giles Alleyn implies
in later litigation. They cared for their father's family as well
as their own and Cuthbert stayed on in his father's house, the
larger of the two homes. Both seemed to have married their
wives in another parish as there is no entry in St. Leonard's
regarding either, and Cuthbert, at least, had children by this
time.

There must have been a good deal of hard thinking done in
Holywell at that time. By 25th March or by 13th April, as
they chose to read it, there was the end of their lease to grapple
with. Neither of the proposed new leases of 1585–6 had been

signed, but as Cuthbert did not know what else to do, he stayed on, paying rent quarterly as usual. No one has suggested the reason of Giles Alleyn's unwonted placidity at this crisis.

It was because a new law-suit had been started against him, and he wanted Cuthbert Burbage to act as a buffer to him, and to save him coming up too often from his home at Haseley in Essex. It was a foolish and unfounded suit, but he knew he could not hope to get a new tenant to the property till it was settled, he knew that no one was so likely to have it so favour-ably settled as Cuthbert Burbage. The Earl of Rutland, his nearest neighbour, had claimed the close on which the Theatre was built, and had given his tenants leave to enter it and enclose part. Cuthbert naturally objected, and Alleyn induced him to sue the aggressors, Powell, Ames and Robinson, in the King's Bench ; so that the owner might rest at Haseley in peace.

The Earl of Rutland was a minor, and beyond the seas, knowing nothing about it. It was a scheme of Thomas Scriven, his steward. But Giles Alleyn well knew that the young nobleman was friendly with the Earl of Southampton, Shake-speare's patron, with the Burbages themselves indeed, and he was more likely to get out of the business easily if Cuthbert had it in hand, than if he himself appeared, or got a new tenant to make a timid and uncertain protest. So Giles Alleyn took Cuthbert's proffered rent and said nothing and each of them waited, warily watching the other.

One comfort the brothers had—their master, Lord Hunsdon, was appointed Lord Chamberlain on 17th March, 1596–7, so once again theirs became " the Lord Chamberlain's company."

In the summer Cuthbert Burbage lost his son, " James Burbage, son of Cuthbert Burbage, buried 15th July, 1597, Halliwell." The small namesake of his grandfather died at a saddening season. Hardly had his father Cuthbert returned from his burial in St. Leonard's than he had to face a cloud-burst.

It was not because that year, 39 Eliz., the Statute against

Rogues, Vagabonds, and sturdy beggars was confirmed and strengthened.

But a letter written by the Lord Mayor on 28th July, 1597, found a new cause of complaint against the theatre. " Divers apprentices and other servantes, who have confessed unto us that the saide Staige-playes were the very places of their randevous appointed by them to meete with such others as wear to joigne with them in their designes and mutinus attemptes, beinge allso the ordinarye places for maisterles men to come together to recreate themselves," so they pray for " the present staie and fynall suppressinge of the saide stage-playes as well at the Theatre, Curten and Banckside, as in all other places in and about the City."[1]

The Privy Council on the same day wrote to the Justices of Middlesex, " Her Majestie being informed that there are verie greate disorders committed in the common playhouses, both by lewd matters that are handled on the stages, and by resorte and confluence of bad people, hath given directions that not onelie no plaies shal be used within London or about the Citty, or in any publique place, during this tyme of sommer, but that also those playhouses that are erected and built only for suche purposes shal be plucked downe namelie the Curtayne and the Theatre nere to Shoreditch, or any other within that county ; theis are therfore in her Majestie's name to chardge and command you that you take present order ther be no more plaies used in any publique place within three myles of the Citty untill All-halloutide next, and likewise that you do send for the owner of the Curtayne Theatre, Theatre or anie other common playehowse, and enjoin them by vertue hereof forth-with to plucke downe quite the stages, galleries and roomes that are made for people to stand in, and so to deface the same as they maie not be ymploied agayne to such use ; which if they shall not speedily performe you shall advertyse us that order maie be taken to see the sam doon, according to her Majesties pleasure and commandment."

[1] " Remembrancia," p. 354.

It was a hard saying, for it meant that all James Burbage's life-work was to be destroyed without compensation, and all the means of support of the family taken from them.

Cuthbert seems to have found some means of postponing the destruction, probably by a "gratification" to some one in power. It does not seem however to have been used. A book, probably *written* in that year, but published as Guilpin's "Skialethia," in 1598, speaks of a character—

> "But see yonder, one
> Who, like the unfrequented Theater
> Walkes in dark silence and vast solitude."

This of course might only have referred to its appearance during the summer months of inhibition.

In February 1597–8, a seemingly contradictory order was issued that none but the servants of the Lord Admiral and the Lord Chamberlain were to be allowed to play, practically making them the Queen's two companies, instead of the defunct company entitled "The Queens."

In the 1598 edition of Stow's Survey he mentions Holywell, and the old priory long since pulled down, as a place "where many houses are built for the lodging of noblemen, of strangers born and other." He speaks of the Church of St. Leonard's, "and near thereunto two publique Houses for the acting and Shewe of Comedies, tragidies and Histories for recreation whereof one is called The Courtein, and the other the Theatre both standing on the Southwest side towards the Field." This was his last printed reference to The Theatre. His next edition came out without mentioning it, for it had departed long before to a better place.

In 1598 appeared another Book, where the Burbages had an "advertisement" of their wares, from an unexpected quarter. Francis Meres, Master of Arts in both Universities, and Professor of Rhetoric in Oxford, in his "Wit's Treasury," classed their poet Shakespeare among the greatest poets, and the greatest dramatists, and gave a long list of his admired plays.

This praise alone must somewhat discount the judgment of the railers at *the Theatre* and its audiences, amongst whom Meres must often have sat to hear the plays he praised. For play-books were not printed then, they lost value by publication, and many a complaint the players made about the wicked pirate printers.

A tragedy took place that year in Shoreditch which may have affected them somewhat. To understand it fully we must, as has never been done, go back to the story of a previous tragedy in the same place. In the Middlesex Sessions Roll it is recorded that at the Coroner's inquest taken at Holywell Street on 10th December, 39 Eliz., i.e. 1596, the body of a certain James Feake there slain was viewed, and it was stated that " a certain Gabriel Spenser, late of London, yeoman " and James Feake had been in the dwelling-house of Richard East, barber, in the said parish, on the 3rd day of December current, between the fifth and sixth hour of the afternoon, and insulting words had passed between them. James Feake had in his hand a candelabrum of copper, which he had intended to cast at Gabriel Spenser, wherefore the said Gabriel Spenser having a sword called a rapiour of iron and steel, of the price of 5s., in the scabbard, beat the said James Feake, and gave him a mortal wound " six inches deep and two inches wide on the face, between the pupil of the right eye called the ball of the eye and the eyebrows, penetrating to the brain, of which the aforesaid James Feake languished and lived in languor at Hallowell Street from the 3rd day of December until the 6th day, when he died." He was buried at St. Leonard's Church, 7th December, 1596. " Thus the aforesaid Gabriel Spenser then and there killed and slew the aforesaid James Feake in the manner aforesaid and no otherwise, nor in any other manner than is aforesaid the said James Feake came to his death." What amount of property Gabriel Spenser had is unknown ; and there is no record of his being condemned, or of reading his neck-verse and being branded in the thumb.[1] It is possible

---

[1] But that he was in trouble may be seen from Henslowe's Diary.

that the three days' delay in his victim's death helped him, and friendly witnesses and relatives might have said that James Feake had been provoking. But it is a witness to the quarrelsome disposition of the time, and also a proof of the fact that in spite of the statute against it, ordinary people did carry about with them weapons of warfare. Spenser was last mentioned in Henslowe's Diary on 19th May, 1598 (42. 24).

It was necessary to tell this story of Gabriel Spenser, one of Lord Pembroke's men, who transferred himself to the Lord Admiral's men, and left Langley for Henslowe on 11th October, 1597 (see Note XI) because of the remarkable manner in which Nemesis came to him in the following year.

There is a full account of it in Mr. Cordy Jeaffreson's book, p. xxxviii. On the 22nd September, 40 Eliz., there was, at the Middlesex Sessions a true bill found against Benjamin Johnson, late of London, yeoman, for killing Gabriel Spenser in the Fields [1] on the said day. G.D.R., 40 Eliz. " The said Ben Jonson with a certain sword of iron and steel called a Rapiour of the price of 3s. gave Gabriel Spenser on his right side a mortal wound of the depth of 6 inches and breadth of one inch, of which he then and there died." [2]   Johnson confessed the indictment at the gaol delivery in Old Bailey in October 1598. He was thrown into prison, and indicted by grand jury, and " arraigned " at the next gaol delivery. The indictment called him the aggressor, he afterwards stated that the quarrel was forced on him. He read his neck-verse, and was delivered according to the Statute, 18 Eliz., C. 7, after being branded in the thumb with the Tyburn " T." Mr. Cordy Jeaffreson says

---

The cause of his becoming connected with Henslowe is not mentioned, but I give it among my new authorities (Note XI). Henslowe however gives the date, " the 11th of October begane my Lord Admirals and my Lord Pembroke's men to play at my howsse " 1597. (27. 15).

[1] Hoggesdon or Hoxton Fields, in parish of St. Leonard.

[2] "Gabriel Spenser being slayne, was buryed the 24th of Sept., 1598, Register St. Leonard's, Shoreditch." There were many Spensers in Shoreditch, probably relatives.

that he must have had some chattels to be forfeited, or the clerk would have noted the fact against his name. Whether he really had his thumb branded is doubtful, it might have been done by a cold iron, or some of his friends at Court might have saved him. None of his enemies ever taunted him with it, not even Dekker.

In Jonson's Conversations with Drummond (" Shakespeare Society's Transactions," 1842, p. 8) he says, " being appealed to the field he had killed his adversarie who had hurt him in the arm, and whose sword was 10 inches longer than his, for the which he was imprisoned and almost at the gallows."

Henslowe was very angry at the loss of his man, as he wrote to his son-in-law about it. He let his spite out by calling Jonson " a Bricklayer " in recording the event.

He would naturally have nothing to do with Jonson's next play, which was offered to the Lord Chamberlain's men and was accepted, it has been said, through the influence of Shakespeare, who acted in it himself (see the printed list in Jonson's works).

The year 1598 as it approached its close, became darker and darker to the Burbages. Weightier matters than plays absorbed them. Poets were as plentiful as blackberries then, it was *theatres* which were scarce. They were suspicious of the mind of Giles Alleyn ; and their patrons had become weaker. The Earl of Southampton had lost favour with the Queen, for secretly marrying her maid of honour, Elizabeth Vernon, and reflected favour fades as the shining from the source of light pales. The Earl of Essex even was not in the same favour he used to be. Perhaps Giles Alleyn reckoned on that, he was sure he could reckon on the support of the Corporation in his plan to pull the Theatre finally down, as the Council had decreed, take possession of the material, and recoup himself for all the losses he fancied he had suffered. He would cut the Gordian knot of the contested lease, get rid of one he called " a troublesome tenant " and start with a new tenant. It is more than probable that he had got one in view at that time ; and he thought that the suit with the Earl of Rutland

might be quashed.   At any rate, he made up his mind to do
the deed, had engaged a party of " housebreakers " to join him
just after the Christmas holidays, on some day then to be fixed
by him.

But Cuthbert was too acute for him, and he lived among
friends who gave him warning.   He realized there was no
further chance of saving his Theatre, the most he could hope
for was the saving of its material.   He turned his eyes southward to the southern Liberty of Bankside.   There were already
two theatres there, but he had no choice.   He found a suitable
enough site near St. Saviour's Church, west of Dead Man's
Place and south of Maiden Lane, and he arranged with its owner,
Nicholas Brend, to take a long lease of it at £14 10s. a year rent,
to run from the December quarter, 1598.   I know that the
final concord was not signed till 21st February, 1598–9, but
as it expressly states that the lease was to commence from 25th
December, 1598, we may be sure that a *lease parole* had already
been assured by that time.   There would be some delay in
preparations for his desperate venture, but as soon as he could
he risked it.

One night after Christmas, on 28th December, 1598, he, with
an army of companions and workmen, under the direction of
Peter Street, a master carpenter, began hastily to tear down
his father's beloved *Idea*.

They did not find it so easy as they expected.   There had
been tale-tellers on both sides, and Alleyn's men, finding their
promised job about to be snatched from them, were there to
disturb, and trouble and hinder, and make an uproar.   It was
probably they who did most to destroy the grass valued afterwards in Alleyn's complaint at forty shillings.

We are accustomed to consider the players as the temporary
element, and " the House " as a comparatively stable one.   But
in this case the Lord Chamberlain's company moved, like the
snail, with their house on their back.   To tear it up was one
task, to remove it was another.   They would never dream of
taking it the easiest way, in a chain of lumbering waggons

across London Bridge. At night the gates there would be shut, at all times there were heavy tolls for " wheelage and passage," and they would lay themselves open to questions and delays at many points. I feel sure they would go by water, and that they would start from Peter Street's Wharf at Bridewell Stairs,[1] or at one engaged by him nearer, whence he probably wafted them by sailing barges at high tide to the other side. Removing the things down to the wharf must have been the hardest part of the work, and much must have been destroyed and probably much stolen in the transit. And when Cuthbert had succeeded in his herculean task of carrying away his dead Theatre to the other side, there it would lie, an unsightly pile of rubbish to the west of Dead Man's Place while the old year passed away and the New Year came in.

They played at Court that Christmas, in spite of their upturning on St. Steven's Day at night, on New Year's Day at night, and on Shrove Sondaye at night.[2] Think of it !

I know that the law-suits give two different dates for the event, the one as above on [3] 28th December, 1598, the other on 20th January, 1598–9.[4] Many have tried to account for this by reckoning two occasions of carrying away the material (I did so myself at one time). But now I believe that old Giles Alleyn *blundered in the date* at his first suit, and corrected it in his later one. He had not been present, he makes it a count in his complaint that Burbage had come " while he was away in the country." But he also says that he had begun his suit against Peter Street the Hilary Term ensuing, and after 20th January he would hardly have time for the processes.

A close study of all the pleadings convinces me that we may take the earlier date as the true one. It was more practicable

[1] Court of Requests, 91 (37), 29th Jan., 39 Eliz.
[2] Dec. Acc., Treas. Chamb., Audit Off. 387, 38.
[3] Star Chamber Proceedings, 44 Eliz. xii. 35, 1601, Alleyn and Burbage.
[4] Coram Rege Rolls, Trinity Term, 42 Eliz. R. 587, Alleyn *v.* Peter Street.

and prudent, it was covered by the date of Nicholas Brend's lease and it was *unexpected*. Quite probably the original plan had been made for 20th January when the "information" came. The Burbages were always short of money. We owe Alleyn a debt of gratitude for telling us of the mysterious friend who helped the transportation of the Theatre in many ways, in money particularly. This was a man called plain William Smith, who has never been noticed in this relation by anybody. But so important did Alleyn reckon him as a helper to Burbage that he included his name in his later "complaint" (Note XXI).

Who was William Smith ? I believe he must have been a player at some time or other, and one of the minor poets of the time, with the confusing initials W. S. (Stat. Reg.), "Amours by J. D., and certain other Sonnets by W. S.," suggest the trace of further details. At least, he then proved himself the friend in need. Another curious thing may be noted, that on 20th January, 1599, Giles Alleyn was drawing up his complaint, *in conjunction with Cuthbert*, against Ames and others, for trespass on his Holywell property (see Note XIII). It may be Cuthbert had withdrawn from it.

This incident of the Earl of Rutland's claim has not been thoroughly worked out by any one ; it bulks more largely in the story than has been estimated. Therefore I give some further details among the "Authorities."

The transportation of the Theatre was a great and novel conception heroically designed, and heroically executed through the dark night and cold grey dawn of midwinter. It cannot be imagined the work would be completed in one round of the clock. But scarcely less heroic than the transportation, would be the rebuilding. Every nerve would be strained to its utmost at the highest speed-limit. Fortune seemed willing to shine on such determined courage at last. The Burbages were not now working alone. They had associated five of their fellows in their enterprise, and practically turned their responsibility for the future of the new theatre into *a company*. We may read in that group the names of their chosen friends, and it is pleasant to know that Shakespeare was one of them. Cuthbert divided the liabilities and prospective profits into two parts, one of which he reserved for his brother Richard and himself in equal shares, because they always seem to have been held as owners of the house, the other to be divided into five equal shares for William Shakspeare, Augustine Phillipps, Thomas Pope, John Hemmings, and William Kempe, who shortly afterwards gave his share up to the other four.

Professor Wallace has found the exact proportions of the shares in the Record Office, which may be consulted independently, but which do not affect my story.[1] Where was William Smith? Peter Street did his best, Burbage did his best, the shareholders were eager, and money-lenders ready. Cuthbert put into the work material and probably all his own savings. At any rate, in a very short time, a much shorter time I imagine than is generally reckoned, a new theatre arose, like a Phœnix from the ashes of the old, and wise in his day and generation, Cuthbert changed its name. All the decrees were out against " The Theatre," and so " The Theatre " disappeared. They called it " The Globe "—was it because they had already heard " All the world's a stage," they did so, or was it from their figure of Hercules carrying the world on his back (as they had so lately done for their world) which adorned their new structure? Truly, as Hercules had done in fable, that they had done in reality; and " The Globe " it was called, and as " The Globe " it was known till the end. There Shakespeare was free to create and Richard Burbage to interpret his creations. Now it was North London (which had watched curiously its exodus) that could see afar its rising again phœnix-like from its ashes, and again it was its own advertisement. The hopes of the Thames watermen were radiant at the prospect. There

---

[1] See Prof. Wallace's " Shakespeare's money interest in the Globe Theatre," " Century Magazine," August, 1910. Also his article in " The Times," Oct. 2nd, 1909—on the Osteler-Hemming case; of which the original may be found in Coram Rege Rolls, Hilary term, 13 James I, 1454, R. 692.

were now three important theatres in Bankside beside the Bear Garden and minor shows.

But neither Henslowe nor Langley seemed to have any animus against the Burbages, at least there are no law-suits between them.   At last, for a time (too short, alas), Cuthbert breathed free from a law-suit.   Myles had given up harassing him after the death of his father, and he did not trouble himself much about the suit he had brought against Roger Ames, John Powell and Richard Robinson, because they had on 1st May, 1596, trespassed on the inner close of Cuthbert Burbage at Holywell, kept it in their own custody from the 1st May till 27th June, and destroyed grass to the amount of forty shillings.   For the close was no longer his even by tenancy, Giles Alleyn, whose interest he had been protecting,[1] had become his foe.   The young Earl had come of age and repudiated the suit and Thomas Scriven, his steward, was in a fix.   He had found that it was quite true that the Close belonged to the " Capital Mansion " but the Capital Mansion did not belong to the Earl of Rutland, but to Giles Alleyn.   The Earl's was a secondary mansion which an ancestor had leased from the Crown and *enlarged* for his own use.[2]

Whether Cuthbert gave himself any further trouble in the matter of Ames, Powell and Robinson, I know not, but in Easter term, 41 Eliz., 1599, Alleyn brought in the bill of complaint, of which he says he had given notice in Hilary term, against Peter Street in an action for trespass and other crimes in the Queen's Bench.   Of course all the expense and most of the trouble would fall on Cuthbert Burbage, not on his employé (who would, however, have trouble enough).   They had leave to " imparl the complaint until Friday next after the morrow of Trinity." [3]

---

[1] See Coram Rege Rolls, Trinity term, 38 Eliz.   Coram Rege Rolls Hilary term, 41 Eliz., R. 320 (see Note XIII).

[2] Exchequer Bills and Answers, Eliz., 369 (see Note XVIII). Exchequer Depositions, Eliz. No. 18, 44, 45 (see Note XIV).

[3] Coram Rege Rolls, Trinity term, 42 Eliz., R. 587 (see Note XVIII).

Alleyn charged Peter Street with coming on the 20th day of January with force and arms to break the close called The Inner Courtyard, formerly belonging to the disused Monastery of Holywell, now belonging to him and his wife. He trod down and consumed the grass, and did other enormities, in pulling to pieces and carrying away a building belonging to the said Giles Alleyn, called the Theatre, worth £700, and the damages, added to the loss, he reckoned at £800. Peter Street denied all wrong-doing except treading down the grass. He acknowledged that he took down and carried away the Theatre, but he acted only as the servant of Cuthbert Burbage, and Giles Alleyn ought not to maintain this action against *him*. But he gave all Burbage's story of the lease and following events, and sought judgment that Giles Alleyn should have no plea.

Giles Alleyn and his wife said that Peter Street's defence was insufficient in law and that they should have their plea. Peter Street said he was able to verify his statements. The Court did not think itself yet fully informed of the cause, and gave a day to both parties, on Thursday next before the Octaves of Michaelmas to plead before a jury.

It is curious to see that Alleyn should content himself with a charge of *trespass*.

But that date was further postponed by Cuthbert Burbage giving notice of a complaint against Giles Alleyn in the Court of Requests, to stay the suit that he had brought in the Queen's Bench. This was heard on 26th January, 42 Eliz., 1599–60, and seems to have been carefully heard. Giles Alleyn answered on 6th February, 42 Eliz. Cuthbert replied on 27th April, 1600. Not only is the whole story repeated here in comparatively simple English (the Coram Rege Rolls are in contracted Latin), and ordinary witnesses heard on 9th April, but a Royal Commission was appointed to hear formal depositions upon Interrogatories on 5th June, 1600. The depositions were taken at Kelvedon, Essex, for the convenience of Alleyn, on 14th August, 1600. There one Robert Vigerous, acquainted with both parties, on Giles Alleyn's side stated that " about four years past " he had drawn up a new lease of Holywell for James and Cuthbert Burbage, who offered to take the Theatre for a new term of ten years at £24 a year, and that he believed an offer of £100 as a consideration accompanied the draft of agreement.   The deponent had drawn it up himself, Cuthbert Burbage had come to his rooms (in the Temple at that time), paid him his fees, and promised him a satin doublet when the agreement was completed.   But he had never had that doublet.[1]

Thomas Neville, of Bricklesea, co. Essex, gent., gave a rather confused statement of the same events, adding that James Burbage had not paid £30 of his rent, and Cuthbert had promised to do so, with the other conditions about 2 *years ago*. But he evidently refers to *Giles Alleyn's lease*, which Cuthbert Burbage had always refused to sign.

Among the uncalendared proceedings of the Court of Requests, Eliz., Bundle 372, I found an imperfect book of " decrees and orders," and therein; under date 11th June, 42 Eliz., one which duly records the order for the *arrest of Giles Alleyn*, for contempt of court, which he describes so bitterly in his later Star Chamber Case (44 Eliz. xii. 35, see Note XXI), and this may be the cause of the delay between the appointment of the Commission on 5th June, and the depositions on 14th August. Poor old Giles Alleyn, he felt himself terribly discredited by having been sent for by a Royal messenger, and in his wrath he did not hesitate to charge Cuthbert with conspiracy, and the deputy registrar even with fraud over the order (ibid.).

We may note that in general Giles Alleyn's papers in his various suits were much *longer* than those of his opponents.   He brought in many irrelevant matters, and tried to prejudice the hearers by charging James Burbage with taking the Theatre from John Braynes, who had really built it, and with various other mal-practices.   However, the Court did not find for him but for Cuthbert Burbage, and ordered Giles Alleyn to stay his suit at the Common Law and to bring no other suits on this count.

[1] See Note XIX.

Halliwell-Phillipps states that the decision has not been preserved. I know that. But I find the fact recorded in Giles Alleyn's own later pleadings in the Star Chamber (see Note XXI), which Halliwell-Phillipps did not study. Nevertheless Alleyn is not afraid to bring a similar suit against " Cuthbert Burbage, in the custody of the Marshall," in Hilary term,[1] 43 Eliz., 1601, under another claim for a " *breach of covenant* " ; and it comes to hearing in Easter term, 44 Eliz. Cuthbert said they had no right to bring the case after the last decision ; Giles Alleyn and his wife said they had.

But they had overreached themselves in their eagerness. They had brought a suit against Cuthbert and Richard Burbage in the Star Chamber, on 23rd November, 44 Eliz., 1601, xii. 35. It is this suit, unstudied by Halliwell-Phillipps, which gives us the greatest amount of information. Giles Alleyn had thought that he saw a chance, now that the Essex conspiracy had thinned the ranks of the friends of the Globe company, when the players had even been touched themselves, of getting what he would call a " true bill " heard without influence being exerted against him. He first states the well-known preliminary arrangements, and adds that " the Theatre was erected at the cost not of Burbage but of Braynes to the value of 1,000 marks " ; gives as a reason why he could not sign the second lease, that the £200 had not been spent, and that the building had been assigned to John Hyde.

The lease was not signed, but Cuthbert remained on the premises after the expiry thereof, and therefore the right to the Theatre clearly remained to the landlord. He seeing that " great and grievous abuses grew by that said Theatre " meant to pull it down to relieve himself from his losses, and the breach of his covenants, and because James Burbage had made a deed of gift in his lifetime of all his goods and chattels to Cuthbert and Richard, who made their mother Ellen, " a very poor woman," administratix in order to *defraud him*. But Cuthbert

[1] The time the world was aghast at the trial of Essex, and the Globe Company excited over the examination of Augustine Phillipps.

"having intelligence of his purpose" unlawfully confederated
with Richard Burbage, Peter Street, and William Smith, and
removed it on and about 28th December, 41 Eliz., 1598.
Whereupon *he* (Giles Alleyn) in the Hilary term [1] following
commenced an action of trespass in the King's Bench, but Cuthbert "maliciously intending to vex and molest your subject,
in the Easter term [2] following, brought a complaint in the Court
of Requests to stay his suit, and he appeared and made answer
in the Trinity term [3] afterwards, 42 Eliz.   An order was published that the suit should be stayed till the cause in Equity was
heard—Michaelmas, 42 Eliz. [4]   Meanwhile, Cuthbert to "entrap your subject, did very maliciously and fraudulentlie"
confederate with John Maddox, his attorney, and Richard
Lane, the deputy registrar, "to draw up an order (which it did
not appertayne to him to do), thereby abusing your Highness'
Court and subject" that he should not draw up a demurrer.
Not knowing this, he drew up a demurrer, and went home to
the country, thinking everything would rest till the hearing of
the cause.   But on the last day of the term Cuthbert made oath
in court that he had broken order by making that demurrer,
and for supposed contempt of court, in the Vacation time was
fetched up to London by a pursuivant, "a man very aged and
unfitt to travell, to his excessive charges in journey and otherwise to his great discredit and disgrace among his neighbours."   He was there bound to Cuthbert Burbage in
£200 to appear at Michaelmas which he did and was discharged.   He had had several witnesses to appear *viva voce*
on his behalf.   But Cuthbert and Richard reviled them for
having spoken untruths and threatened to stab them if they
did it again.   "By which furious and unlawful threats your

---

[1] Hilary term from 23rd or 24th January till 12th or 13th February.

[2] From seventeen days after Easter Day, till four days after Ascension
Day.

[3] From Friday after Trinity Sunday till Wednesday a fortnight after.

[4] From 9th or 10th of October till 28th or 29th November.

said servant's witnesses were terrified and durst not testifie the truth on behalf of your subject." He said Cuthbert had maliciously bribed Richard Hudson and Thomas Osborne to commit perjury about the costs of £200 promised to be spent on repairs by James Burbage. " *By which unlawful practices your said subject did then lose his cause.*" Further, all the suits had been prosecuted against your subject by the " Malicious unlawful maintenance of William Smith," who spent money in acquiring illegal proof.

Giles Alleyn had excelled himself in vituperation this time. The charges were serious, and that against a deputy-registrar (so far as I know) unparalleled. The legal profession would prick up its ears.

The defendants said they had no reason to answer but they explained that Alleyn had, in the Hilary term, after the removal complained against Peter Street and Cuthbert Burbage, that Cuthbert had sued in Court of Requests against the unjust proceedings, that he knew he was in danger by Common Law, but that it was through Alleyn's own wrong and breach of covenant the second lease was not signed, that they had proved James Burbage *had fulfilled all* the conditions and Cuthbert had perfect right to remove the Theatre as had been agreed if conditions fulfilled. That the Court of Requests gave order on 18th October, 42 Eliz., that the suit at Common Law should be stayed, that Alleyn should never again be able to commence any other action for the same cause, and that Cuthbert could take his remedy at Common Law against Alleyn for not sealing the new lease. That if it had been true that Cuthbert had committed any *fraud* it might have been showed while the case was pending, and it would have been redressed. But Alleyn caused great scandal to Your Majesties Counsel to raise such a case again after such an order in another court.

On 12th June, 44 Eliz. (1602) Richard Lane indignantly repudiated any favour, or any forgery.

On 31st May, 41 Eliz., an order had been issued that the case should be heard on 5th June of next term, and that Alleyn should stay his suit and should be free to examine his witnesses till 2nd day of next term, that he (Richard Lane) had taken notes of the proceedings in his ordinary way, without partiality, and they were signed by some of her Majesty's Counsel, that Alleyn had slanderously and untruly charged Burbage, Maddox and himself with confederating to draw an order illegally, and that every part of Alleyn's bill was untrue.

On 17th June, 44 Eliz., Richard Hudson and Thomas Osborne said that *none* of the matters with which Giles Alleyn charged them were true and demurred against his bill being brought against them.   The Court therefore referred the case to the consideration of the right worshipful Francis Bacon, Esq., and "he reporteth that the said Bill is very uncertain and insufficient, and that *no further answer needeth to be made thereto.*"

Here at last I have found a real association of Francis Bacon with the Theatre, and I am glad to find he supported its owners and friends.   But it was only, as we have seen, in his *legal capacity*, not a poetic one at all.   This case, it may be seen by the dates, was running concurrently with Alleyn's second case at Common Law against Cuthbert Burbage for breach of covenant, which was brought in Hilary term, 43 Eliz., heard in Easter term, 44 Eliz., 1602, on the Quindene of Easter. Cuthbert had defended himself, Giles and Sara threw themselves on the country and demanded a jury—which was not named— and no decision was come to because this Star Chamber case decision of June 1602 covered the proceedings in that court, as well as in all others.

So, at last, by midsummer 1602, Cuthbert Burbage cast the millstone of Alleyn's law-suits from his neck.   The gall must have remained in him for long, for much trouble and anxiety had been spent, and much more money than would appear on the surface   It would be a little alleviation to him that Giles Alleyn would have to pay costs in both of the latter courts of Star Chamber, and King's Bench.   But it would not cover the losses to the family, or to the Globe Company, for the output and the actor Richard's time and strength must have been occupied considerably also. It is quite possible that Giles Alleyn might have tried to run another case somewhere on some pretext under the new King. But from the beginning of James' reign favour was shown to the Globe Company, their star was in the ascendant, and Giles Alleyn's had set for ever.

I thought it necessary to go on till this date with the law-suits, so as to get the story of *The Theatre* finished before I turned to other things.

We must go back to understand. By 28th December, 1598, we found that the Lord Chamberlain's company were homeless. With a beautiful theatre, "curtained and closed and warm," ready for their winter work, waiting them at Blackfriars, it must have been peculiarly galling that they should have been forbidden to use it. It is quite probable that the Company risked playing a few times there or played for a time at the Curtain when the Globe was rising. Unfortunately, there was no parallel to Henslowe in charge at the Curtain, and we only know fragmentary facts from stray notices as to what happened there. Halliwell-Phillipps gives some of these—under "The Theatre and Curtain." But I am convinced that the Globe did not take so very long to build as is supposed. Just a year after it was commenced a curious incident occurred. Henslowe and Edward Alleyn, of the Rose Theatre, engaged Burbage's "Peter Street" to build for them a Theatre after the model of the Globe in Golden Lane, afterwards called "The Fortune." It would almost seem as if the rivalry had affected them, and that they wanted to secure the northern contingent of theatre-goers now that they had two rivals in the south.

The Burbages, though removing their theatre to the south, continued to live in Shoreditch. We know this not only from the Parish Register, which records the births and deaths in their family, but from the Subsidy Rolls. James Burbage's house in Holywell Street, afterwards Cuthbert's, may be supposed to have been larger than Richard's, as Cuthbert was rated on £4 goods—and Richard on £3. Shakespeare did not live in Shoreditch itself but he was not far off. He lived in the parish of St.

Helen's in Bishopgate. It is curious to realize that he was assessed on £5, which implies that he lived in a larger and better house than either of the brothers Burbage. That again suggests a possibility, which has never been suggested, that his family was with him during some years of his life in town. There is a curious point about Shakespeare's house to note. The Subsidy Roll for St. Helen's, Bishopsgate, in October 1598, 146 / 369, which assesses William Shakespeare on £5 goods was discovered by Joseph Hunter in 1845, though many others have claimed the discovery since. The levy was for 13s. 4d. and the marginal reference *affd.* means that he did not pay but made an affidavit as to his reason for not paying.[1]

About twenty other names out of seventy-two in the same roll had also " affid." against them, so the collector had had some trouble that year. Of course the natural suggestion was that he had followed the fortunes of the transported theatre, and gone to live in Bankside. Fortunately for us, Professor Hales has been able to prove this supposition true.

In an article in " The Athenæum," 26th March, 1904, p. 401, Professor Hales now tells us that Shakespeare's name appears in the same Subsidy Rolls for 1595–6, and 1596–7 with smaller levies in proportion, but they had not been collected, the 13s. 4d. was therefore cumulative. The curious point is that in the great Roll of the Pipe of 40 Eliz., 1598, in " Residuum, London " is the entry, " William Shakspeare in the Parish of St. Helen's, Bishopsgate Ward, owes 13s. 4d. of the subsidy," and he answers in the following Roll 41 Eliz. In " Residuum Sussex," is the entry, " William Shakspeare in the parish of St. Helens, 13s. 4d. of the whole subsidy granted in the said 39th year which is required upon the same roll there," Against this is the entry " O. N." or " oneratur nisi " unless he show cause, and in the margin " Episcopo Wintonensis " and a

---

[1] See Excheq. Lay. Subs. London, 35 Eliz. $\frac{146}{354}$

      ,,   ,,   ,,   39 Eliz. $\frac{146}{369}$

Roll of the Pipe Residuum, Sussex, 41 Eliz.

" t " which the sheriffs mark against names they collect fiom. Now Sussex and Surrey had only one sheriff between them, the Bishop of Winchester owned the Liberty in which the theatre and Shakespeare now found themselves. The subsidy must have been at last settled then and the Bishop of Winchester accounts for a sum of money from payments of various persons.

The summer after the transplantation of the Theatre was a fortunate one for the company. Their poet was enriching their repertoire by his inimitable plays. Curiosity made Londoners row over to see their new attractions.

Many came often. We know that the Earl of Southampton, still out of favour at Court, because he had married the Elizabeth of his choice, along with his friend the Earl of Rutland, undisturbed by his steward's suit with Cuthbert Burbage " went to see plays every day." [1]

In the early days of the Globe, Shakespeare's " Henry V " was produced, a play which gives many traces of the poet's feelings. His views of the relations of the audience to the actors are there explained, " You must work, work your *thoughts*." *Your imagination* must make up for us the deficiencies in our stage setting ; *you* must *give*, as we give though in a greater degree. Thus only can you understand the suggestions and generalizations of a dramatist. He loved his subject on this occasion. There is no doubt that in describing the personal charm of the young King, his will to rough it among his subjects, his patriotic praise of England, and his power of infusing his subjects with courage, he had made the Earl of Essex sit as his modern model. The words in the chorus to Act v. also reflect the personal influence of the Earl on Londoners especially. The Mayor, his brethren, the plebeians may

> " Go forth and fetch their conquering hero in
>   As by a lower, but loving likelihood,
>   Were now the general of our gracious empress
>   (As in good time he may) from Ireland coming . . .
>   How many would the peaceful city quit
>   To welcome him." Chorus, Act V.

---

[1] Winwood's " Memorials."

A happy proclamation of the popularity of his friend's friend, too soon, alas! to sink in gloom. Separation ensued, when Southampton went over to join Essex in Ireland, and then came the Queen's wrath, the Council's underhand policy, discontent, planning of strong remedies for sore needs, failure, return, rising and death, a tragedy enacted on the world's stage which poured a new tragic sense into the soul of the Globe's *Poet*, and coloured the after output of his brain.

How very near had the sympathies of the players drawn them to the maelstrom of Essex's evil fortunes! Augustine Phillipps was examined [1] by the Privy Council over the suspicious performances of " Richard II," the play which Elizabeth hated and feared. Either his astute " confessions," or the influence of the Lord Chamberlain, saved them then. Essex's enemies, it is true, had no wish to increase the number of their enemies, or to destroy more than the principals. But there is no doubt that sorrow and doubts and fears hovered around the hearts of every player in the Globe Theatre from the consequences of Essex's so-called *Treason*.[2] A time of suspense, during which their sore hearts did not prevent them from being called to complete their engagement to perform before the Queen, and then the grand head of Essex rolled in blood from the block in the Tower! His friend was left there, long expecting a similar fate. His followers were heavily fined for their complicity, while the Lord Chamberlain's men thought it their wisest course to go and travel in the country. Did they travel as far as Scotland then? and did Shakespeare go with them? A fascinating question arises over that, when we meditate over the suggestions of personal knowledge of the country given in " Macbeth," of St. Colme's Inch, of the blasted heath on the way to Forres, of the unexpectedly mild climate of Inverness.

[1] State Pap., Dom. Ser., Eliz. 278 (85).

[2] I have just noted Sir Walter Raleigh's letter to Cecil dated 5th July, 1597, " I acquainted the Lord General with your letters and kind acceptance of your entertainment. He was wonderful merry at the conceit of Richard II." What can this mean? Dom. Ser. State Pap., Eliz. 264 (10).

Shakespeare might have read the whole of Holinshed's history of ancient Scotland, but where did he get, " How far *is't called* to Forres ? " a pure Scotch idiom which could not have flowed by nature from the lips of a man of English birth. At that same season we know that a man afterwards so mysteriously associated with their fortunes was in the North of Scotland, and that the King favoured him above measure, Laurence Fletcher by name, " The English Comedian." Of him no English records are available, but there are several notices among Scotch public records. " Payment to certain English Comedians, February 1593–4." Treasurer's accounts Register House. The first mention of Fletcher is in a letter from George Nicolson [1] to Mr. Bowes, dated 22nd March, 1595, in which it is said, " The King heard that Fletcher the player was hanged and told him and Roger Aston so in merry words, not believing it, saying very pleasantly " that if it were true, he would hang them too."

The second entry is a much more serious one. George Nicolson, in his usual despatch to Sir Robert Cecil on 12th November, 1599, said that the King had given the English players permission to play. But " the four Sessions of this town (without touch by name of our English actors Fletcher and Mertyn with their company) and not knowing the King's ordinances for them to play and be heard, enacted yt their flocks were to forbear and not to come or haunt profane games, sports or *plays*." The King was in a towering passion, summoned the Sessions before him and threatened them with punishment. At first the ministers would not yield an inch, later they agreed to be silent as to the action of their congregations. The next day the King " by proclamation with sound of a trumpet hath commanded the players liberty to play, and forbidden their hinder or impeachment therein " (St. Pap., Scotch Ser. lxv. 64). He also ordered the ministers " not to restrain or censure those that repair to comedies and plays on pain of rebellion. Holyrude House, 8th November, 1599."

[1] St. Pap., Scotch Ser., Eliz. lv. 59.

The third notice is even more interesting. It shows us the
English Players in 1601, as far north as Aberdeen, where the
Town Council on the request of the King granted " The Freedom of the City " to Fletcher, Martin, and their fellows (see
Dibdin's " History of the Edinburgh Stage " and Kennedy's
" Memorials of Aberdeen ").   That was the very year Shakespeare's company was travelling.   Was it possible that, through
the known sympathies of the Scotch King for the Earl of Essex,
the players who had performed for him " Richard II " thought
themselves safer for a while under his protection ?   Was it
there, in the far north, Laurence Fletcher forged the links of
association between himself and the Lord Chamberlain's
players, which were afterwards to be bound more closely in
the south ?

When the Chamberlain's company returned to the Globe,
there was for them an end of the Essex Conspiracy, except for
the memory of the prisoner immured in the Tower.   An
interesting notice in a contemporary University play shows
somewhat of the position they had attained.

(Written 1601, printed 1606.)

In " The Returne from Pernassus," Part II, Act iv. Scene 3,
Philomusus and Ingenioso are driven to try the stage, and
interview Burbage and Kempe, who are willing to consider
them because they would work cheaply.

" *Kemp*.   Few of the University pen plaies well, they smell
too much of that writer Ovid, and that writer Metamorphosis
and talke too much of Proserpine and Juppiter.   Why, here's
our fellow Shakespeare puts them all down, I, and Ben Jonson
too.   Oh that Ben Jonson is a pestilent fellow, he brought up
Horace giving the poets a pill, but our fellow Shakespeare hath
given him a purge that made him beray his credit.

" *Bur*.   It's a shrewd fellow indeed.

" *Kemp*.   Be merry, my lads, you have happened upon
the most excellent vocation in the world for money : they
come north and south to bring it to our playhouse, and for
honours, who of more report, than Dick Burbage, and Will

Kempe, he is not counted a gentleman that knows not Dick Burbage and Will Kemp. . . .

"*Phil.* Indeed, Mr. Kempe, you are very famous.

(After suggestions as to acting, and teaching it.)

"*Kemp.* Thou wilt do well in time, if thou wilt be ruled by thy betters, that is by myself, and such grave Aldermen of the Playhouse as I am.

"*Bur.* I like your face and the proportions of your body for ' Rich. III."

In " Returne from Pernassus," Part I, there are allusions to Shakespeare and his poems.

But new trouble arose to them all through Richard's inheritance.

When in the year 1597 James Burbage's heart had been broken by his failure to work the Blackfriars as a theatre, it seems to have been left unused. Perhaps it may have been borrowed for private entertainments, for fencing classes, or other purposes, we may surmise, but we know nothing. On the death of William Hunnis [1] the Master of the Children of the Chapel Royal, on 6th June, 1597, he was succeeded by Nathaniel Giles. He received the patent of appointment and privilege and the patent to take up singing children for the Queen's Chapel, similar to those generally granted to his predecessors. He also in pursuance of custom set about to prepare the children to perform plays before the Queen if invited to do so.

It is probable that from the very first he set his eyes upon Burbage's theatre (compulsorily vacated by the Lord Chamberlain's company) for the rehearsals of his children, and that gradually, by the convenience of things, wider ideas took shape. He associated himself with one Henry Evans, who took a lease of the premises from Richard Burbage at £40 a year, and they began to run what was afterwards called " a private theatre," at which the children performed. It became very fashionable and successful. The rougher elements were shut out entirely,

---

[1] See my book, " William Hunnis and the Revels of the Chapel Royal," the first book written about the man.

prices were high, the luxuries designed by James Burbage for audiences to come to see his son, came to hear the children instead. They attracted the better classes away from the Globe, and other *public* theatres, where *anybody* could go by payment. The "Globe" players were wounded as by an arrow feathered from their own wing by the successes of the children actors. Then trouble came to the managers at the Blackfriars Theatre. Mr. Greenstreet discovered what is known as the Clifton Case, which has been fully published in Fleay's "History of the Stage." Nathaniel Giles' patent to take up children had a proviso, "not the sons of gentlemen," but Giles or Evans or their assistants disobeyed the limitations, and "took up" children who had no "singing voices," for their aptitude as players, "took up," (unfortunately for them) by main force a lad called Clifton, son of a gentleman, who very indignantly appealed at once to Court authorities, secured his son, and instituted proceedings against Giles and Evans, which must have put both of them in a very unpleasant position. Evans made over his lease to his son-in-law, paid a visit to the country, a new directorate was formed and the children at Blackfriars went on as a Company as popular as ever.

Ben Jonson, Marston, Chapman and others wrote plays for the children, plays that held music, singing, dancing, masques, with less depth of feeling, more sparkle, more Court gossip, wit and satire, till the audience became attracted, not only for the refinement and the prettiness of the things, for the lightness of the touch, but for the news of the day. It took less thinking, less imagination than "the strong meat" presented by Shakespeare at the Globe. Jealousies arose between the companies; courtiers accustomed to bearbaiting fanned these jealousies for their own amusement, and hence arose a curious Theatre-War. The story has been frequently told. The main point of interest in it all is the consideration of the meaning of the words in Shakespeare's "Hamlet" (his greatest tragedy, created for Richard Burbage, the greatest actor), when the two great men felt their popularity begin to fade before the meretricious charms of the children.

It is worth re-reading as a chapter apart.

" *Hamlet.* What players are they ?

" *Ros.* Even those you were wont to take such delight in, the tragedians of the city.

" *Ham.* How chances it they travel ? [1] Their residence both in reputation and profit, were better both ways.

" *Ros.* I think their inhibition comes by the means of the late innovation.

" *Ham.* Do they hold the same estimation they did when I was in the city ? Are they so followed ?

" *Ros.* No, indeed, they are not.

" *Ham.* How comes it ? Do they grow rusty ?

" *Ros.* Nay, their endeavour keeps in the wonted pace ; but there is, sir, an aery of children, little eyases, that cry out on the top of question, and are most tyrannically clapped for't ; these are now the fashion ; and so berattle the common stages (so they call them) that many wearing rapiers are afraid of goose-quills, and dare scarce come thither.

" *Ham.* What ! are they children ? Who maintains them ? How are they escoted ? Will they pursue their quality no longer than they can sing ? Will they not say afterwards, if they should grow themselves to common players (as it is most like if their means are not better) their writers do them wrong, to make them exclaim against their own succession ?

" *Ros.* 'Faith there has been much to do on both sides ; and the nation holds it no sin, to tarre them to controversy ; there was, for a while, no money bid for argument, unless the poet and the player went to cuffs in the question.

" *Ham.* Is it possible ?

" *Guil.* O ! there has been much throwing about of brains.

---

[1] The title page of the edition of Hamlet licensed in 1602, notes that the Chamberlain's men had been travelling to Oxford and Cambridge.— *Fleay.*

" *Ham.*   Do the boys carry it away ?

" *Ros.*   Ay, that they do, my Lord.   Hercules and his load too.

" *Ham.*   It is not strange." [1]

The betraying phrase in the passage is in Rosencrantz's description, " They   dare   scarce   *come   thither.*"   Shakespeare acknowledges they of the Globe are the losers, through the triumphs of the children and the children's poets.   " The pity of it," to turn to gall what might have been good fellowship, for the pleasure of those who were not ashamed " to tarre them " on, and to provide them with quarrelsome plays against players. But he does not acknowledge defeat.   The real conclusion of the poet's thoughts requires further reading.   The players, driven to travel, are the real *artists.*

" *Ham.*   Come, give us a taste of your quality ;   come, a passionate speech !

" 1*st Player.*   What speech, my good Lord ?

" *Ham.*   I heard thee speak a speech once :—but it was never acted ;   or if it was, not above once ;   for the play, I remember, pleased not the million ;   'twas caviare to the general, but it was (as I received it and others, whose judgments in such matters cried in the top of mine) an excellent play, well digested in the scenes, set down with as much modesty as cunning.   I remember, one said, there were no sallets in the lines to make the matter savoury, nor no matter in the phrase that might indite the author of affectation, but called it an honest method, as wholesome as sweet, and by very much more handsome than fine.   One speech in it I chiefly loved :   'twas Æneas' tale to Dido ;   and thereabouts of it especially where he speaks of Priam's slaughter.   If it live in your memory, begin at this line." . . .

" *Polonius.*   Look whe'er he has not turned his colour and has tears in his eyes !   Prythee no more !

" *Ham.*   'Tis well, I'll have thee speak out the rest of this soon. . . .

[1] Dr. Furnivall's Leopold Shakespeare, " Hamlet," Act ii. Sc. 2.

> " *Ham.*   O ! what a rogue and peasant slave am I !
> Is it not monstrous that this player here,
> But in a fiction, in a dream of passion,
> Could force his soul so to his whole conceit
> That from her working, all his visage wanned ;
> Tears in his eyes, distraction in's aspect,
> A broken voice, and his whole function suiting
> With forms to his conceit ? and all for nothing !
> For Hecuba !
> What's Hecuba to him, or he to Hecuba
> That he should weep for her ? "

And that is the distinction the poet (Shakespeare) would draw between plays fit for " the tragedians of the city," between the passion and power of these tragedians, and the little eyases and their plays.   We may think of it as if Richard Burbage himself had spoken the words, a challenge to the greatness in the souls of men, which he and Shakespeare had done so much to foster.   Oh Mayors, Aldermen, Recorders, Sheriffs, what preacher of his time had done more for his kind than this player-poet Shakespeare had done by this time ?

The old year of 1602 died in gloom.   A failing Queen, uncertain succession, rumours and realities of plague, and the spirit of Hamlet was in the air.

> " O cursed spite
> That ever I was born to set it right."

The New Year of 1603 opened no better.   The Queen's sister Mary had said that when she died the word " Calais " would be written on her heart.   The loss meant so much to her, for she was patriotic and proud of her country, though she had so little chance to show *herself*.   More truly might Elizabeth have said, and all knew, though she never spake the words, that the word " *Essex* " would be written on her heart. The bright life quenched by her, she the mere tool of enemies, as she had discovered when too late, it burned into her soul.

The years being then reckoned from the 25th March, it was a curious coincidence that Elizabeth should die on the 24th March, the last day of the old year, 1602–3, and that a King saw the New Year in.   And even amidst the terrors of the plague time, in the hearts of the players at the Globe his coming awakened a dawn of hope.   They did not pretend to mourn. Their poet Shakespeare made no sign.   Others did.

" A MOURNFUL DITTIE ENTITULED ELIZABETH'S LOSSE.

" You poets all, brave Shakspere, Jonson, Greene,
Bestow your time to write for England's Queene.
Lament, Lament, Lament you English peeres,
Lament your losse, possest so many yeares,
Return your songs and sonnets and your layes
To set forth sweet Elizabetha's praise.
          Lament, Lament."   1603.

Many noted this.   Chettle in his " England's Mourning Garment " wrote—

" Nor doth the silver-tongued Melicert
Drop from his honied muse one sable teare
To mourne her death, who graced his desert,
And to his laies opened her Royall eare.
Shepherd, remember our Elizabeth,
And sing her rape. done by that Tarquin, Death."

In vain.   The Poet's memory was with Essex.   His heart was in the Tower, where his chief patron lay, left there by the departed Queen.   Drayton hastened too much to welcome James, others just hit the time.   The players made no sign.   But the coming King scattered joy and peace and freed Southampton on 10th April.   Hardly had James reached the Metropolis, and begun to touch State business, than he changed many things.   He took from noblemen the power to select and patronize players. Henceforth that was to be a Royal privilege alone.   He chose as his own royal company the company of the Lord Chamberlain, who had just retired sick unto death, but with this peculiar condition, that the Laurence Fletcher who had delighted his heart in Scotland was to be at their head. We do not know how the Burbage Company dealt with this intrusion, and how they fitted him among their ranks at the Globe. He does not seem to have been up to their mark, and little more is heard of him. But he led in the Royal Patent. The King came to London on 7th May, the Privy Seal for their patent was signed on 17th May, 1603. The patent was granted on the 19th.

"Pro Laurentio Fletcher et Willielmo Shakespeare et aliis.

"James by the Grace of God, etc., to all Justices, Maiors, Sheriffs, Constables, Headboroughs, and other our Officers and lovinge Subjects, Greetinge. Knowe ye that wee of our Speciall Grace, certeine knowledge, and mere motion, have licensed and authorized, and by these presentes doe license and authorise these our Servaunts, Laurence Fletcher, William Shakespeare, Richard Burbage, Augustine Phillippes, John Hemings, Henrie Condell, William Sly, Robert Armyn, Richard Cowly, and the rest of their Associates, Freely to use and exercise the Art and Facultie of playing Comedies, Tragedies, Histories, Enterludes, Morals, Pastoralls, Stage Plaies and such others, like as these have alreadie studied or hereafter shall use or studie, as well for our Solace and Pleasure, when wee shall thincke good to see them, during our Pleasure ; and the said Commedies, Tragedies, Histories, Enterludes, Moralls, Pastoralls, Stage-playes, and suche like, to shewe and exercise publiquely to their best Commoditie, when the Infection of the Plague shall decrease, as well within their nowe usual house called the Globe within our countie of Surrey, as also within anie Towne Halls, or Moote Halls, or other convenient places within the Liberties and Freedom of anie other Cittie, Universitie, Toune or Boroughe whatsoever within our saide Realmes and Dominions.

"Willing and commaunding you and everie of you, as you tender our Pleasure, not onelie to permit and suffer them herein, without anie your Letts, Hindrances, or Molestations, during our said Pleasure, but also to be aiding and assistinge to them

H

if anie Wronge be to them offered, and to allow them such
former curtesies as hath been given to men of their Place and
Qualitie ; and also what further Favour you shall shewe to
theise our servaunts for our sake, Wee shall take it kindly at
your handes.   In witnesse whereof, etc.

" Witnesse our selfe at Westminster the nynetenth Daye of
Maye in the first year of our reign.

" Per Breve de Privato Sigillo."

It is interesting to compare this patent, the first player's
patent of the new King, with the first Royal patent granted
Burbage's men by Elizabeth by the persuasion of the Earl of
Leicester in 1574.

With all their faults, the Stuarts were the first real patrons
of the Drama in this country, as they were the first patrons of
art and science.

The difference made thereby in the players' *status* was enor-
mous.   They took rank as grooms of the Royal Chamber
(though without fee), wore the King's livery, held certain
privileges, as freedom from arrest while on the King's service
(except for Treason or great crimes).   The Lord Chamberlain
dealt with the minor questions of debt, duty and recognizances.   Their patent carried them all over the country, and
protected them in London from Civic interference.

The Earl of Southampton, safe now himself, and in attendance on the King (though his affairs were not all settled) would
doubtless have a good word to say for them in the Royal ear.

In the Royal Progress that year, necessitated by a recurrence
of the Plague, the King visited the Earl of Pembroke on 30th
August, and held his court at Wilton, Winchester, and Basing
during the most of October, November and December, as may
be seen by following the dating of Letters and Proclamations
from thence among the State papers of the time.   Apparently
the King was not inclined to wait till Christmas to see his
players, so he summoned them to come to him.   "John
Hemynges one of his majesties players " received a warrant

for a play at the Court at Wilton on 3rd December, 1603, " for the paynes and expense of himself and the rest of the company coming from Mortlake in the Countie of Surrey unto the Courte aforesaid, and there presenting before his Majestie one play on the second of December last, . . . by way of his Majesty's reward £30." They would think that liberal in those days even after their long journey.

But even more liberal would the company feel it, when in February they had at last some compensation made them for their loss through their inhibition on account of the plague.[1] " To Richard Burbage, one of his Majesties Comedians, upon a warrant dated at Hampton Courte 8th Feb., 1603-4, for the maintenance and reliefe of himselfe and the rest of his company being prohibited to present any plaies publiquely in or neare London by reason of the great perill that might growe through the extraordinarye concourse and assemblie of people to a newe increase of the plague, till it shall please God to settle the city in a more perfect health, His Majesties free gift £30."

In the same month they were also paid for two plays.[1] " John Hemyngs one of his Majesties players by a Warrant dated at the Courte at Whitehall on the last day of February, 1603, for two playes presented before his Majestie on Candlemas Day at night, and on Shrovesunday at night . . . £20."

Henceforth all the *nagging* lawsuits against the Burbages were closed, all the Giles Alleyns and his like had to hide their diminished heads. The King's company went from glory to glory. Early in the New Year the plans were being arranged for the King's Coronation, which had to be postponed, and the details of the Royal Procession through the city, which took place on 15th March, 1603-4.

In the Lord Chamberlain's accounts ii. 4. (5) are noted between the Fawkeners and the Officers of the Household the King's players, to receive each for their Livery 4½ yards of Scarlet Cloth (they knew their rank by the amount of cloth given), the same as the other Grooms of the Chamber. There

---

[1] Declared accounts Treasurer of the Chamber, Pipe Office, 542.

is something new in the order of the players themselves as written in that volume.   This list is commenced *currente calamo*, right across the page—

" William Shakespeare (*sic*)
  Augustine Phillipps
  Laurence Fletcher
  John Hemminges
  Richard Burbidge
  William Slye
  Robert Armyn
  Henry Cundell
  Richard Cowley."

I know not if it be a sign of a deposing of Laurence Fletcher in the King's favour.   The *spelling* of the first name is important, for it is spelt in the way it *always* is in Court records when it is intended to represent the player of Stratford-on-Avon, giving no support to the nonsensical theory of the Baconians that when spelt so it represents the *nom de plume* of their man.   Their fellow, Thomas Pope, had lately died —was it of the plague ?

After the Players and their liveries comes the Clerk of the Closet, Mr. Doctor Neale.

It may be interesting to add that in the Queen's Expenses also come her players, among the officers of her household.

I know that many believe that though receiving red cloth, among the others in preparation for the Procession, that the players did not go on that procession, because they were nowhere mentioned *as players* in accounts of the Coronation.   I do not myself see that there is any force in the argument, because since they had received their patent, they were the King's *Servants*, before being his *players*, and as such, would march among other *Servants*.   In the temper of the King at the time, I am inclined to think he would have made it a personal matter that they should do so.   If we are not absolutely sure they did not, we have a right to suppose they did.   But it is true that the grant of the cloth was not in itself an invitation to the Coronation. It was to be their ordinary livery, given in future "every other year," with a bit of red velvet for a cap.

There have been doubts suggested that they were really appointed Grooms of the Chamber, doubts that they were paid. Of course not—they were of the class called extraordinary Grooms of the Chamber and they were paid only when they rendered services. In the general hospitality offered to foreign ambassadors that summer something occurred to show that their royal service was a real office.[1] In August 1604 they were appointed to attend on the Spanish Ambassador at Somerset House, and were *paid* for the occasion. Some one must have told this fact to Halliwell-Phillipps and he had forgotten the reference,[2] which had troubled him, and he invited his readers to contribute it if they knew, but none replied during his life. I believe I was the first to find it many years ago anew for myself, and after keeping it for a suitable setting, I interwove it into my "Shakespeare of the Court,"[3] fortunately for me before Mr. Law brought out his little book, "Shakespeare as Groom of the Chamber."

"To Augustine Phillips and John Hemynges for th' allowance of themselves and tenne of their fellows his Majesties Groomes of the Chamber and Players, for waytinge and attendinge in his Majestie's Service by commandmente, upon the Spanishe Embassador at Somersette House, for the space of 18 dayes, viz. from the 9th day of Auguste, 1604, till the 27th day of the same, as appeareth by a bill thereof signed by the Lord Chamberlayne £21 12.[3]

It is interesting to think of Shakespeare and his fellows learning Spanish Court Etiquette from the Ambassador's own Major Domo. We wonder in vain whether they performed any

---

[1] See my "Shakespeare's Fellows and Followers," "Shakespeare Jahrbuch," 1910.

[2] "Athenæum," July 8th, 1871.

[3] "Athenæum," 12th March, 1910. Declared Acc. Treas. Chamber, Audit Office R. 41, Bundle 388, and Pipe Office, 543.

plays before him or no. There is just a straw, blown by the breezes of the time, which gives a suggestion that they did. This is the fact that six months after they spoke of having lately revived " Love's Labours Lost," a play which they might have supposed fit to suit a Spaniard. This play is noted in three references. The one is the 1605 forged list of plays performed at Court during the winter of 1604–5, preserved among Cunningham's Extracts from the Accounts of the Revels at Court. There are many other reasons to suspect this list, but the main one is the inclusion of an entry, " By his Majesties Plaiers Betwin Newers Day And Twelfe day A Play of Loues Labours Lost." Now the clerks of the Treasurers of the Chamber always knew their dates (which they were paid to do). Nothing would come " between " two things.

The Dec. Acc. Treas. Chamber, Pipe Office, 543, show that the King's company *did not play* at Court that year between Innocent's Day at night and 7th January, and if they did not do so, no other company would have dared to perform this ' Love's Labours Lost," for the play *belonged* to the King's company. I am not going to discuss the honesty of Peter Cunningham, but to get to the real story of the performance. Just after the New Year 1604–5, Sir Robert Cecil, then Viscount Cranborne, and the Earl of Southampton were planning festivities in their own houses in honour of the Queen and her brother. Each was going to give a play. Sir Walter Cope was helping Lord Cranborne to arrange his when he wrote the following letter dated only " 1604," but which may be dated 11th January, 1604–5, by the context.

" From your Library.[1]

"Sir, I have sent and bene all thys morning huntyng for players, juglers and such kinde of creatures, but fynde them harde to fynde, wherefore leaving notes for them to seeke me, Burbage ys come, and says there is no new playe that the Queene hath not seene, but they have revyved an olde one cawled " Loves Labore Lost," which for wytt and mirthe he sayes will

[1] Cecil Papers.

please her exceedingly. And thys ys apointed to be playd tomorowe night at my Lord of Sowthamptons, unless you send a wrytt to remove the *Corpus cum causa* to your howse in Strande. Burbage ys my messenger ready attendyng your pleasure.

" Yours most humbly,

" WALTER COPE."[1]

Apparently Cranbourne did not do anything so ungenerous as to change arrangements at the last, but likely got Burbage to revive another play for him. Carleton writes, in one of his gossippy letters, dated 15th January, 1604–5 :—

" Last nights revels were kept at my Lord of Cranborne's . . . and ye like two nights before at my Lord of Southampton's." They played several times at Court that season, as may be seen in the Treasurer's Declared Accounts, though unfortunately no names of plays are given at that date. It is certain they were successful at the Globe, now that they were distinguished above their fellows, until they had been unwise enough to produce " The Tragedy of Gowry," in which the King himself was represented on the stage. Something in the rendering probably was the real cause, but the ostensible reason given was that it was not fit to represent events or people of the time, when the play was ordered to be suppressed. We do not know the author, but it evidently was not Shakespeare.

The incident would, however, determine him in the idea he had conceived. Shakespeare was composing a new form of Laureate poem—a Laureate Play to please the King who had done so much for them. " Macbeth," a story from Scotch history, at one of the rare times when Scotland was at peace with England, in which Scotch characters and incidents are combined, yet not a true story. The reverse of his " Hamlet," who, unlike the real history, became christianized and through conflicting feelings became a man of thought, and not of action, who did not kill his father's murderer, and who did not succeed to his father's throne ; a different Hamlet entirely from the truth. Here otherwise the reverse of this picture the best king that early Scotland had, has all the crimes of his predecessors for ninety years poured on his head, to create a generalized idea of his race, a pagan at heart, utilitarian of creed, but a man of action. And this to glorify Banquo, from whom the King supposed he had descended.   The King's book, and the King's opinions are skilfully interwoven in " Macbeth," which was we know, a popular tragedy.   We can see the little suggestion of the witches in Holinshed ; but there was also the little play produced at Oxford on the subject by Matthew Gwynn when the King went there in 1605.   There is no doubt the King would be pleased with " Macbeth."   Of Shakespeare's genius and of Shakespeare's plays I cannot now speak, but I may later say a word about them in relation to the career of Richard Burbage.

Little seems to have disturbed the King's company at the Globe during the early years of James, save the loss of members of their company, Augustine Phillipps in particular.   He left remembrances to his " fellows " in his will.   His unwise widow made a foolish second marriage with John Witter, who brought her and her children to ruin,[1] and instituted legal proceedings which give a good deal of information about the history of the company.

The pin-pricks of the children at Blackfriars continued to a certain degree, but there were great changes there.   The " Children of the Chapel " had been discontinued as actors.

Richard Burbage had leased his house to Henry Evans for twenty-one years from Michaelmas (Sept. 29), 1600, at £40 a year. It must be remembered this rent was for *the house ;* at the Globe the £14 10s. rent was only for the *ground* on which they built their house.   The Clifton Case had practically ruined Evans in credit.   He handed over his lease to his son-in-law, Hawkins, let half the profits to Kirkham, Rastell and Kendall in consider-

---

[1] See Prof. Wallace's " Shakespeare's Money Interest in the Globe Theater," " The Century," August 1910.

ation of their taking over the bond of £400 he had assigned to Burbage for the fulfilment of covenant.

Then came the plague of 1603–4 ; the changed relations with the new King. After the plague was over Evans began to treat with Burbage about surrendering the lease, but instead of this the company was reconstituted as the Children of the Queen's Revels, under Kirkham, Hawkins, Kendall, Payne. They were still lively and audacious, but more solemnly satirical than ever. The troubles arising from the performance of " Eastward Hoe " in 1605 were serious. Some of the children were sent to prison and Chapman had to hide. The Queen's patronage was withdrawn, changes took place among the managers, but the children continued to act as the Children of the Revels. Though the lightness and brightness had gone from their boards, the poets still remained unwise in treating contemporary matters satirically, and the children did not mince matters in their methods of performing them. Finally Chapman's " Tragedy of Biron " offended the French King, and to pacify him the children were suppressed. On 9th August, 1608, the lease of Blackfriars was surrendered to Richard Burbage, as owner, and as Cuthbert said in 1635 " it was considered that house would be as fit for ourselves." Doubtless it would be a relief to them to get rid of their "eyases." Richard Burbage made a company of seven sharers from his partners at the Globe, and took over some of the children who had grown up, Underwood, Field and Ostler. The other children ran a new career at Whitefriars later, independent of the Burbages.

The King's company strengthened themselves in the new venture of the Blackfriars Theatre.[1] At last old James Burbage's second " *Idea* " was fulfilled, and his son Richard was able to hold his own in a theatre of which he was the landlord, and the King himself the Lord in Chief. With two stages at his command, he could vary his parts and his performances, in

---

[1] It is strange that just then Laurence Fletcher dropped out of their lives. He was buried in St. Saviour's that year.

a way few actors then could do. He could work both summer and winter, both by daylight and by candlelight. He had still his " Poet " by his side, a fellow and fellow-actor, ready to find themes and characters suited to his genius, and for the remaining years of his life he was the pride and joy of his fellow-countrymen. Not that he was always at peace. Litigation pursued him, but it was a litigation not overwhelming in its magnitude, or fundamental in its bearings, arising over second-ary questions, the claims of disappointed individuals as to profits and shares in the ventures which he, above all others, made a success, questions in which the company bore a share of the trouble and expense, and in which he won his suits.

The suits of Evans *v.* Kirkham, 1612,[1] and of Kirkham *v.* Painton, however,[2] caused a good deal of trouble. Besides being a witness, Richard Burbage was dragged into giving an " answer " to Kirkham, " The joint and several answers of John Hemings and Richard Burbage to Edward Kirkham, 2nd November, 1612," by order of the Master of the Rolls.   Richard acknowledged that being seized in the Blackfriars he had let it to Henry Evans for a lease of twenty-one years to erect a com-pany of playing boys.   But he asked some security that Evans would be able to pay the rent, and then Alexander Hawkins, his son-in-law, became bound with him in a bond of £400 in conditions for paying that rent of £40.   He thinks it true that Evans treated with Edward Kirkham, William Rastall and Thomas Kendall about setting up the company of boys, which they did.   And he thinks they spent money on it and became sharers.   He thinks that it was the great visitation of the plague which was the cause that they earned less than had been ex-pected.   Alexander Hawkins did not like the notion of the heavy bond, and so the lease was cancelled, and Evans' interest in the playhouse ended. Hemings agreed with Burbage and believed that the complainant did spend money, but not on the house but on apparel. They denied that Evans assigned the

[1] Chanc. Bills and Answers, Bundle E, 4–9.
[2] Ibid., K. 5, No. 25.

house to Hawkins on trust, but believed the complainants were to be partners. *They* themselves never got any profit and denied that they confederated with Evans to defeat the complainant's claim.

Edmund Kirkham replied, repeating the fact that Alexander Hawkins deceased had half the property and the other half assured to him and his fellows, that Evans had no right to give up the lease, and that Hemings and Burbage and their company made by playing in " the fryers " in one winter by a thousand poundes more than they were used to get at the Bankside. He wonders Evans could claim any interest in the premises after the decision in the Clifton Case, when he was censured and all his engagements cancelled,[1] that they did not make so much money as they expected. Edward Painton in his answer says he married Margaret Hawkins, widow of Alexander Hawkins, and daughter of Henry Evans—and she says that the interest and residue of the lease is her own as it was sold to Alexander Hawkins though the deed remains with Evans, Hemings and Burbage.

Mr. Greenstreet found all the papers long since, and they appear nearly in full in Mr. Fleay's " History of the Stage."

Robert Keysar had also brought a suit against Richard Burbage, John Hemmings and Henry Condall in the Court of Requests, complaining that he had bought a share in the Company from Marston, the Poet, for £100, before the Children of the Revels had been suppressed, and he had not been indemnified. He also had maintained many of the boys, he said, to his great loss. His extravagant reckonings, his unfounded charge of fraud, were easily rebutted by the King's company. Professor Wallace discovered this case and gives the details of the law-suit in " The Century Magazine " for September 1610.

The law-suits lead us on to busy years. The Corporation had become more friendly with players, since the King's steady favour allowed them to see the men as they really were. On

---

[1] Chancery Bills and Answers, James I, K. 5, 25.

one occasion, indeed, they enlisted his services to do honour to
Prince Henry on his installation as the Prince of Wales.
Anthony Monday wrote the speeches, and designed the pageant,
and we may be sure that Burbage did all the honour he could
to his part, for the sake of his prince.

" Martis quinto die Junii Anno regni Regis Jacobi Anglie
etc. octavo. . . .

" Item, it is ordered that Mr. Chamberleine shall pay unto
Mr. Burbage and John Rice the players that rodd upon the twoe
fishes and made the speeches at the meetinge of the high and
mighty prince the Prince of Walles upon the River of Thames
on Thursday last seventeene pounds tenne shillinges and six-
pence by them disbursed for robes and other furniture for
adorning themselves at the same meeting.   And that they
shall retaine to their own use in lewe of their paynes therein
taken such Taffety, silke and other necessaryes as were provided for that purpose without any farther allowance.   And
this shalbe Mr. Chamberlain his warrant in their behalfe Guildhall."   (Letter Book DD. f. 184b).

One talent of Richard Burbage I have not yet discussed
He was deeply interested in *Art*, to the extent that he had
somehow acquired the art of *painting*.   There are specimens of
his work preserved at Dulwich College even yet.   Perhaps
we would not pass on them the high encomiums that his con
temporaries did, but they have some power, and we must remember the rarity of native painters at his time.   It was said
that he had painted one of the portraits of Shakespeare, a fact
possible, but hardly complimentary to his skill.

It is probable that his artistic knowledge enabled him to
visualize the effects of the grouping of characters on the stage
in producing pleasing pictures to be remembered by the
audience.

But about this time he is noticed as earning money in a new
way, fringing on art, in an interesting record at Belvoir Castle
It occurs in the expenses of the Steward, that very Thomas
Scriven who had plagued Cuthbert Burbage so, by bringing a

suit in the name of the Earl of Rutland for the possession of the close in which his Theatre stood ; the same Thomas Scriven who became a benefactor to the Church of St. Leonard's to the extent of £10 (for the good of his soul, no doubt). The entry occurs among the expenses in preparation for his master the Earl of Rutland's masking suit and tilting suit, and runs : " 31 Martii, *Paid* To Mr. Shakspeare in gold, about my Lordes impreso, 44/- To Richard Burbage for paynting and makyng yt, in gold, 44/— —£4. 8." This had been discovered by Mr. Stevenson while calendaring the Belvoir MS. But I discovered it for myself among these MSS., when I was kindly allowed to see them at Belvoir Castle. The decoration was not intended for the Earl Roger of the Shoreditch lawsuit, who in 1599 with his friend the Earl of Southampton " went not to the court, but only to plays every day," the Roger of the conspiracy. He had died, it was his brother Francis who now reigned at Belvoir and was going to court and to tilt.

Now a *crest* was intended to reveal in a figure the name of the visored knight, but an *impresa* was intended to do just the opposite—to veil the name of the knight under some special device, known only to a few. This entry was of course at once accepted by the public as referring to the poet and his actor. It is quite possible the poet was interested in heraldry. But there is an alternative possibility. There was in court at the time another of the name, who was in the habit of preparing decorations for tournaments, Mr. John Shakespeare, the Prince's, afterwards the King's, bitmaker. If, as I suppose, this John was Shakespeare's cousin of Snitterfield, there need be no surprise at his being associated with Richard Burbage in related work.[1]

In later years Richard Burbage was employed again. " 25th Martii 1616, given to Richard Burbidge for my Lorde's shelde

---

[1] See my article, " Mr. Shakspeare about my Lorde's Impresa." " Athenæum," 16th May, 1908.

and for the embleance £4 18/-." It may be supposed that it would be a painted shield with devices thereon, as an artist painter was employed.

The events which stand out in the general history of the time, were the coming of the Prince Palatine in October 1612, the death of Prince Henry on 6th November, 1612, and the marriage of the Princess Elizabeth in February 1612–13. For her and her betrothed, the Prince Palatine, many performances took place. The succession to the Blackfriars Theatre had helped to modify Shakespeare's later plays. The introduction of masques, songs and dances was an inheritance from the " Children," made possible by the different stage, and Shakespeare wrote " The Tempest " to show that he could command in that vein also. There was long a question as to the date of " The Tempest," there is so still. It cannot very well have appeared before the news arrived of Sir George Somers' wreck on the Bermudas, 1610, we know it was presented before the Princess Elizabeth in 1613. On the authority of the doubtful papers in Cunningham's " Extract " it was entered as having been performed in 1611. Even if a forgery, it *may* still speak the truth. If it appeared in 1611 it can hardly be read as the poet's last play, as so many consider it to be. Ben Jonson, his greatest rival, who had so often satirized him on the Blackfriars boards, in his Prologue to " Every Man in his Humour," brought with his Collected Works in 1616—while he satirizes plays which let years pass in their Acts, made use of stage-tricks and unreal imaginations, speaking of himself as author—

> " He rather prays you will be pleased to see
> One such to-day, as other plays should be
> Where neither Chorus wafts you o'er the seas.
> . . . nor rolled bullet heard
> To say it thunders ; nor tempestuous drum
> Rumbles to tell you when the storm doth come,
> But deeds and language such as men do use.
>
> .   .   .   .   .
>
> Which, when you heartily do, there's hope left then
> You, that *have so graced monsters*, may like *men*."

To a certain extent, a classic scholar whose work was limited by the dramatic unities of time, place and action, his strictures were just of the work of the great master of the Romantic School of Drama. But we cannot conceive that Ben Jonson meant his Prologue to appear in the very year of his friend's death. That it did so appear, is no doubt partly the reason that he tried so eloquently to put his position clear, in his enthusiastic appreciation of Shakespeare before the first folio in 1623.

London had calmed down after the festivities of the Royal Wedding in the spring of 1613, when another *event* excited every inhabitant of the city.

The Globe Theatre was burned to the ground on St. Peter's Day, 29th June, 1613, burned, too, without warning, in the middle of a performance ! Yet it speaks much for the building and the management of the time, much for the common-sense and self-control of the audience, that *all* should have escaped [1] by "two small doors." The performance was "Henry VIII," or "All is True," and some of the cannon used to express the rejoicings caught some of the drapery, and instantly the whole wooden shell seemed to ignite. Many contemporary allusions show regret for the loss and wonder at the escapes. (See Reliq. Wotton, 165, 425–6 ; Howe's "Continuation of Stowe," 1003–4 ; Winwood's "Memorials," iii. 469 ; Lorkin's "Letter to Puckering," Harl. MS. 7002 ; Taylor's "Collected Works," Epigram 33, 265.)

Ben Jonson in a poem called "An Execration of Vulcan" for his mad pranks, reproaches the God for destroying

> "The Globe, the Glory of the Bank,
> Which, though it were the fort of the whole parish,
> Flanked with a ditch, and forced out of a marish
> I saw with two poor chambers taken in

---

[1] "It was a marvel and fair grace of God that the people had so little harm, having but two narrow doors to get out."— Winwood's Mem. iii. 469.

And razed, ere thought could urge this might have been.
See the World's ruins ! Nothing but the piles
Left, and wit since to cover it with tiles.''

But a more graphic, if more homely description is preserved in some verses from an old MS. printed by Haslewood ; and also by Halliwell-Phillipps :—[1]

" Now sitt thee downe Melpomene
Wrapt in a sea-cole robe,
And tell the direfull tragedie
That late was played at Globe.
For never man that can singe and saye
But was scard upon St. Peters daye.
    Oh sorrow ; pitifull sorrow, and yett all this is true.

" All you that please to understand
Come, listen to my storye
To see Death with his rakeing brand,
'Mong such an auditorye ;
Regarding neither Cardinall's might
Nor yett the rugged face of Henry theight.
    Oh, sorrow, etc.

This fearfull fire began above—
A wonder strange and true—
And to the Stage howse did remove
As round as taylor's clewe
And burnt downe both beame and snagg,
And did not spare the silken flagg.
    Oh, sorrow, etc.

" Out runne the Knightes, out runne the Lordes
And there was great adoe,
Some lost their hattes, and some their swordes,
Then out runne Burbidge too,
The Reprobates, though drunck on Munday,
Prayed for the Foole and Henry Condye.
    Oh, sorrow, etc.

---

[1] Stat. Reg. A dolefull Ballad of the general conflagration of the Globe.

" The perriwigges and drummeheades frye,
Like to a butter firkin
A wofull burneing did betide
To many a good buff jerkin.
Then with swolne eyes like druncken Fleminges
Distressed stood old stuttering Heminges.
    Oh, Sorrow, pitiful sorrow, and yet all this is true."

This would be a great and special loss to the Burbage brothers, and an indirect loss to all the Company.   Yet doubtless they made shift to have performances in their winter house of Blackfriars, or elsewhere.

Then there was the new toil and trouble of building, and it is said that the King and Court helped them liberally, and they built their Globe House fairer than before.   Court letters witness the satisfaction with the restoration.   Sir Matthew Brand, son of Nicholas Brand, from whom they had leased the land, extended the original lease for them, and they were once more in working order early in 1614.   (In February of that year there were burglaries committed in the Burbages' houses—with the gruesome conclusion of the execution of the principal (see Note IV).

It has seemed to me that this " Fire " would be the determining factor in Shakespeare's complete separation from the acting stage.   We know that he had made a home for his wife, himself and children in Stratford, and that he spent there more and more of his time as the years went by.   But he was often up in London, once at least in 1615, as his cousin, Thomas Green, says in his Diary, " My cosin Shakespeare coming yesterday to town I went to see him how he did."   Their talk was chiefly of the Stratford enclosure.   He might have brought in his pocket something for others than Greene a new play for Burbage.

Richard Burbage was still to the front.   On 29th March, 1615, a Royal Messenger was sent for John Hemmings and him, with the chiefs of the other companies to come before the Council, because they " have presumed, notwithstanding the commandment of the Lord Chamberlain, signified unto them by the Master of the Revels, to play this prohibited

I

time of Lent." They were to appear " on Friday next at 8 of the clock in the forenoon, without any excuse or delay. And in the meantime that neither they, nor the rest of their company presume to present any playes or interludes as they will answer the contrary at their perils." The results were not preserved. The Register of the Privy Council had been destroyed by fire from the beginning of the reign of James up till 1613 ; and after that date they are in manuscript but have not been published. I extracted the points relating to the players and published them in the " Shakespeare Jahrbuch," 1911.[1]

There is also an interesting account of a rival theatre in Blackfriars, which came to grief that year. Philip Rosseter had really got permission to build in Blackfriars under the great seal of England. He had already pulled down the Lady Sandars house, but the Lord Mayor and Aldermen complained of it and said it would be so near the church in Blackfriars that it would disturb the congregation at divine service. The Lord Chief Justice ruled that Rosseter's licence applied to building a theatre in the liberties but not in Blackfriars. So the Lords told Rosseter and his workmen that if they continued the work they should be sent to prison.

Rosseter and his friends, however, seem to have been undismayed by the threats and continued the building, unluckily for themselves. On 26th January, 1616–7, the entry is made :

" Whereas his Majestie is informed that notwithstanding divers commandments and prohibitions to the contrary there be certain persons who goe about to sett up a Play-house in the Blackfriars neere unto his Majesty's Wardrobe, and for that purpose have lately erected and made fit a building which is almost, if not fully finished. You shall understand that his Majesty hath this day expressly signified his pleasure that the same shall be pulled down soe as it be made unfitt for any such use, whereof we require your Lordship to take notice and per-

---

[1] Shakespeare Jahrbuch, " Dramatic Records from the Privy Council Register," 1912.

formed accordingly with all speede, and thereupon to certifie us of your proceedings."

So Richard Burbage and his company were saved from what might have proved a dangerous rival.

This Philip Rosseter was one of the Royal Musicians, but he had occasionally presented plays at Court by the Children of the Chapel, as for instance,[1] " To Philip Rosseter, on a warrant dated 24th November, 1612, for presenting a play by the Children of the Chapel before the Prince, the Lady Elizabeth and the Prince Palatyne, £6 13s. 4d. More to the said Philip Rosseter, for presenting before them two other plays by warrant, dated 31st May, 1613, £13 6s. 8d."

A new crop of law-suits arose around the Company, the one of them personal to Hemmings, the other relating to the Company in general. Hemmings' daughter had married William Osteler, one of the Blackfriars " children " who had been received into the King's company, and he had died. She sued his father for the full control of his shares, and John Witter, who had married the widow of Augustine Pope, one of the original shareholders, sued the Company for more profits. (See Professor Wallace's paper in " Century," August, 1910.)

Shakespeare was out of it all now—away in the quiet Stratford Church he lay. And Richard Burbage, having a son at the end of the year, in memory of him called the child by the name of " William." It has often been noted by enemies that the world did not seem very much distressed about the death of Shakespeare. No one seems to have grasped the true reason. Shakespeare had retired from the stage, as an actor, some time before he died. His personal appearances in London were rare.

And when the end came, and the *creation* of plays from that source ceased, we have every reason to believe that there was an *increase in the number of the performances* of his plays. For in the characters Shakespeare wrote for him Richard Burbage attained his greatest glory. Men did not realize that Shake-

---

[1] Dec. Acc., Treasurer of the Chamber, p. 543.

speare was dead while Burbage lived.   His power of impersona-
tion was so great that he *became* his characters.   An illustration may be given from Bishop Corbet's poem, " Iter Boreale,"
p. 193.   Speaking of his Host at Bosworth Field—

> " But chiefly by that one perspicuous thing
> When he mistooke a player for a King.
> For when he would have cryd King Richard dyed
> And call'd A Horse ! A Horse ! he ' Burbidge ' cryde."
> (This shows that he acted " Richard III.")

We have only to turn to the poems referring to Richard Burbage to realize that it was in the death of Burbage that to the
world our Shakespeare died.   Hardly three years later was it,
when the nervous system of Richard Burbage broke down.   It
seems from one of the poems to have been a shock, or an acute
attack of paralysis which took him away.   Queen Anne of
Denmark had died on 2nd March, 1618–9, Richard Burbage
died on the 13th of the same month (not on the same day, as the
D.N.B. says), and sorrow for his loss seems to have made men
forget to show the sorrow due to a Queen's death.

" Exit Burbage." [1]

The city and the Stage were clothed in gloom.   He was
buried in St. Leonard's, probably in the churchyard.   Men
poured forth their mourning for the loss of their great dramatist.

Chamberlain writes : " The funeral (of the Queen) is put off
to the 29th of next month, to the great hindrance of our players,
which are forbidden to play so long as her body is above
ground : one special man among them, Burbadge, is lately dead,
and hath left, they say, better than £300 land."

A touching tribute to his charm comes from the pen of the
great Lord Pembroke himself, to whom and to his brother,
Hemmings and Condell afterwards dedicated Shakespeare's
plays—reminding them how much they had honoured the
writer living.   The letter is new to literature, and is worthy of
being preserved (Egerton MSS., 2,592, f. 81).

[1] See Camden's Remains, also Ashmol. MS. Bodleian.

Letter of William, Earl of Pembroke, to Viscount Doncaster, Ambassador to Germany, at Middleburg.

" MY LORD,—

" I could not let my cousin Berkley go without this small testimony of my unceremonious respect unto your Lordship. . . . This day the French Ambassador took leave . . . we shall put off our blacks at St. George's tyde, and be laught at for it by all Christendom at Midsummer . . . now you have all that I know that past since your departure but that my Lord of Lenox made a great supper to the French Embassador this night here and even now all the company are at the play, which I being tender-harted, could not endure to see so soone after the loss of my old acquaintance Burbadge. . . . Your Lordships most affectionate friend and Servaunt,

" PEMBROKE.

" WHITEHALL,
    " 20*th May*."

Thomas Middleton writes lines, published among his poems, " On the death of that great Master in his art and quality, painting and playing, R. Burbage :

> " Astronomers and Stargazers this year
> Write but of four eclipses, five appear,
> Death interposing Burbage and there staying
> Hath made a visible eclipse of playing."

De Burbagio et Regina.

" Hung be the Heaven's with black, yield day to night,
    Comets importing change shoot through the sky.
Scourge the foul fates that thus afflict our sight,
    Burbadge the player has vouchsafed to die ;
    Therefore in London is not one eye dry :
The deaths of men who act our Queens and Kings
Are now more mourned than are the real things.
The Queen is dead ! To him now what are Queens ?
    Queans of the Theatre are much more worth.
            *   *   *   *   *
Dick Burbage was their mortal God on earth.

When he expires, lo ! all lament the man,
But where's the grief should follow good Queen Anne ? ''

An epitaph upon Mr. Richard Burbage, the player.

'' This Life's a play, sceaned out by Nature's Arte,
  Where every man hath his allotted parte.
This man hath now (as many men can tell)
  Ended his part, and he hath acted well
The Play now ended, think his grave to be
  The retiring house of his sad Tragedie,
Where to give his fame this, be not afraid,
  Here lies the best Tragedian ever played.''

Sloane MS., 1786

The longest Epitaph is worth inserting.

'' On ye death of ye famous actor R. Burbage.

'' Some skillful limner aide mee, yf not soe
Some sad Tragedian to expresse my woe :
But (oh) hee's gon, yt could ye best both limne
And act my griefe, and it is only him
That I invoke this strange assistance to't,
And on ye point call for himselfe to doe't :
For none but Tully Tully's praise could tell,
And as hee could, no man could doe so well
This part of sorrow for him, nor can drawe
So truely to ye lyfe this mapp of woe.
This griefe's true picture, which his losse has bred
Hee's gon, and with him what a world is dead.
(Which he revived to be renewed soe.
No more young Hamlett, ould Hieronymoe,
Kind Lear, the grieved Moore, and more besyde
That lived in him, have now for ever dy'de,)
Oft have I seen him leape into a grave
Suiting ye person (which he seemed to have)
Of a sad lover, with so true an eye
That then I would have sworn he meant to die ;
Oft have I seen him playe his part in jest,
So lively, yt spectators, and the rest
Of his sad crewe, while hee but seemed to bleed
Amazed thought that he had died indeed.
Oh ! did not knowledge check me, I should sweare

Even yet it is a false report I heare,
And thinke that he who did so truly faigne
Is only dead in jest to live againe:
But now this part he acts, not playes, 'tis knowne
Others hee plaide, but now hee acts his owne.
England's great Roscius, for what Roscius
Was more to Rome than Burbadge was to us;
How to ye person hee did suit his face,
How did his speech become him, and his face
Suit with his speech, whilst not a word did fall
Without just weight to balance it withall.
Had'st thou but spoke to Death, and used ye power
Of thy enchaunting tongue, but ye first hower
Of his assault, hee had let fall his dart
And charmed bene by all thy charming art.
This he well knew, and to prevent such wrong
First cunningly made seizure of thy tonge,
Then on ye rest 'twas easy, by degrees
The slender ivy toppes ye tallest trees.
Poets! whose glory 'twas of late to heare
Your lines so well exprest: henceforth forbeare
And write noe more, or if you doe't, let't bee
In comic scenes, for tragic parts you see
Die all with him, nay, rather sluice your eyes
And henceforth write naught else but tragedies,
Moist dirges, or sad elegies, and those
Mournfull laments, which may expresse your woes.
Blurr all your leaves with blotts, yt what is writ
May bee but one sad blacke, and upon it
Draw marble lines, yt may outlast ye sun
And stand like trophies when ye world is done.
Or turn your ink to blood, your pens to spears
To pierce and wound the heaven's hearts and eares;
Enraged, write stabbing lines yt every word
May be as apt for murder as a sword,
That no man may surmise after this fact
Of ruthlesse Death, either to hear or act.
And you, his sad companions, to whom Lent
Becomes more lenten yn this accident,
Henceforth your wavering flag no more hang out.
Play now noe more at all, when round about
Wee looke and misse ye Atlas of ye spheare,
What comfort thinke you have wee to bee there;

And how can you delight in playing when
Sad mourning soe affecteth other men ?
Yf you will hang it out, yt let it weare
No more light colours, but death's livery beare.
Hang all your house with black, ye eaves it beares
With icicles of ever melting teares :
And yf you ever chance to play againe
Let nought but tragedies affect your scene.
And thou dear earth yt enshrines yt dust yt must
By heaven now committed to thy trust
Keepe it as precious as ye richest mine
That lies entombed in ye rich wombe of thine
That after times may know yt much loved mould
Fro' other dust, and cherish it as gold.
On it bee laid some soft but lasting stone,
With this short epitaph endorst thereon ;
That every one may reade, and reading weepe,
' 'Tis England's Roscius, Burbage, whom I keepe.' "

Em. H.

There are five transcripts of this Elegy, one at Warwick
Castle ; one in Mr. Huth's collection, which calls it " A funerall
Elegy on the death of the famous Actor Richard Burbage :
who died on Saturday in Lent, the 13th of March, 1618–9."
It was first printed in " The Gentleman's Magazine," 1825 ;
and Collier prints from some other MS. some extra verses.
This copy is from " The Gentleman's Magazine," corrected
from Halliwell's with one of Collier's verses included within
brackets.

Collier says he has found another MS. which enlarges the
list in his " New Particulars."

An elegy on our late Protean Roscius Richard Burbage.

(After a few couplets, the same as above, it continues) :—
" No more young Hamlet though but scant of breath
    Shall cry revenge for his dear father's death :
    Poor Romeo never more shall tears beget
    For Juliet's love and cruel Capulet ;
    Harry shall not be seen as King or Prince,
    They died with thee, Dear Dick—
    Not to revive again.   Jeronimo

Shall cease to mourn his son Horatio ;
They cannot call thee from thy naked bed
By horrid outcry ; and Antonio's dead.
Edward shall lack a representative,
And Crookback, as befits, shall cease to live.
Tyrant Macbeth, with unwash'd bloody hand
We vainly now may hope to understand.
Brutus and Marcius henceforth must be dumb,
For ne'er thy like upon our stage shall come
To charm the faculty of eyes and ears,
Unless we could command the dead to rise.
Vindex is gone, and what a loss was he !
Frankford, Brachiano and Malevole
Heart-broke Philaster and Amintas too
Are lost for ever ; with the red-haired Jew,
Which sought the bankrupt merchant's pound of flesh,
By woman-lawyer caught in his own mesh.
What a wide world was in that little space,
Thyself a world, the Globe thy fittest place !
Thy stature small, but every thought and mood
Might thoroughly from thy face be understood,
And his whole action he could change with ease
From ancient Lear to youthful Pericles.
But let me not forget one chiefest part,
Wherein beyond the rest, he moved the heart,
The grieved Moor, made jealous by a slave
Who sent his wife to fill a timeless grave,
Then slew himself upon the bloody bed.
All these and many more with him are dead,
Thereafter must our poets leave to write.
Since thou art gone, dear Dick, a tragic night
Will wrap our black-hung stage. He made a Poet,
And those who yet remain full surely know it ;
For having Burbadge to give forth each line
It filled their brain with fury more divine.''

Another outburst of praise came after the Restoration, printed
in Collier's " New Particulars " from an MS. of time of
Charles I :—

" Dick Burbage, that most famous man,
    That actor without peer,

> With this same part his course began
>   And kept it many a year.
> Shakespeare was fortunate, I trow,
>   That such an actor had,
> If we had but his equal now
>   For one I should be glad."

Richard Flecknoe in his Epigrams gives—

The praises of Burbage, or an excellent Actor.

> Who, by the best and noblest of the age
> Was held the chiefest ornament of the stage,
> And Actor's clearest Light in no dark time
> To shew them what to follow, what decline.
> Who knew, by rules of the Dramatic Art,
> To fit his speech and action to his part,
> And of an excellent orator had all
> In voice and gesture which we charming call ;
> Who a delightful Proteus was that could
> Transform himself into what shape he would
> And finally did on the stage appear
> Beauty to th' Eye, and Musick to the Ear.

Richard Flecknoe in his " Short Discourses on the English Stage," printed 1664, inserted the description of an excellent actor, versified in his Euterpe restored 1672—

The praises of Richard Burbadge

> " Who did appear so gracefully on the stage
> He was the admired example of the age,
> And so observed all your dramatic laws
> He ne'er went off the stage but with applause."

Sir Richard Baker, " Theatrum Redivivum " answering Prynne's " Histriomastix," 1662, " Scurrility." " Yet he shall never give that contentment to Beholders as honest Tarlton did, though he said never a word. And what scurrility was ever heard to come from the mouths of the best actors of our time, Alleyn or Burbidge ? Yet what plays were ever so pleasing, as where their parts had the greatest part."

Sir Richard Baker's Chronicle, 1643, continues :—

" After such men (Statesmen, Writers, Divines), it might be thought ridiculous to speak of Stage-players ; but seeing Excellency in the meanest things deserves remembering and Roscius the Comedian is recorded in History with such commendation, it may be allowed us to do the like with some of our nation. Richard Bourbidge and Edward Allen, two such actors as no age must ever look to see the like ; and to make their Comedies compleat, Richard Tarleton, who for the part called the Clown's part, never had his match, never will have. For writers of playes, and such as have been players themselves, William Shakespeare and Benjamin Johnson have specially left their names commended to posterity " (p. 120).

We might go even further to behold how Richard Burbage became an example to succeeding ages, and men moulded their art on his conceptions.

When Burbage Played.

When Burbage played, the stage was bare
Of fount and Temple, Tower and Stair,
Two backswords eked a battle out,
Two supers made a rabble rout
The Throne of Denmark was a chair !

And yet, no less the audience there
Thrilled through all changes of Despair,
Hope, Anger, Fear, Delight and Doubt,
  When Burbage played.

This is the Actor's gift, to share
All moods, all passions nor to care
One whit for scene, so he without
Can lead men's minds the roundabout,
Stirred as of old these hearers were
  When Burbage played.
                    (*Austin Dobson's Poems*, 1897, p. 473)

CHAPTER III

WHAT WAS LEFT OF THE BURBAGES

CUTHBERT BURBAGE, whose material, whose work and whose brains were built into the first Globe Theatre, does not appear much during the course of its history. There were no insurance companies then, and he and his brother must have lost much more than the others. But it seemed to have been made up to them somehow. The brothers put their brains into the building of the second Globe Theatre, but the " Shares " by that time necessarily changed much in value and in condition. Cuthbert remained a sharer in the House, as may be seen later. It is to be supposed that he followed some other profession, such as that of a Scrivener or an Attorney, by which he could help the Company in their business affairs.

He comes into our notice, performing such duties, when, in that ill-starred month of March 1618–9 his brother Richard was seized by his last illness. The picture rises before us. Richard had lost his power of writing, lost his power of clear speech, but seated by the bed Cuthbert drew up in his fair clerkly hand the nuncupative will of his brother on 12th March, 1618–9. Richard appointed his well-beloved wife Winifred sole executor of his goods and chattels and his will was signed by Cuthbert Burbage his brother, Elizabeth his wife (made her mark), Nicholas Tooley, Anne Lancaster, Richard Robinson,[1] Elizabeth Graves (made her mark), and Henry Jacksonne. The widow proved it on 22nd April. She had a daughter after her

---

[1] Richard Burbage's widow afterwards married Richard Robinson.

husband's death, whom she baptized Sara.   She had lost many children, but her son William survived.   To him his father's lands in Kent and elsewhere would pass by law.

Before the month was out, on 27th March, 1619, the King granted a new Patent by Privy Seal to his servants, still including the name of Burbage second in the list.

The names of the members of the King's company re-patented in 1619 show how few of the old men still remained. John Hemmings, Richard Burbage, Henry Condell, John Lowen, Nicholas Tooley, John Underwood, Nathan Field, Robert Benfield, Robert Gough, William Ecclestone, Richard Robinson, John Shancks and the rest of their associates.   The first was evidently manager, as we may see from various references in public papers.

The apparently friendly relations of all the company to each other might have been noted throughout.   They remembered each other in their wills, they trusted each other as overseers. And Cuthbert Burbage was still reckoned as one of their band privately.   This may be seen in his relation to Nicholas Tooley, who had been the " servant " or apprentice of Richard Burbage.   He had lived in Shoreditch and he died in Cuthbert Burbage's house there.   He made his will on 3rd June, 1623. For some unexplained reason he seems to have been called Nicholas Wilkenson alias Tooley, though he used the latter name, made his will, signed it, and then added a codicil as " Nicholas Wilkenson alias Tooley," that he wished all the items in his will signed " Nicholas Tooley " to be faithfully carried out.   He left £80 to the Church of St. Leonard's for the distribution of 32 penny wheaten loaves every Sunday to the poor ; and Howe in his continuation of Stowe, duly enters him among the benefactors of the parish, and notes the fact that the parish had invested the money in a rent-charge " issuing out of the George in Holywell Street " for the true performance of the will.   He seems to have died single and had no heirs.   He forgave most of his debtors.   What Richard Robinson owed him (over £29), he desired to be paid to Sara the daughter of his late master, Richard Burbage. He left £10 as a remembrance of his love to Mrs. Elizabeth Burbage for her motherly care of him, and £5 to Alice Walker, sister of his late master. He then left Cuthbert Burbage and John Hemmings his executors, and after they had paid all his funeral expenses and legacies they were to share the remainder between them. He was buried in St. Giles without Cripplegate.

When John Hemmings made his will, it was " Mr. Burbage his loving friend, to be overseer," and Mr. Rice also.

He was buried 12th October, 1630. Condall had already gone in 1627.

In 1633 there was a definite attempt to suppress the Blackfriars Theatre, on account of the great inconvenience to the inhabitants ; not as was attempted in Elizabethan times without redress to the owners or the Players.   In the yet unpublished volumes of the Privy Council Register there is entered a letter dated " 8th Oct., 1633. Upon consideration this day had at the Boarde of the greate inconvenience and annoyance occasioned by the resort and confluence of Coaches to the Playhouse in Blackfriars, whereby the Streets being narrow therabouts are at those times become impassable to the great prejudice of his Majesties subjects passing that way upon their severall occasions and in particular to divers noblemen and Councillors of State whose houses are in that way, whereby they are many times hindered from their necessary attendance upon his Majesty's person and service. Their Lordships calling to mind that formerly upon complaint hereof made the Board was of opinion that the said Playhouse was fitt to be removed from thence, and that an indifferent recompense and allowance should be given them for their interest in the said house and buildings thereunto belonging, did therefore thinke fit and order that Sir Henry Spicer and Sir William Becher Knights, the Aldermen of the Ward, Laurence Whitacker Esq. and William Child citizen of London, or any three of them, be hereby required to call such of the parties interested before them, as they shall thinke fitt, and upon hearing of their demands and view of the place, to make an indifferent estimate and valewe of the said house and buildings, and of their interests therein and to agree upon and sett down such recompense to be given for the same as shall be reasonable and thereupon to make report to the Board of their doings and proceedings therein by the 26th of this present month."

In the course of the inquiries, it was found that Cuthbert Burbage and William Burbage the son of Richard were the owners ; and they estimated its value as £700. They were owners also of 4 adjacent tenements, and their estimation of its business value raised it to a very high figure. Collier says the Report was subscribed by William Baker, Humphrey Smith, Laurence Whitaker and William Childe, and in consideration of the loss to the shareholders and the players the surveyors estimated it at £2,400. Probably this was thought too much to spend for the purpose, and further correspondence and arrangement ensued but nothing definite seems to have been done then. Arrangements were attempted.

" 20th November, 1633. Whereas the Board hath taken consideration of the great inconveniences which growe by reason of their resort to the Playhouse of the Blackfriars in coaches, whereby the Streetes neare thereunto are at the Play time so stopped that his Majesties Subjects going about their necessarie affayres can hardly finde passage and are oftentymes endangered. Their Lordships remembering that there is an easie passage by water unto that Playhouse without troubling the Streetes, and that it is much more fit and reasonable that those which goe thither should goe thither by water or else on foote, rather than the necessarie businesses of all others and the public commerce should be disturbed by their pleasure, doe hereafter order, that if anie person, man, or woman, of what condition soever repaire to the aforesaide playhouse in a Coach, so soon as they are gone out of their coaches the Coachmen shall departe thence and not retourne till the end of the play, nor shall stay or retourne to fetch those whom they carried anie nearer with their coaches, than the further part of St. Paules

Churchyarde on the one side, and the Fleet conduit on the other syde, and in ye tyme betweene their departure and returne shall either returne home, or else abide in some other streetes lesse frequented with passengers, and to range their coaches in these places that the way be not stopped, which order if any coach-man disobey the next Constable or officer is hereby charged to commit him presently to Ludgate or Newgate : And the Lord Mayor of London is required to see this carefully performed by the Constables and officers to whom it apperteynethe, and to punish every such Constable or officer as shall be found negligent therein.   And to the ende that none may pretende ignorance thereof it is lastly ordered that Copies of this order shall be set up at Paules Chaine, by direcion of the Lord Mayor also at the West end of St. Paules Church at Ludgate, and the Blackfriars gate and Fleete Conduit."

In order to strengthen this resolution of keeping the streets clear, the Privy Council wrote on 29th November, 1633, to the Lord Mayor, etc. : "Wee send your Lordship herewith an order of this Board, for redressing of the inconveniences that growe by reason of the great resort in Coaches to the Playhouse in the Blackfryers which orders we doe hereby pray and earnestly require your Lordship to see fully and diligently executed in every point thereof, and so much the rather in regard it is of noe lesse unsemeliness to the City, than of trouble and annoy-ance to his Majesties subjects.   So expecting your Lordship's performance of these our directions, etc."

One can imagine the outcry that wealthy women, going to the Playhouse in fine clothes, would make about uncertainty as to the whereabouts of their carriages in wet weather.   There were no umbrellas then.   The husbands and friends on the Privy Council could not have spent a happy month, between their first order, and the succeeding one—

" 29th December, 1633.   Ordered this day, the King present, upon informacion this day given to the Board of the dis-commoditie that divers persons of great quallity, especially ladies and gentlewomen, did receive in going to the Playhouse

of Blackfriers by reason that noe coaches may stand within
the Blackfryers gate, or returne thither during the play, and of
the preiudice the players, his Majesties servants, doe receive
thereby.   But especially that the streetes are soe much the
more encumbred with the said Coaches, the Board, taking into
consideration the former order of the 20th November last concerning this business, did thinke fitt to explaine the said order
in such manner, that as many coaches as may stand within
the Blackfriers gate may enter and stay there, or retourne
thither at the end of the play, but that the said former order of
the 20th November be duly observed in all other partes.
Whereof as well the Lord Mayor, as all other his Majesties
officers who are prayed and required to see the said order
observed, are to take notice, etc."

The Lord Mayor and Corporation, even then, would have
thought it easier and wiser to suppress the theatre altogether,
but their time was not yet.

There was trouble also at the Globe.   For the second time
in his life Cuthbert had trusted his landlord in a verbal promise concerning a lease, and for the second time was driven to
strong measures.   Sir Matthew Brand, son and heir of the
Nicholas Brand from whom he had taken the site in Maiden
Lane, had respected the original 31 years lease, but had been
very uncertain about further extension.   His principle began
more and more to go against theatres, and his interest, in this
case pulled in the same direction as his principle ; for there
seems to have been no saving clause as to the builder's right to
carry away the material when his lease expired.   Cuthbert and
the others went to law against their landlord.   I have not been
able to find the proceedings in the case, but I have found the
note in the Decree and Order Books of the Court of Requests.
" 6th February 9 Charles I, Hilary Term, 1634.   Burbage *v.*
Brend.   In the Cause at the suit of Cuthbert Burbage, Richard
Robinson, William Hemmings and others, plaintiffs, against Sir
Matthew Brand, Knt. defendant.   Upon the motion of Mr.
Richard Lane of Counsaill with the said Complainants, it is

K

ordered that the Council on both sides shall attend this Court
upon Monday next to be heard upon the case this day delivered
into the said Courte by the said complainants under their
counsells hands of Richard Lane and John White Esquiers
of Counsaill severally with the said parties, and thereby such
further direction shall be given in the case as shall be moved.
And the said defendant forthwith to have notice of this present
notice." The names above mentioned rouse memories. Cuthbert, the oldest survivor of the whole concern ; Richard
Robinson, witness to Richard Burbage's will, who had married
his widow, and stood, *jure marito* in her place, and as representative of his stepson William, not yet of age, William Hemmings,
the unlucky son of old John Hemmings of the First Folio. And
Mr. Richard Lane their Counsel, was the very same Deputy
Registrar in the Court of Requests, whom Giles Alleyn had
charged with confederacy, fraud and acceptance of bribes, in
the last year of Elizabeth, when Francis Bacon, Esq., found the
charge fit only to be dismissed. (See Note 21.) Sir Matthew
Brand seems to have come round at the time, probably through
the influence of the Court of Equity.

But Cuthbert Burbage was to have one more blow, of the
same nature as he had so often endured, but in a new court,
under conditions more trying to him than ever. In his long life he
must have seen many changes in the *personnelle* of what through
all its various names had remained the Burbage Company.
New actors had risen round him and grown old, and men newer
still had grown up and had become popular. We see their
names in the payments of the Lord Chamberlain's books, and
Eyllardt Swanston, one of these, was the leading actor of the
company when he brought Cuthbert Burbage's last trouble to
him. He was of the modern school, the *worker* is *everything*,
the Inventor, the Creator, the Supporter, is nothing ; there is
no meaning in inheritance, no right in Landlords. Such
thoughts, hazily enough shaped, no doubt, were in Eyllardt
Swanston's mind when he persuaded Robert Benfield and
Thomas Pollard, who had been one of the boy-actors in the

early Blackfriars, to complain along with him to the Lord Chamberlain, that the bulk of the shares of the Theatre were in the Burbages' hands, they being no actors.   He wanted shares in *the house*, and there being none to sell just then, he wanted the Lord Chamberlain *to force the Burbages* to part with some of their shares, and to sell them to him and Pollard.   It must be remembered that this Lord Chamberlain was not William, Earl of Pembroke, whose touching tribute to Richard Burbage's memory I have recorded above.   He had died in 1630. The Lord Chamberlain in 1635 was his brother Philip, of a denser brain, and a coarser heart-fibre.   It was he who, on the petition of Swanston and Pollard, probably because they were the best actors in the King's company at the time, granted their petition before he heard what the Burbages had to say, and supported his decision after he had heard the old survivor's " *answer.*"   There seems some rough justice in the decision, but it was hard on the man, at the close of his life, who had inherited his father's Idea, had carefully tended it, sacrificed himself for it, and expected comfort in his old age as the result of the labours of his youth.   His speech has a dramatic power.   It is the fourth act of his Tragedy.

I can only here give a few phrases from it, as it appears in extenso at the end :—

" RIGHT HONOURABLE. . . .   Wee your humble suppliants Cuthbert Burbage, and Winifred [1] his brother's wife, and William his son . . . wee ought not in all charity to be disabled of our livelyhood by men so soone shott up, since it hath been the custom that they should come to it by farre more antiquity and desert than these can justly attribute to themselves. . . . shewing the infinite charges, the manifold lawsuits, the lease's expiration, the restraints in sickness times and other accidentes that did cutt from us the best part of the gaines. . . .

" The father of us Cuthbert and Richard was the first builder of playhouses, and was himself in his younger yeres a Player.

---

[1] She was by this time Mrs. Robinson.

The Theatre he built with many hundred pounds taken up at interest, the Players that lived in these first times had only the profits arising from the dores, but now they (the players) receave also the cominge in at the dores to themselves, and half the galleries from the Housekeepers. Hee built this house upon leased grounds by which meanes the Landlord and he had a greate suite in lawe, and by his death, the like troubles fell on us his sonnes. We then bethought us of altering from thence, and at like expense built the Globe, with more summes of money taken up at interest which lay heavy on us many yeares, and to ourselves we joined those deserving men Shakespeare, Hemmings, Condall, Phillipps and others partners in ye profitts of that they call the house.

" The Blackfriers that is our inheritance, our father purchased it at extreme rates, and made it into a play-house with great charge and troble which after was leased out to one Evans that first sett up the Boyes commonly called The Queen's Majesties Children of the Chappell. In processe of time, the boyes growing up to bee men, which were Underwood, Field, Ostler, and were taken to strengthen the King's service, and the more to strengthen the service, the boyes daily wearing out, it was considered that house would be as fitt for ourselves, and soe purchased the lease remaining from Evans with *our* money, and placed men-players which were Hemmings, Condall, Shakespeare, etc. And Richard Burbage who for 35 years pains, cost and labour, made meanes to leave his wife and children some estate (and out of whose estate soe many of other players and their families have been mayntained) these new men that were never bred from children in the King's service, would take away with oathes and menaces that wee shall bee forced, and that they will not thank us for it. . . .

" Against their sayinges that wee eat the fruit of their labours, we referre it to your Honours judgment to consider their profitts, which wee may safely maintain . . . each of these complainants gained severally, as he was a player and noe Housekeeper £180. Besides Mr. Swanston hath received from the Blackfriers this year, as he is there a Housekeeper, above £30, all which accompted together, may very well keep him from starving. Wherefore your honours most humble suppliants intreate they may not further bee trampled upon then their estates can beare, seeing how dearly it hath been purchased by the infinite cost and paynes of the family of the Burbages, and the great desert of Richard Burbage for his quality of playing, that his wife should not starve in her old age.

"Mr. Hemming and Mr. Condall had theirs (shares) of the Blackfriers of us for nothing, *It is only wee that suffer continually.*" That may be taken as the last known words of Cuthbert Burbage, indeed of the whole family.

The Lord Chamberlain, in spite of all, held to his earlier decision and the scornful Eillardt Swanston triumphed over the others.

How little did it all matter in the light of the short leases yet to run. Yet how much it seemed to matter to the old shareholders.

The new Shakespeare Society's Transactions of 1886 give some dates concerning the Shakespearean Actors, and John Shancke is said to have been buried 27th January, 1635–6, so soon after his pleadings with Burbage, against Eillardt Swanston before the Lord Chamberlain.

Cuthbert Burbage died not long after. Did the Lord Chamberlain's decision, and the inevitable bad feeling stirred up by it help to hasten the end ? Or was it a swift visitation in the Plague of 1636 which carried Cuthbert Burbage away in September 1636 ? The Register does not notify the cause. It says :—

"Cuthbert Burbardge was buryed ye 17th day of September 1636" (no address given). And within a fortnight his wife followed him : "Elizabeth Burbadge, widow. First day of October, 1636" (no address). They were buried in the same tomb in the Chancel of St. Leonards'. Strype's continuation of Stow records it, and if we read the words aright, the inscription ran, " Cuthbert Burbage and Elizabeth his wife.   They departed in Sept. 1636.

Venimus, Vidimus, Redivivimus, Resurgemus."

This memorial is gone now, as well as that which must certainly have been set up to James and Richard Burbage, of whose last resting-place no definite account has been preserved.

Cuthbert left no son alive.   If there are any descendants it must have been through Elizabeth.   We know too little of any.

Cuthbert had secured at some time before his death a coat of arms, entered in the Visitation of London, 1634, " Crest, a Boar's Head ; and three Boars' Heads on a Shield."   He claims no long pedigree.   The family began and ended in father and sons.

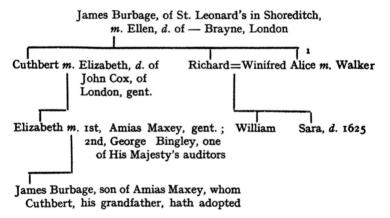

James Burbage, of St. Leonard's in Shoreditch,
m. Ellen, *d*. of — Brayne, London

Cuthbert *m*. Elizabeth, *d*. of   Richard=Winifred Alice *m*. Walker [1]
John Cox, of
London, gent.

Elizabeth *m*. 1st, Amias Maxey, gent. ;   William   Sara, *d*. 1625
2nd, George   Bingley, one
of His Majesty's auditors

James Burbage, son of Amias Maxey, whom
Cuthbert, his grandfather, hath adopted

In Wood's " Fastı Oxoniensis," I, 303, Robert Burbage is described as a great professor of divinity "nearly related to the famous Richard Burbage."

Among the numerous records I have searched at the Record Office to find any information concerning the family I was often confused by a Richard Burbage [2] of Somerset.

[1] I include Richard's name.   There may be descendants.
[2] In searching the Registers of South Stoke, Oxfordshire, or the

William Burbage, twenty years old at death of his uncle, evidently had not the genius of his father or his name-father, not even the talent ; or perhaps he was affected by the fresh wave of disapproval of the stage.

I have found nothing definite of William, but there are two little suits which may, or may not, refer to him.

In the Records of the Middlesex Sessions for 9th September, 27 Charles II, at Whitechapel, complaint was made that John Rudd, late of the same parish, yeoman, assaulted John Hewlett, the apprentice of William Burbidge, Taylor, and sent him off to Virginia and sold him there.   Also in Chanc. Proc. Reynardson, 399–66, Burbage *v.* Burbage, 16th Feb. 1669, complaint that Henry Burbage in his minority claims a small property in Barrow-on-Soar, Leicester, which had been bought by Richard Burbage, 2 Jan., 9 Jas. I, by deed from Henry Earl of Huntingdon and it had come to William Burbage his son and heir, who had gone to the Barbadoes for fifteen years.   This Henry was his son born in this country who had also gone to the Barbadoes and was now of the age of twenty years.   On the other hand, he is said to have given the property to his brother Hugh.

It is difficult to know how the Burbage " inheritance " went.   The Globe Theatre was entered as " the inheritance of Sir Matthew Brand and worth £20 a year in 1637."   Dr. Furnivall found in the Phillipps Collection at Cheltenham a copy of the 1631 edition of Stow, with manuscript notes at the end regarding the fate of the playhouse : " The Globe Playhouse on the Bank side was burnt down . . . built up again . . . and now pulled again to the ground by Sir Matthew Brand on Monday, the 15th April, 1544, to make tenements in the room of it."   (Through the transfers of these tenements we learn the boundaries of the old site.)   The Blackfriars estate

notices of the Rev. James Stopes there, I found " Richard Burbidge, son of Richard Burbidge, baptized 30th March, 1577—buried 1578." " Thomas Burbidge, baptized 2nd Dec., 1579," " buried 16th March, 1608."

was held in fee simple, and it is difficult to imagine how the property was dealt with, and whether there was any compensation or not, to anybody. The same authority notes, " The Blackfriars Playhouse pulled down on 6th August, 1555," and the other playhouses finished their career shortly before or after.[1]

The Stage sank to a lower level after the death of the greatest poet and the greatest player. Yet a reflected light from their glory still hung for awhile about their successors until 1640.

We know something of their names and of their Court performances from the Lord Chamberlain's Books,[2] and less from other books of Court expenses.

Only those who have long been searching in that later period for minor details, can estimate the difference in the bulk of material information concerning the stage which has come down to us from the later years of James, and the beginning of Charles' reign, compared with those to be had of Elizabeth's reign. There was a dearth of the old gossippy Court letters, which told us so much in the sixteenth century. Histories dealt with things more serious than the fortunes of playhouses and the fate of players. Yet we are allowed the pleasure of " looking backwards " later, and think of the diatribes of the preachers when Richard Burbage was a boy.

Wright in his " Historia Histrionica " says, " The reader may know that the Profession of Players is not so totally scandalous, nor all of them so reprobate. . . .   We have indeed poets of a different genius, so are the plays . . . as much inferior to those of former times, as the actors." He had seen before the wars Lowen, Taylor, Pollard and some others, " all who related to the Blackfriars, where they acted in perfection." In the

[1] " The Fortune between White Cross Streete and Golding Lane burned 1619, rebuilt 1622, pulled down 1649." " The Hope on Bankside commonly called the Bear Garden, a playhouse on Mondays, Wednesdays, Fridays and Saturdays and for the Baiting of Bears Tuesday and Thursday, built 1610, pulled down 25th March, 1656."

[2] See my paper reprinted from the Shakespeare Jahrbuch, 1910, " Shakespeare's Fellows and Followers."

conversation Lovewit asks, "What master parts can you remember the old Blackfriars men to act in Johnson's, Shakespeare's and Fletcher's plays?"

"Shakespeare (who, as I have heard was a much better poet than player), Burbage, Hemmings, and others of the older sort were dead before I knew the town. . . . Lowen used to act with mighty applause Falstaffe." "Taylor acted Hamlet, incomparably well," "Swanston used to play Othello, Pollard and Robinson were comedians, so was Shank. These were of the Blackfriars. . . . The Blackfriars and the Globe on the Bankside, a winter and a summer house belonging to the same company, called the King's servants . . . all these got money and lived in reputation, especially those of the Blackfriars who were men of grave and sober behaviour."

"The prices were small (there being no scenes) and better order kept among the company that came, which made very good people think a play an innocent diversion for an idle hour or two, the plays being then for the most part more instructive and moral," and a great contrast to the present. "The private houses were small, and the acting was by candlelight. The Globe, Fortune and Bull were large houses, and lay partly open to the weather." "When the stage was put down, most of them except Lowen,[1] Taylor,[2] and Pollard (who were superannuated) went into the King's army, and like good men and true served their old master." Robinson was killed at the taking of Basinghouse by Harrison.[3] Hart was a Lieutenant of Horse, Allen of the Cockpit a Major at Oxford. "I have not heard of one of the players of any note that sided with the other party, but only Swanston, and he profest himself a Presbyterian, took up the trade of a jeweller and lived in Aldermanbury. . . . The rest either lost or exposed their lives for the King."

Collier gives some particulars of the other actors. Notices of the greater ones appear in the "Dictionary of National Biography."

[1] Buried 18th March, 1659.   [2] 1653.   [3] 23rd March, 1647.

Of these some were born in Shoreditch, some lived, some were buried there, some both born and buried.

It would make this volume too long to dwell even on all of these, the Shoreditch players.   They were men of the same profession, it is true, but not to them was given the inspiration of pioneers, the courage of champions, the provident skill of commanders.

Not to any but to the Burbages, so interwoven with the whole history of the Dramatic Art in *their* century, can we ascribe the honour of being the discoverers and fellow-workers of Shakespeare, and the Founders of the British Stage.

SELECTIONS FROM ST. LEONARD'S REGISTERS, SHOREDITCH.

Burials.

William Somers was buryd the 2nd day of Julye, 1560, Shordiche

Joan Dowle, wife of Isaac Dowle, 19th Feb., 1580, Curtayn.

John Aynsworth, a player, Sept. 28th, 1581.

Joane Burbidge, daughter of James Burbage, 18th August, 1582

Richard Torrelton, 3rd September, 1588, Halliwell Street.

Augustine Fletcher, 24th June, 1596, Goddards.

James Feake, 7th Dec., 1596, Halliwell Street.

James Burbidge, 2nd Feb., 1596–7, Halliwell.

James Burbage, son of Cuthbert Burbage, 15th July, 1597, Halliwell

Gabriell Spencer being slaine was buryed ye 24th September, 1598
  Hoggeslane.

Francis Burbedge, the daughter of Richard Burbadge, 19th Sept.
  1604, Halliwell Street.

Augustine Beeston, son of Christopher Beeston, 17th Nov., 1604
  Halliwell Street.

Richard Burbage, son of Richard, 16th Aug., 1607.

Jane Beeston, daughter of Christopher, 22nd Sept., 1607, Halliwell

Mary Condell, daughter of Henry Condell, 24th March, 1607
  Hoxton.

William Slye, gent, 16th Aug., 1608, Halliwell Street.

Juliet Burbege, daughter of Richard Burbage, 12th Sept., 1608
  Halliwell.

Thomas Cowlie, 19th March, 1608, Peckham's Rents.

Elizabeth Keysar, widow, 23rd June, 1609, Churchend.

Christopher Beeston, son of Christopher Beeston, 15th July, 1610

Thomas Greene, 29th April, 1613, Peckham's Rents.

Hellen Burbadge, widow, 8th May, 1613, Hallywell Street.

George Wilkins (poet and player), Aug. 9th, 1613.

Julia Burbadge, daughter of Richard Burbadge, 15th Aug., 1615, Halliwell Street.

Robert Beeston, son of Christopher Beeston, Clerkenwell, 26th Dec., 1615.

Elizabeth Cowley, wife of Richard Cowley, 28th September, 1616, Holywell Street.

Wynefryd Burbadge, daughter of Richard Burbadge, 14th Oct., 1616, Holywell Street.

Sylvanus Skory, Esq., 15th Oct., 1617, St. Peeter's Hill.

Richard Cowley, Player, 12th March, 1618, Halliwell Street.

Richard Burbadge, Player, was buried the 16th March, 1618-9, Halywell Street.

Etheldred, wife of William Johnson, 20th Jan., 1622-3, Halliwell.

Margaret Cooley, widow, 24th Oct., 1623.

Thomas Ainsworth, son of Robert Ainsworth, 10th Nove., 1625, Halliwell Street.

John Hide, 14th Maie, 1624, Swan Yard.

Sara Burbadge, 29th April, 1625, Hallywell Street.

Robert Wilson, 27th July, 1625, Church End.

Elizabeth, servant to Mr. Shoncke, Aug. 2nd, 1625.

Other two servants same place, Garden Alley.

Sara, daughter of — Shoncke, 16th August, 1625, Garden Alley.

John Pollard, 26th August, 1625, Halliwell Street.

John Batcher, servant to Mr. Shoncke, 16th Sept., 1625, Garden Alley.

Joane Johnson, wife of William Johnson, 11th June, 1627, Halliwell.

Margery Wilkins, 1st April, 1635, Halliwell.

Cuthbert Burbardge was buryed ye 17th day of September, 1636.

Elizabeth Burbadge, widow, first day of October, 1636 (no address).

Winifred, the wyfe of Mr. Richard Robinson, 2nd May, 1642.

There were Gossons, Quyneys, Taylors, Lamberts, Somers, Greenes, Sissells, Newtons, Kemps, Jaggards, etc.

Baptisms.

Alice Burbage, d. of James Burbage, 17th March, 1575-6, Halliwell Street.

Oliver Stiddard, sonne of Thomas Stiddard, bapt. 17th Feb., 1582, Curtayne.

Samuel Heming has many children, and also the Bassanos.

Henry Lawes, son of Henry, 14th Jan., 1592.

Cuthbert Cowley, son of Richard Cowley, 8th May, 1597, from Allin's.

John Hart, son of John Hart, 19th June, 1597, Talbot Alley.

Cuthbert Cowley, son of Richard Cowley, 8th May, 1597.

Richard Cowley, son of Richard Cowley, 29th April, 1599, Halliwell St.

Robert Wilson, son of Robert Wilson, 15th Jan., 1600.

Elizabeth Burbedge, daughter of Cuthbert, 30th Dec., 1601, Halliwell.

Elizabeth Cowley, daughter of Richard Cowley, 2nd Feb., 1601.

Julia Burbedge, daughter of Richard Burbedge, 2nd Jan., 1602–3, Halliwell.

John Field, son of John Field, 26th Feb., 1603–4.

Frances Burbadge, daughter of Richard Burbadge, 16th Sept., 1604.

Augustine Beeston, son of Christopher, 16th Nov., 1604, Halliwell Street.

Christopher Beeston, son of Christopher Beeston, 1st December, 1605, Halliwell Street.

Anne Burbadge, daughter of Richard, 8th August, 1607, Halliwell Street.

Christopher Ames, son of Richard Ames, 25th Oct., 1607.

Mary Wilson, daughter of Robert Wilson, 17th Jan., 1607–8.

Robert Beeston, son of Christopher Beeston, 2nd April, 1609.

Albone Sly, daughter of John Slye, 11th June, 1609.

Winifred Burbadge, daughter of Richard Burbadge, 10th Oct., 1613, Halliwell Street.

Julia Burbadge, daughter of Richard Burbadge, 27th Dec., 1614, Halliwell Street.

William Burbadge, son of Richard Burbadge, 6th Nov., 1616.

Elizabeth Burbadge, daughter of Cuthbert Burbadge, baptized 30th December, Halliwell Street.

Sara Burbedge, daughter of Winifred Burbadge, widow, 5th Aug., 1619, Halliwell Street.

Richard Cooly, son of John Cooly and Sara his wife, 29th April, 1621, Hoxton.

Marriages.

John Cooke and Joane Larinor, 14th July, 1589.

John Cooke and Elizabeth Norland, 5th Sept., 1591, Halliwell.

Francis Langley and Hester Saule, 15th Jan., 1594–5, Bp. Cant. Lic.

John Donne and Dorithy Dale, 11th May, 1619, Licence fac.

Francis Goldingham and Alice Lawless, widow, 13th Oct., 1619, Lic. Bp. of London.

Peter Street and Elizabeth Wooten, wid., 12th Feb., 1628.

Samuel Johnson and Anne Lane, wid., 1st Feb., 1634, from Church-end.

Many Somers, Spensers, Robinsons, Greens, Fields, Slys, Shaws, Cookes, Jubyes, Beestons, Hemings, Miltons, Griffins, Johnsons.

(I only spent four long days on the Registers, and had not a list of all the players with me.)

AUTHORITIES FOR
THE FACTS IN THE
STORY OF THE BURBAGES

AUTHORITIES

NOTE I.—Queen Elizabeth's Proclamation as to Licences for Interludes, and their not Touching Religion or Politics.

By the Queen, 1559.

"Forasmuch as the tyme wherein common Interludes in the English tongue are most usually to be played is now past untyll All Hallowtyde, and that also some that have been of late used, are not convenient in any good ordered Christian Common Weale to be suffered." The Queen's Majistee forbids any to be played openly or privately, without notification and licence, by the Maior, Chief Officers, or Lieutenants for the Queen, and none to be permitted, where matters of religion or the governance of the estate of the commonweale shall be treated. If any attempt to do to the contrary, they are to be arrested.

Westminster, 16th Maye, 1 Eliz.

This proclamation was the cause of Sir Robert Dudley's letter in 1559, see page 7.

NOTE II.—1572. "The danger of Conventicles of people at playes in hot weather. Martis xx Die Maij, 1572 ("Repertory," 17, 316).

"Item this Daie, after the readyng of the Lordes of the Queenes Maiesties most Honorable Counselles Lettres, writen in the favor of certein persones to have in theire howses, yardes, or backe sydes, being open or overt places, such playes, enterludes, Commedies and Tragedies as maye tende to represse vyce and extoll vertewe, for the Recreacion of the people, and thereby to draw them from sundrye worser exercises, The matter thereof being first examyned, sene, and allowed, by such discrete person or persons as shalbe by the Lord Maiour thereunto appoynted, and taking bondes of the said Housekeapers not to suffer the same playes to be in the tyme of devyne service, and upon other condicions in the same Letters expressed.

" Item, it was agreed that Master Town Clark shall devyse a letter for answer of thother, to be sent unto my Lord of Burleighe, signifying to his honour, that it is thought very perillous (considering the tyme of the year, and the heat of the weather) to have such conventicles of people by such means called together, whereof the greatest number are of the meanest sorte, beseeching his Honour, yf it may so seeme him good, to be a meane wherbye the same for a tyme, may be forborne." (See p. 11.)

Football playing is also forbidden in the city shortly afterwards.

NOTE III.—THE LORD MAYOR'S ORDERS OF 1574

are printed in Stow's " Survey," v. 245, but I give the copy in Lansdowne MS. xx. 10, where on 6th December, 17 Eliz. (1574), the Lord Mayor, Council, and Recorder William Fleetwood were present.

" Whereas hearetofore, sondrye great disorders and Inconveniences have beene found to ensewe to this cittie by the inordynate hauntynge of great multitudes of people, speciallye youthe, to playes, enterludes and shewes namelye, occasyon of frayes and quarrelles, eavel practizes of incontinencye in great Innes, having chambers and secrete places, adjoyning to their open stayres and gallyries, inveglyinge and allowynge of maides, speciallye orphanes, and good cityzens children under age to previe and unmete contractes, the publishynge of unchaste uncomelye and unshamefaste speeches, and doyinges, with drawing of the Queenes Majesties servantes from dyvyne service on sundaies and hollydayes, At which tymes suche playes weare chefelye used, unthriftye waste of the moneye of the poore and fond persons, sondrye robberies by pyckinge and cutting of purses, utteringe of popular busye and seditious matters, and manie other corruptions of youth and other enormityes besydes that allso sondrye slaughters and mayheminges of the Queenes subjectes have happened by ruines of Skaffoldes frames and stages, and by engynes weapons and powder used in plaies.   And whear in tymes of Godes visitacion by the plaigue suche assemblies of the peoplc in thronge and presse have beene very dawngerous for the spreadynge of Infection, and for the same and other greate cawses, by the Aucthoritie of the honorable Lords Mayors of this cyttie and thaldermen theire Bretheren and especially upon severe and earneste Admonition of the Lords of the most honorable councell with signifyinge of her Majesties expresse pleasure and commandemente in that behalfe, suche use of playes, Interludes and shewes hath beene duringe this tyme of syckenes forbydden and restrayned, And for that the Lorde Mayor and his brethren thaldermen together with the goode and discrete citizens in the comon councell assembled, doo doughte and feare leaste uppon Goddes mercyfull withdrawinge his hand of sickness from us (which God graunte) the people, speciallye the meaner and most unrewelye should with sodayne forgettinge of his visitacyon withowte feare of goddes wrathe and withoute deowe respecte of this good and politique meanes that he hath ordeyned for the preservacion of the comen weales and peoples in healthe and good order retourne to the undewe use of suche enormyties to the great offence of god, the Queenes Majesties commandment and good governance. We therefore to the intent that such perilles maie be avoyded and the lawfull honest and comelye use of plaies pastymes and recreacions in good sorte onelye permitted, And good provision hadd for the saeftie and well orderynge of the people there assemblyd. Be yt enacted by the Aucthoritie of this comen councell That from henceforthe, no playe, comodye, Tragedye, enterlude nor publyke shewe, shall be openlye played or shewed within the liberties of the cittie, wherein shalbe uttered anie wourdes, examples, and doyinges of anie unchastitie, sedicion, or suche lyke unfytt and uncomelye matter upon paine of Imprisonment by the space of 14 daies, of all persons offendinge in anie suche open playings or shewinges, and £5 for everie other suche offence And that no Inkeper Tavernkeper nor other person whatsoever within the liberties of the said cittie shall openly shewe or playe, or cause or suffer to be openly shewed or played, within the hous yarde or anie other place within the liberties of this cyttie anie playe enterlude comodye, Tragidye, matter, or shewe which shall not be first perused and allowed in suche order and forme and by such persons as by the Lord Maiour and Courte of Aldermen for the tyme beinge shalbe appoynted, nor shalle suffer to be enterlaced added mynglyed or uttered in anie suche playe enterlude Comodye Tragidie or shewe anie other matter then shalbe first perused and allowed as ys abovesaid, And that no person shall suffer anie playes enterludes comodyes Tragidies or shewes to be played or showed in his hows yarde or other place, wheareof he then shall have rule or power, but onely suche persons and in such plaies as upon good and reasonable consideracions shewed shalbe theareunto permitted and allowed by the Lord Maior and Aldermen for the tyme beinge neither shall take or use anie benifitt or advantage of suche permission or allowing before or until suche person be bound to the Chamberlaine of London for the tyme beinge with suche sureties and in suche Summe and suche fourme for the keeping of good order and avoidinge of the disorders and Inconvenyences abovesaid as by the Lorde Maior and courte of Aldermen for the tyme being shall seeme convenyent neither shall use or execute anie suche lycence or permission at or in anie tymes in which the same for anie reasonable consideration of Syckness or otherwise shalbe by the Lorde Maior and Aldermen by publique proclamacion or by precept to suche persons restrayned or commanded to cease to playe, nor in anie usuall tyme of dyvyne service in the Sondaie or Hollydaie nor receyve anie to that purpose in tyme of service to se the same upon payne to forfeit for everie offence £5.   And be yt enacted that everie person so to be lycensed or permitted shall duringe the tyme of such contyneuance of suche lycens or permission paye or cause to be paid to the use of the poore in hospitalles of the cyttie or of the poore of the cyttie visyted by the sycknes by the discretion of the saide Lord Maior and Aldermen suche sumes and paymentes and in suche forme, as betweene the Lord Maior and Aldermen for the tyme beinge on thonne partie and suche person so to be lycensed or permitted on thother partie shalle be agreed upon payne that in waunte of everie suche paymente, or if suche person shall not firste be bound with good suerties to the Chamberlaine of London for the tyme being for the trewe payment of suche sommes to the poore That then everye suche lycense or permission shalbe utterlye voide and everie doinge by force or cullor of suche lycence or permission shalbe adiuged an offence againste this Acte in suche manner as if no such lycense or permission hadd benne hadd nor made anie suche lycence or permission to the contrarye notwithstanding.

And beyt lykewise enacted that all somes and forfeytures to be incurryd for anie offence against this Acte and all forfeytures of Bonds to be taken by force meanes or occayson of this acte shalbe ymployed to the relief of the poore in the hospitalles of this cittie of London as the Lord Maior and courte of Aldermen for the tyme being shall adiudge meete to be distributed, And that the chamberlayne of London shall have and recover the same to purpoyes aforesaid by Bill, plainte, accion of Dett or ynformacion to be commenced and pursewed in his owne name in the courte of the utter Chamber of the Guildhall of London called the Maiors courte in which sute no Essoine nor wager of lawe for the defendants shall be admitted or allowed. Provided allways that this Acte (otherwise then touchinge the publishinge of unchaste sedycious and unmete matters shall not extend to anie plaies, Enterludes, comodies, Tragidies or shewes to be played or shewed in the pryvate hous dwellinge or lodginge of anie nobleman, citizen, or gentleman who shall or will then have the same thear so played or shewed in his presence for the festivitie of anie marriage assemblye of frendes or other lyke cawse, Withoute publique or comen collection of money of the Auditorye or behoulders thereof, referringe alwaies to the Lorde Maior and Aldermen for the tyme beinge the judgment and construction According to equitie what shalbe counted suche a playinge or shewing in a pryvate place, anie thinge in this Acte to the contrarie notwithstanding.

Acte for Plaies *tempore Hawes Lord Maior.*

NOTE IV.—(*Résumés of following.*)

MIDDLESEX COUNTY RECORDS, ed. by Cordy Jeaffreson. Vol. ii., p. xlvii.

See also " Athenæum," 12th February, 1887.

These are recorded in Latin, but a free translation is published.

Middlesex, to wit ; The Jurors for the Lady the Queen present John Braynes of Shorditche in the Countie of Middlesex yeoman, and James Burbage of the same yeoman, on the 21st day of February in the 22nd year of the reign of Elizabeth, etc., etc., because that they on divers other days and occasions before and afterwards brought together and maintained unlawful assembles of the people to hear and see certain colloquies or interludes called plays or interludes exercised and practised by the same John Braynes and James Burbage, and divers others persons not known at a certain place called The Theatre in Hallywell in the aforesaid county By reason of which unlawful assembly of the people, great affrays, assaults, tumults and quasi-insurrections and divers other misdeeds and enormities having been there and then done and perpetrated by very many ill-disposed persons, to the great disturbance of the peace of the Lady the Queen and the overthrowing of good order and rule, to the danger of the lives of divers good subjects of the Queen being there, and against the form of the Statute in that respect published and provided. Result not given. . . . .

On 6th Dec. 38 Eiiz. Gabriel Spencer had killed James Feake with a sword costing 5s. by a wound in the eye at the barbers in Holywell Street, parish of St. Leonards, Shoreditch. Inquisition, 10th Dec., 39 Eliz., see page 71.

(It does not say how he got off.)

Vol. i. R.Ac. 8108, arraigned in Oct.

The Jurors for the Lady the Queen present that Benjamin Johnson late of London, yoman, on the 22nd day of September in the fortieth year of the Lady Elizabeth by God's grace Queen, etc., made an assault with force and arms against and upon a certain Gabriel Spenser, when he was in God's and the Queen's peace, at Shoreditch in the aforesaid county of Middlesex in the fields there, and with a certain sword of iron and steel, called a rapiour, of the price of 3s., which he then and there held in his right hand drawn, feloniously, and wilfully struck and beat the same Gabriel then and there with the aforesaid sword, giving to the same Gabriel Spenser, in and upon the same Gabriel's right side a mortal wound of the depth of 6 inches and of the breadth of one.inch, of which mortal wound the same Gabriel Spenser then and there died instantly, in the aforesaid Fields at Shordich in the said Countie of Middlesex. And thus the jurors said upon their oath that the said Benjamin Johnson feloniously and wilfully slew and killed the aforesaid Gabriel Spenser at Shordiche in the said county and fields, in the yeare and day above stated against the peace of our Lady the Queen. Endorsed " True Bill." But at the beginning is written, " He confesses the indictment, asks for the Book, reads like a Clark, is marked with the letter " T," and is delivered according to the Statute 18 Eliz. c. 7. Mr. Jeaffreson Cordy adds, " had he had no chattels to forfeit, the Clerk would have written ' ca null'. "

See also " Athenæum." 6th March. 1886.

28th Oct., 40 Eliz., at Hoxton.

Three yeomen of London " broke burglariously into the dwelling house of Jerome Bassano gentleman and stole therefrom a gold cheyne worth £24, a pair of bracelets of gold worth £32 ; eight gold rings worth £40, a jewell of gold worth £6 13, and £17 in numbered money."

II, 62, 3, March 18th, 7 James I.

John Lockewood, late of London Clerk, made a priest by the see of Rome, traitorously and feloniously regardeth not the statutes. He puts himself on a jury of the Country, and is found guilty, and has no goods and chattels. He was to be executed at Tyburn by the traitor's death, but he was reprieved by the court after judgment. (Among the 12 jurors, was " Cuthbert Burbage.")

II, 108, 19th Feb., 12 James I.

True Bill That at Hollowel Street in Shoreditch co. Middlesex about 12 o'clock of the night of the said day Henry Elliot yeoman, and his wife Emma Elliot, and Thomas Pierson yeoman all three late of the same street, broke burglariously into the dwelling house of Cuthbert Burbage gentleman, and stole therefrom a French russet-coloured cloake worth sixty shillings, another russet coloured cloake worthe forty shillings, and another cloake " color Daroye " worth twenty shillings and a green sage apron worth five shillings, of the goods and chattells of the said Cuthbert Burbage gentleman.

On the same file is a true bill against the same culprits on the same night, about the same hour, who broke burglariously into the dwelling house of Richard Burbage gentleman, in Hollowell Street, and stole thence a "darinxe carpet worth six shillings and eight pence, a fowling piece worth twenty four shillings, forty pieces of pewter worth twenty shillings, three holland aprons worth eight shillings, a smock worth four shillings, eleven falling bands worth twenty five shillings, seven cuffs worth five shillings, a handkerchiefe worth twelve shillings, three other handkerchieves worth seven shillings, two cambric headbands and biggens worth ten shillings, five cross cloathes worth seven shillings, five children's aprons worth eight shillings, three women's bands worth eighteen shillings, two laced handkerchiefs worth six shillings ; two cross clothes worth twelve pence, " duo alia capitalia vocata a Call and a Quoife " worth two shillings, one " diaber starching clothe " worth fourpence and divers pieces of linen worth twenty shillings of the

goods and chattell of the said Richard Burbage.   On his arrayne-
ment, Henry Elliot stood mute, and was sentenced to the " peine
forte et dure."   Emma Elliot put herself " not guilty " and was
acquitted.   Thomas Pierson was found not guilty of burglary,
but guilty of felony.   He received benefit of clergy, was branded
and delivered."   G. D. R. 29th March, 13 James I.   See page 113.

MIDD. CO. SESSIONS ROLLS, 2nd Nov., 5 Mary.

True Bill.   That on the said day Robert Burbage gent of Heisse
co. Midd. together with 16 others assembled in the close of Roger
Green at Heisse, and beat the said Roger Greene ; so that life was
despaired of.

II, 5, 3 Feb., 1 James I.

Robert Burbage of London yeoman to inform against Margaret
Whytten of Finchley.

II, 158, 18 James I.

Robert Burbage of Fulham gent, for his appearance at next sessions, and in the mean time for good behaviour, tried 12 Jan., 18
James I.

6 April, 34 Eliz.

Recognizances taken before Sir Owen Hopton Knight, J.P.,
of Henry Bett of St. Leonards' Shoreditch, gent, and — Burbage
in the Strond yeoman, in the sum of £10 each, and James Burbage
of Shoredich gent in the sum of £20, for the said James Burbage's
appearance at the next Sessions of the Peace for Co. Middlesex,
G. D. R., 34 Eliz. p. 47.

11 September, 35 Eliz.

Recognizance taken before Richard Young, Esq., J.P., of James
Burbage of Hallywell Street yeoman, for the appearance of the said
James Burbage at the next session of the Peace at Middlesex.
Then and there to answer, etc.   G. S. P. R. Michaelmas, 35 Eliz.

April, 37 Eliz.

Recognizances for the appearance of John and Edward Burbage,
both of London, gents, at the next general Session of the Peace
Easter, 37, G. S. P. R.

I. 259.

William Hawkins charged with a purse taken at the Curten, with
26/6 in it.   11 March, 42 Eliz.

Vol. ii., p. 83, 1 Oct.   10   James I.

An order made at the General Session of the Peace at Westminster " That all Actors of every Playehowse within this citie and Liberties thereof, and in the Countie of Middlesex, that they, and everie of them utterly abolishe all jigges Rymes and Dances after their plays, and not to tollerate permit or suffer any of them to be used upon payne of ymprisonment and putting down and suppressing of their plays.

(This was specially intended for the Fortune.   If after this order the players persevered in dancing their jiggs the offenders were to be imprisoned.)

NOTE V.—*The Queen's Players in* 1588.

" The Subsidies granted 29 Eliz.

" Sir Francis Knollys, Knight, Treasurer of the Privy Chamber, Sir Thomas Heneage, Knight, Vice Chamberlain, and Gregory Lovell, Cofferer.

" To certifie the Lord High Treasurer," mention a few officers of the household, gentlemen ushers, trumpeters, etc., who have not paid their subsidies.

" The Players, viz., Richard Tarleton, 8s. 4d. ;   John Laneham, 8s. 4d., William Johnson 5s., John Towne, 8s. 4d., John Addams 8s. 4d., John Garlande 8s. 4d., John Dutton 8s. 4d., John Singer, 8s. 4d., Lyonell Cooke 8s. 4d. (and another crossed out, who had either died or paid his subsidy.)

" The Collectors say these have not, nor at any time since the coming of the astrete to their handes have not had which they could come bye to distraine, any landes or tenements, goods or chattells, wages, or fee within the limittes of their collection to their knowledge," and Sir Francis Knollys and Gregory Lovell sign this declaration to free the collectors.

Lay Subsidies Household, 29 Eliz., 69/97.

See p. 36.

A soldier's opinion of plays and players, 1586.

(I here insert the first half of an unsigned letter to Walsingham on this subject.)   Harl. MS. 286, f. 102.

" The daily abuse of stage plaies is such an offence to the godly, and so great a hindrance to the Gospell as the papists doe exceedinglie reioice at the blemisshe thereof and not without cause, for every daye in the week the players' billes are sett upp in sundry places of the Cittie, some in the name of her Majestie's menne, some the Earl of Leicester's, some the Earl of Oxford's, the Lord Admyralles and divers others, soe that when the bells tole to the Lector The Trumpetts sound to the Stages whereat the wicked faction of Rome lauvgheth for ioy, while the Godly weepe for sorrowe. Woe is me, the playhowses are pestered, when the churches are naked, at the one, it is not possible to gett a place, at the other voyde seates are plentie, the profaning of the Sabbaoth is releesed. But as badde a custome entertayned, and yett still our long-suffering God forbaireth to punisshe yt is a wofull sight to see two hundred proude players iett in their silkes, wheare fyve hundred pore people sterve in the Streetes, but yf needes this mischiefe must be tolerated whereat, (no doubte) the highest frowneth, yet " for God's sake sir) let every Stage in London pay a weekly portion to the pore."

It continues as much again even more in earnest : " I see your honor smyle and saye to yourself theise things are fitter for the pulpit than a souldier's penne. 25th Jan. 1586.

"To Sir Francis Walsingham."

See p. 26.

NOTE VI.—*James Burbage against Mrs. Braynes.*

Burbage *v.* Braynes. Chancery Proceedings. Bills and Answers, Series II., 222/83.

(About one-fourth of this is burnt off at left side, date nearly gone, only final 8 remains of the 1588.)

" To the Rt. Hon. Christopher Hatton, Knt., The Lord Chancellor of England.

"Complaineth unto your good Lordship James Burbidge . . . Cuthbert, Richard, Alice and Ellen Burbidge, the children of the said James and Ellen his wief, that whear your said orator . . . one Giles Allen, gent . . . of the Queen's most excellent Maiestie that now is in certain decayed barnes, vacant ground, and garden plottes scituat . . . for a term of certaine years at a rent of £14 to be quarterlie paied and in the said lease did promise and covenant . . . to and with the said Giles Allen, to build in and upon the demised . . . building for tenements to be erected upon the premises, the some of £200 and the same to be done and finished in a certaine tyme . . .

for the accomplishment whereof the said James your said orator, was constrayned to borrow divers somes of money, and to impawn his said . . . erecting of a plaiehouse or Theatre, and other the buildings for tenements as is aforesaid, The which one John Brayne late of White . . . practised to obteyne some interest therein presumynge that he might easily compass the same by reason that he was naturall brother . . . somes of money he made meanes to your said orator James Burbedge that he might have the moietie of the above-named Theater . . . that in consideration thereof he would not only beare and paie half the chardges of the said building then bestoed, or thereafter to be bestoed . . . orator aforesaid her children should have the same moitie so to him to he conveyed and assured making semblance that his industrie was . . . of his sister as is aforesaid. Whereupon your orator⁵James Burbedge who did become bound to the said John Brayne in £400 . . . That your said orator should at the request of the said . . . John Braine his executors or assignes convey to him the said John Braine his . . . erected upon the premises demysed by the said Giles Allen to your said orator with such covenants and warranties as your orator might . . . lease made by the said Giles Alleyn was then or thereafter should be chardged with by any acte then done or thereafter to be done by your . . . money borrowed by your said orator, as by the same obligacion and condicion more at Lardge yt doth and may appeare And after the . . . exceeding chardge about the said building then of habilletie to support the same, and having gotten your said orator to he bound . . . to redeem the said lease nor had wherewith to proceed in those manner of buildings wherein he had procured your orator to enter into . . . chardge any somes of monye growen due for the said building, nor paie the moietie of the rent aforesaid, but with your orator's money. The profitts . . . of the said Brayne before being conveyed and weyed with the costs. . . . upon the said Inne by him bestoed after, yt manifestly appeared And . . . the furnishing of the said building, to his gret hinderaunce, as is well to be proved And after for that your said orator James Burbedge had no bond . . . him to be receved out of the premises from thensforthe upon the said building and maintainance thereof he the said Brayne and the said James Burbedge your . . . arbitrament of certain arbitrators who thereupon, according to the said submission, did deliver up an Award or Arbitrament in wrightinge dated about the—yere

. . . Braine should not be comprised within the compasse of the said arbitrament, but that as well by force thereof as by vertue of said Arbitrament your said orator . . . Theatre and buildings and of the moitie of the profits thereof, whensoever Braine would demaund the same, with sutche exceptions of Acts as is aforesaid . . . which arbitrament your said orator did content himsealf, and did permit and suffer the said John Braine to receve the moitie of the profits of the said Theatre and . . . on his parte.   But the said John Brayne being a very subtell person and confederating himsealf with Robert Myles of London, Gouldsmith,——Tomson of . . . might impoverishe your said orator and to depryve hym of his interest and tearme of yeres in the said Theatre and Building, and to bringe him into the damage . . . same he the said Brayne, not meaning to gyve the said moietie, nor his interest to your said orators the children aforesaid nor the lease of the said Geordg . . . moitie of the profitts of the premises, as is aforesaid, the which promise was made as well before as after the said Arbitrament as is aforesaid, but practising to depryve . . . made a deed of gift to the said Tomson, and thereby did gyve and grant to him all his goods and chattells wherein he was then or thereafter should be possessed.   Whereby your . . . for the recoverie of the bond of £200, to hym forfeyted by the said Braine, for the not performynge the said arbitrament, nor to levie the same out of his goods and chattells . . . against the bodie of the said Brayne for the same, the which during his life he was loathe to do, for that he was his brother-in-law as is aforesaid.   The benefitt . . . the said Tomson the said Brayne for the mayntenance of his said fraude and devise, procured the executors or administrators of the said Tomson to convey to the said Robert . . . so granted to the said Tomson by the said Braine with the lease of the said Inn called the Geordg, And also at his owne deathe or not long before, he fearing . . . conveyance of all his goods and chattells, which he then had to the said John Gardiner and others, to the intent that he or they by force thereof should or might enter in . . . the premises, or that the said Myles by vertue of the same deed of gift made to the said Tomson should challenge or demand the same or to incur the damage . . . in the tyme of his sickness and not long before his death promised, confessed and agreed with your said orator James Burbage and his wief, in the presence . . . of the said Myles that as well the moitie of the premises, and all matters whatcoever concerning the said Theatre and buildings and his moitie therein to be assuered and . . . receved of and by the premises as namelie the lease of the Geordge in Whitechapel were and should be and remain yf he died, (or that he had no children and for . . . premises to your orators the children aforesaid, whose advancement he then seemed gretlye to tender. And further promised to your said orator that his said bonds should be . . . of your said orator James Burbage. And after the said John Braine died in 1586, by meanes whereof. . . . Nowe so yt ys, yf it may please your Honor the . . . Administracion of the goods of her said late husband, (the which she practised then to have) by the said John Gardenor and Robert Myles, by reason yt they claymed the same goods and chattells . . . conveyance under the collour of a will supposed to be made by the said Braine long before the said conveyaunce, so made to the said Gardiner and Tomson the which is supposed to be rased . . . any sutch will should be mayntayned or produced, yet by vertue thereof, and being therein nominated to be executor, goeth about to arrest your said . . . that he did not performe the said arbitrament as in truthe he did, and for the said bond of £400, pretending your orator hath also forfeited the same, as in truth he hath not, And . . . husband denying that her said husband made any sutche promise as is aforesaid ether for the cancelling or conveying of the premises to your orator aforesaid. And the said Robert Myles by . . . sue your said orator, James Burbage for the said bonds, but hath entered into and upon the said Theatre and buildings and troubleth your orator and his tenants in the peaceable possession . . . the yssues and profits thereof by vertue of the conveyances made to him thereof and the Administrators of the said John Gardiner, who deceased in 1587 to whom the said bond . . . made to the said Gardiner, demand and go about to sue your said orator James Burbage for the said two severall bonds. And amongst them by reason of multiplicitie of . . . conveyances and (sometime denying the same to be good) they all do joyne together to imprison your said orator James Burbage, therby to enforce him to yeld to their requests And . . . accions only to procure him to gret chardge and to his impoverishment for ever, the rather because by thes devices, he cannot have the said £200 due to him by the said . . . Braine.

In tender consideracione of the premisses And for that the said Margarett Braine, Robert Myles and — Gardiner, the administrator of the said John Gardiner, . . . so being mortgaged and forfeited as is aforesaid, and have the said lease to them reconveyed, they do demand the same moitie, and will not permit the children aforesaid . . . the said premisses the which now your said orators are unhable to do, by reason that the same premisses were done in secret, and in the presence of the said Robert . . . or gone beyond the seas, so that your orators can not have their testimony in the premisses, by which means your orator James Burbage is without . . . the said bonds or to enforce them to cancell the same nor the children aforesaid by the ordinarie course of the common law aforesaid can not procure the . . . the premisses so promised to them by the said John Braynes, the which to do the said Braine was bound in conscience to see performed and that the said bonds should . . . the said John Braine and by your said orator James Burbedge ioynes them in contradiction of the matters conteyned in the said bond and arbitrament, so . . . be performed yf thei or any of them had lawfull interest therein (as thei have not) Maye it therfore please yor honor to grant to yor said . . . the said Margarett Braine, Robert Myles and — Gardener commaunding them and everie of them personallie to appere in the court of Chancerie . . . and ther to make answer to the premisses. And further to command the said Margarett Braine, Robert Myles and — Gardenor to . . . other their said conveyances so to them made only to perturbe your said orators as is aforesaid, and to the end the same may be ther . . . suche further order as to your Honor shall be thought to agree that equytie and conscience And all your said . . . in all felicitie.

FRANCIS MORGAN.

(No date.)[1] The answer . . . Margaret Brayne, Wydowe and Robert . . . complainte of James Burbeidge and other . . . that the said Bill of Complaint is very untrue and insufficient in the . . . imagyned of set purpose to put the said defendents to wrongfull . . . he the said complaynant wrongfully might shadowe his bad and unconscionable . . . defendants shalbe compelled to make any further answere to . . . and insufficiency thereof now and at all tymes . . . that the said complainants in their tedious and untrue Bill do . . . Gyles Allen unto the complainant, neither what . . .

---

[1] The last numeral of the date is 8, and we know from the book of Decrees and Orders, the suit took place in 1588.

the said complainant as in the said Bill is also set down . . . certaine date or tyme of any such bonde wherein he and . . . hundreth poundes to abyde a certain awarde and arbitrament . . . when they yielded upp any such arbitrament, And further setteth out . . . with this defendant Robert Myles and John Gardyner, who is not nowe . . . neither doth the said complainant set forth any sufficient consideracion . . . of the said leasses in the said Bill mencioned upon the children of the . . . The said Margaret Brayne, the other defendant being his wief without . . . divers other in the said Bill mencyoned. The . . . over tedious to be recyted the . . . of this honorable Courte yf they or either of them shall be compelled . . . insuffycient bill. And for the insufficiency thereof they pray to be dismissed out of this honorable courte . . . so wrongfullie sustained.

Scott.

(Since I copied these injured papers in fragments, they have been mounted and somewhat restored, so that there may be slight differences at the edge of burnt portions.)

NOTE VII.—*The Litigation between Burbage, Braynes and Myles.*

The cases are not all preserved. But through the Chancery Decrees and Orders (preserved in duplicates in what are called the A. Books and the B. Books) we can have some idea of the hearings in Chancery.

" Chancery Proceedings, Decrees and Orders, Easter 29 Eliza., 6th May, 1586. A. Book, 384.

Margaret Braynes, Widow, Plaintiff, Robert Miles, defendant. This day sevennight is given to the defendant to make answer or els an attachment is awarded against him.

The same case in *B*. Book, p. 372.

Chancery Proceedings, Decrees and Orders, 1588, A. Book, 30–31 Eliz., 454. 22nd Feb., Hilary Term 31 Eliz.

James Burbage and others, plaintiffs.

Margaret Brayne, widow, Robert Miles and John Gardyner, defendants. " Forasmuch as this Court was this present daye informed on the plaintiffs' behalf that the defendants have put in a very insuffycent demurrer to the Plaintiffs Bill of Complaint, without showing any good or sufficient causes thereof.

It is therefore ordered that the consideration of the said Bill and demurrer be referred to Mr. Dr. Carewe one of the M^{rs}. of this court to thend he may reporte unto this court whether the same demurrer be sufficient or not, if not, then a subpoena is awarded against the Defendants, without further money, to answer directly to the plaintiff's Bill of Complaint, and to all the material points thereof and the defendants Attorney to be warned hereof.

ROBT. POWLE.

This is practically the same as B. Book, 1588, p. 449, Monday, 17th February, except as to the phrase added " without further money."

D. & O., Book A. 21st May 1589, p. 610.

Margaret Brayne, plaintiff, James Burbage, Cuthbert Burbage and Richard Burbage, Defendants.   Forasmuch as this court was this present day informed on the plaintiffs behalf that the defendants have put in an insufficient demurrer to the plaintiff's Bill of Complaint without shewing any good or sufficient causes thereof, It ys therefore ordered that the consideracion of the said Bill or demurrer be referred to Mr. Dr. Cesar one of the M^{rs} of this Court, to thend he may reporte unto this Courte whether the said demurrer be suffycient or not.   If not a subpoena is awarded against the defendants to answer directly to the plaintiff's Bill of Complaint, and to all the materyal points thereof, and the defendant's attorneys to be warned when the premises shall be considered off.

A. Book, 32 and 33 Eliz., 1590, 4th Nov., p. 109.

Margaret Braynes, widow, exor. of John Braynes, deceased, Plaintiff, James Burbage, Richard Burbage and Cuthbert Burbage defendants.   Forasmuch as the Court was this day informed by Mr. Scott, plaintiff's councell that having exhibited a Bill against defendant for the moietie of The Theatre and other tenements, for which the said James Burbage had made an agreement with the plaintiff's late husband to assigne to the Executors of her late husband, and to suffer him and them to enjoy the moietie during the whole term to come of a lease made to the said James Burbage by one Gyles Allen.   But the plaintiff Brayne said that James Burbage hath not only put in an ill demurrer to that bill which hath been over ruled by order of the court, but also doth by himself and the other defendants take away the whole gaynes and benefits of the said

Theatre and other premises, albeit shee and her husband have been at very great charges in building the Theatre, to the sum of £500, and did for a time enjoy the moietie of the premises according to the meaning of the said agreement. It is therefore ordered that if the defendants shall not by this day sennight shew good cause to the contrarie the sequestration shall be granted of the moietie of all the issues and profitts of the premises until the matter be heard and determined.

D. & O., A. Book, 32–33 Eliz., 1590, p. 145, 13th November.

Margaret Brayne, widow, plaintiff, James Burbage, joiner, Cuthbert Burbage and others defts. Forasmuch as upon the opening of the mater this present day Mr. Sergeant Harrys for the defendant, speaking for stay of sequestration, prayed consideration of a former order on plaintiff's behalf in the cause of Burbage con Braynes. There was an arbitrament made between her husband and Burbage, 12th July 20 Eliz., by one Richard Turner and one John Hill, and that neither of the parties shewed reason why the arbitration should not be performed. The Court finds for the arbitration to be truly observed, as well by the plaintiff as by all claiming under her, and also by the defendant, The Sequestration stayed.

Decrees and Orders, 32 and 33 Eliz., A. Book, 270, 1590–1, 20th Jan., 1590–1.

Margaret Brayne, con James Burbage and others. This day in Court Robert Miles made othe that the said James Cuthbert and Richard Burbage have broken an order made in this court on the 13th of November last, therefore an attachment is awarded against the said parties to the Sheriff of Middlesex.   Also B. Book, 280.

D. & O., 32 and 33 Eliz., A. Book, 317, 30th Jan., 1590–1.

Margaret Braynes con James Burbage, Cuthbert Burbage hath made his personal appearance in this Court upon his letter, for the saving of the bond made to the Sheriff of London.

Decrees and Orders, Book A., 32–33 Eliz., 1590–1, 23rd March, p. 456.

Margaret Brayne, plaintiff, Cuthbeard Burbage and James Burbage, defendants, Whereas the defendants have been examined upon interrogatories at the plaintiff's suit touching the breach of an order made in this court. It is ordered by the Right Hon. Master of the

M

Rolls that the consideration of their examination be referred to Mr. Doctor Caesar, one of the Masters of this Court, whether the said defendants or either of them have committed any contempt or not, that further action be taken, etc.   See also B. Book, 455.

Decrees and Orders, A. Book, 33–34 Eliz., 1591–2, 24th April, 493.
James Burbage con Margaret Brayne and Robert Myles.   The Court is informed that defendant put in a very frivolous and insufficient demurrer to the plaintiff's bill without shewing cause, Both are referred to Mr. Doctor Carew to the end he may consider and report whether the demurrer be sufficient or not, if not, then a subpoena is awarded against the defendant to make a perfect answer to the plaintiff's bill, and to all the materiall points, and defendant's attorney to be warned.   Also B. Book, 497.

Decrees and Orders, A. Book, 1591–2, 15th June, 720.
Burbage con Brayne, The Plaintiff appeared this day in court, forasmuch as the insufficient demurrer of the defendants referred to Mr. Dr. Carew has not yet been satisfied.   He asks a subpoena that the material facts be answered.

Decrees and Orders, 1591, A. Book, p. 818.
20th July.   Margaret Brayne v. Cuthbert and James Burbage. The defendants appeared in Court this day.   The master into whose hands the case was given for contempt, cannot attend, and prays that the Master of the Rolls might give his opinion of the contempt. It is put into the hands of another, and he decides that Mr. Dr. Hone of this court shall consider and report on it.   See also B. Book, 831.

Decrees and Orders, 33–34 Eliz. 1591, p. 16 A. Book, 18 B. Book.
12th Oct., 1591.
That they had committed no contempt.
Margery Brayne, compl., James Burbage, Joiner, and Cutbart Burbage and others, defendants.   Upon the opening of the matter this present day Mr. Sergeant Harris, council for the defendants coming to shew cause wherefore an attachment should not be awarded against them, from a report made by Mr. Dr. Hone, one of the M^{rs}. of this Court on a contempt supposed to be committed.   Ordered by this court, that no advantage or further proceedings shall be had upon that report, but that Mr. Dr. Stanhope and Mr. Dr. Legge

shall consider and report to this court whether the defendants or either of them committed any contempt in breach of a former order laid to their charge upon whose reporte order shall be peremptorily taken without further delay.

Decrees and Orders, A. Book, 1591–2, p. 151 ; B. Book, 163.
13th November.   Margaret Brayne con. James Burbage, joiner, and Cuthbert Burbage and others.   Upon the opening of the matter, the Right Hon. Master of the Rolls, by Mr. Scott for the plaintiff stated that it appeared that before this time it had been referred to Mr. Dr. Stannop and Mr. Legge who have heard cause and council on both sides.   By order of 12th Oct. last, and entering into the consideration of the contempt alleged to have been committed. We do finde that we could not well proceede to examine them, before John Hyde of London, grocer, and Ralph Myles of London, sopemaker, were examined touching the cause, and one Nicholas Bushop and John Allen, upon the contempt in the interrogatories, against the defendant pretended.   Therefore both sides agreed that the court should give us power to give othe to the parties to answer the interrogatories, that upon the depositions, we could better proceed to examine the contempt, that the matter be again referred to Mr. Dr. Stanhope and Mr. Dr. Legge to call all persons concerned and to examine them.

Decrees and Orders, A. Book, 36–37 Eliz. (1594), 14th March, 857.
James Burbage con. Robert Myles.
The plaintiff states by Mr. Borne that they have cross cases, and the plaintiff Burbage now appears to state that the plaintiff Myles has his case down for hearing on the 28th day of May next at the Rolls Chapel.   He desires to know if he and his witnesses may be heard first, Their cause was first, and they are ready.
Agreed, if the defendant does not shew cause to the contrary.

Decrees and Orders, A. Book, 36–37 Eliz., f. 274, 7th June.
Burbage con. More.
James Burbage, plaintiff, con. Gregory More defendant.   The defendant presents an insufficient answer, and plaintiff gives sufficient proof of his surmise of the truth of his bill for the maintenance of his *certiorari*, for removing of his action out of London into this court.   It is ordered that the consideration of this proof and the

answer be referred **to** Mr. Dr. Carew to report upon ; and if the answer
be insufficient then the defendant to answer directly.
    B. Book, f. 277.

Decrees and Orders Chancery, 1595, A. Book, 150, 28th May.
    Robert Miles, Plaintiff, James Burbage and Cuthbert Burbage
defendants.   The matter in question between the saide parties,
touching the moytie of the lease of the Theatre in the Bill mencioned, and the profit thereof comming.   This present day to be
heard in the presence of the Councill learned in the law, on both
parties.   It was alleged by the defendant's council that the said
plaintiff had not only a bond of £400 made unto him by the defendant for the assigning over of the same moytie unto him, whereupon
demurrer ys now joynde at the Common Law, but also another
bond of £200 made for the performance of an arbitrament made
between the said parties, which the said plaintiff pretendeth to be
also forfeited by the defendant.   And therefore, as the said Counsell
alledged, the plaintiff hath no need of the ayde of this court for the
said lease and profitt.
    It ys therefore thought fit, and soe ordered by this court that
the said plaintiff shall proceed at the Common Law against the
defendant upon the said bonde, to thend it may be seen whether
the plaintiff can relieve himself upon the said bondes or not.
    But if it fall out that the plaintiff cannot be relieved upon the
said bondes, then the matter shall receive a speedy bearing in this
court, and such order shall be given thereupon, as the equity of the
cause shall require, and in the mean time the matter is retained in
this court.

Myles *v.* Bishop.

Chancery Proceedings Ser. II, Bundle 245, 85 (*much faded*).

    Complaint of Robert Myles of the George Inn in Whitechapel,
        13th Nov. 1594.   (*A resumé.*)
    That Nicholas Bishop, a very poor man and greatly indebted
asked for his stables to make a boyling house for sope, and he said
it would utterly waste his inn.   But the said Bishop having
his son Raulph Myles to join him, he was persuaded of the great
profit to come of the making of sope, and he provided timber and

other materials to the value of £7. 18s. with workmen, to make the said Office or workhouse. George Harrison backed up this Bishop, but they did not succeed.

Now "so it is, etc." his Inn is spoiled and they give him no redress.

The answer of the defendants Nicholas Bishop and Ralph Myles, 22nd November, 1594.

They said that the complaint was uncertain and insufficient, and of malice and set purpose to injure the defendants. Nicholas Bishop said that it was true that the complainant was possessed of the tenement, and did keep an Inne for some small time, but he never profited much by it and was not of abilitie to stock and furnish the Inn, and for that and other causes the guests did so leave and forsake the house so that he did not long continue that course of housekeeping. It is true that the defendant was not rich, but he had been apprentice for 7 years to a master for soap-boiling, who was willing to lend him money. There was familiarity between him and Ralph Myles because they had been servants together, but he never made proposals to Ralph to get rooms in the Complainant's house, but Ralph proposed it, and there was a lease for a term of years, but it was between the father and son. The complainant did not find timber and material, nor did he find the workmen meate, and the complainant came into the Sope house and took sope to the value of over £7 to pay the chief Landlord. Complainant said the said shop was convenient to sell soape and other things, but he had not used it to do so, and Nicholas Bishop prays to be dismissed.

Replication of Robert Myles, complainant.

That it was true that he was in possession of the tenement or Inne called the George in Whitechapel for a number of years to come and that Nicholas Bishop and Raulph Myles his son begged him that they might have some rooms in the Inn for an office and to make sope. That he had agreed on hearing so great promise of success, so that he had the 3rd part of the profits, and he spent much money in timber, brick and building chambers to make sope in. He entreats consideration of his case.

See p. 51.   SCOTT.

NOTE VIII.—Edmund Peckham against Giles Alleyn.

Hil. 30 Eliz. B. 29.   Court of Wards and Liveries, 1589.
Peckham v. Alleyn.

9th June, 1589. An *Information* was laid before the Court by
Richard Kingsmill, Esq., the Queen's Attorney-General for Wards
and Liveries on behalf of George Peckham, son and heir of Edmund
Peckham, Esq. and her Majesty's Ward. (*All much contracted.*)

That whereas Henry Webbe sometime of Hallowell Co. Middle-
sex was seized in fee of the dissolved priory of Hallowell with its
lands tenements and hereditaments by the grant of King Henry
VIII, and he had only one daughter Susan his heir, And after Henry
Webbe died, and the lands descended to her, she took to husband
George Peckham, now called Sir George Peckham one of the sons of
Sir Edmund Peckham, which marriage was solemnised about
All Hallowtide 1554, and she had issue Edmund Peckham late
deceased, father of your Highness' Ward, and the said Susan died
in December 1555, leaving her son Edmund her heir, he being not
above one day old.

And the said Sir George Peckham in the lifetime of Susan did
bargain and sell the site of the said Priory to one Christopher
Bumpstead and his heirs, which Bumpstead did continue the possession thereof until the said Edmund Peckham came to his full
age, and then, understanding of the sale of the lands and of his
title in the same which descended to him, did, within 5 years after
coming to his full age, that is in 22 Eliz. enter into the said Priory
which was lawful to do, and did commence this action against Giles
Allen, then tenant and occupier of the same, and by verditt re-
covered the same, and died, leaving his said son George of tender
years, after whose death the right came to the said George, your
Majesty's Ward.

But so it is, may it please your Majesty that the said Gyles Allen
by pretence and colour of some fayned and unlawful title, and
having by some sinister means obtained the deeds and writings
concerning the premises, and the assurance of the estate of the site
and Priory of Hallowell to your Majesty's Ward, into his hands,
has now, of late, by that colour, entered into the Priory and expelled
your Majesty and her Ward from the possession thereof, pretending not only to defraud her Majesty of the Wardship and custody

of the Priory, but to disinherit the said George Peckham and his heirs of the inheritance of the Priory, etc.

May it therefore please your good Lordship to grant a writ of Privy Seal directed to the said Gyles Allen Esq. to appear and answer the premises, etc.

This is granted.

Hil. 30 Eliz. 20th Oct.,

1589. The answer of Gyles Allen. (*Very long.*)

It is true that Henry Webbe, Gentleman Porter of the King's Tower of London, in an indenture bearing date 28th Feb. 6 Ed. VI in consideration of a marriage to be had between his daughter Susan and George Peckham son of Sir Edmund Peckham, did make an agreement that he, the said Webbe, should, before Easter following make a grant to certain persons to be named by Sir Edmund, of a good estate of the site of the Priory, to the use of the said Henry Webbe, during his natural life, and after his decease to the said George and Susan, and their heirs, and for lack of these to the heirs of Susan and for lack of these to the heirs of George, and after that, namely on the last day of February 6 Ed. VI, he confirmed to Thomas Mynd and Francis Dorrell, by the Act of Parliament 4th Feb. 27 Hen. VIII for the transferring of uses, the said estate. And after this Webbe died and George and Susan married. And so being seized, by their deed, dated 16th August 2 & 3 Philip and Mary, by an agreement between the said George and Susan, and one Christopher Bumpstead, citizen of London, for the sum of £533 6s. 8d. sold the said site and afterwards there was a fine levied in the Court of Common Pleas, in the Michaelmas Term 2 & 3 Philip and Mary, before the Justices of Peace, between Christopher Bumpstead, and the said George Peckham and John Raignolds and Christian his wife deforciants of the said site, 22 messuages, 40 cottages, 4 Barns, 4 dove houses, 20 gardens, six orchards, and 2 acres of pasturage, with appurtenances and acknowledged all these to be the right of Christopher, and proclamations made thereof, to the *sole use* of Bumpstead and his heirs.

Within six months thereafter, in consideration of £600 payed to him by Christopher Allen Esq. deceased, late father to this defendant, and by this defendant well and truly paid, the said Bumpstead did bargain and sell to them to hold forever and the said Christopher, about 34 years past died and the defendant did receive the premises by right of survivorship, and he has held himself owner. About 23 Eliz., Edmund Peckham, hoping by sinister means to oppress the defendant, or to wrest from him some piece of money, did pretend to the premises, and did execute an action of trespass, and by reason of the great partiality of the jurors through their being suborned and also by reason that they did not understand the nature of the fine, which was levied by George without Susan, but was sufficient to bar the said Edmund ; the jury found the defendant guilty of trespass but it was of no force to bind defendant to any loss in the suit. Neither did the said Edmund proceed to any further trial with the defendant, as he neither could nor did have any right or title touching the estate. Gyles Alleyn denied any claim of the Peckhams altogether resting on his clear right and prayed to be dismissed from further answer in the case.

SMALLMAN.

31st Oct., 1589.

Replication of James Morris Esq. Attorney-General of the Court of Wards and Liveries, to the answer of Giles Alleyn, gent., defendant.

James Morris, in right of George Peckham her Majestie's Ward maintains all the points filed in the Bill of Information. He believes it true that indentures were made bearing date 28th Feb. 6 Ed. VI between Sir Edmund Peckham and Henry Webbe, concerning the limitation of uses for the said Priory of Hallowell, and the landes belonging thereto, but there was a proviso, that if the said marriage between Susan, the daughter and heir of Henry Webbe, and the said Sir George Peckham, then called George Peckham, do not take effect by the disagreement or refusal of Sir George Peckham, that the lands should be assured to the persons assured at the death of the said Henry Webbe, to the use of Susan and her heirs with remainder to the heirs of Elizabeth Trudge, and if the lady refused the marriage, then Peckham's heirs were to succeed to the property after her death. Now Sir George Peckham misliked the marriage, and only by the persuasions of his father fulfilled it, and he did not marry before the feast of St. Michael as agreed ; the deed supposed to be granted to Francis Darrell and Thomas Mynde to the uses aforesaid, with a letter of attorney to the said John Ward and Nicholas Clark to deliver possession, was not sealed by Henry Webbe, nor was any seisin given to the feoffees, as by depositions of the persons sworn at the Examination remaining of Record proveth, so that neither of the bargains mentioned in the answer, nor yet the fine, supposed to be levied of the lands by the said Sir George Peckham unto the said Christopher Bumpstead, whereunto the said Susan was not made party, the said Edmund Peckham her son (father to George Her Majesty's now Ward), then being within the age of one and twenty years, and having made his claim to same lands within five years after he came to his full age so it is untrue to say that the delay shall or may bar the said George Peckham her Majesty's Ward to demand the said lands or exclude her Majesty's title.

And James Morris further saith, that the verdict mentioned in the Bill, in the Court of Exchequer, against the defendant, concerning some parte of the lands in question, was delivered by Jurors then sworn upon full process of the matters, and upon other special processes for the maintaining of the issue on behalf of the said Edmund Peckham against the said defendant, as also through default of sufficient matter provided by defendant to maintain his title, which verdict was without any subornation, or evil practise by or to the jurors, as in the answer is most falsely and untruly suggested.

JA. MORRIS.

28th Nov., 1589.

The Rejoinder of Giles Alleyn gent, to the Replication of James Morris Esq., her Majesty's Attorney of the Court of Wards and Liveries.

The defendant, not confessing anything in the Replication contained, maintained his answer. The Replication is uncertain and insufficient. He denied that Sir George Peckham utterly refused to take to wife the said Susan, and was only enforced to it by his father ; he denied that the marriage did not take place before Michaelmas ; denied that the facts surmised were proved by oaths of credible witnesses or by Sir George ; denied that the deed of Henry Webbe containing a grant to Francis Dorryll, and Thomas Mynd to the uses mentioned, was not sealed and delivered, or that possession was not granted ; denied that there was any insufficiency in the bargain nor sale, nor fine levied of the land by Sir George Peckham unto Christopher Bumpstead ; or that anything material should enable the said George Peckham, her Majestie's ward to

demand the lands ; denied that Edmund Peckham his father made
a claim 5 years after coming of age, or that it is anything material
if he had so done, as he had not any title to the same, or that the
said verdict had in the Court of Requests against the defendant
concerning part of the lands, did pass, on such causes as the Replication surmises, and denied anything else in the same replication
to be true. See p. 52.

SMALMAN.

NOTE IX.—*James Burbage's Purchase of Blackfriars*, 1596.

> Endorsed.   Sir William More to James Burbage.
> James Burbage touching houses in Blackfriars.

This Indenture made 4th Feb. 38 Eliz. (1595–6) betwene Sir
William More of Loseley in the county of Surrey, Knt., and James
Burbage of Hollowell in the County of Midd., gentleman . . .
witnesseth that the said Sir William More for and in consideracon
of the some of Sixe Hundreth Poundes . . . att and before then-
sealinge of these presents truly paid wherewith he the saide Sir
William More doth acknowledge and confesse himself fully satisfied
and paied . . . and doth fully and clerelie Bargayne sell alyen,
enfeoffe, and confirme to the said James Burbage his heirs and
assignes for ever, All those seaven great upper Romes as they are
now devided being all upon one flower, and sometyme beinge one
great and entire rome with the roufe over the same covered with
Leade. . . .   And also all the stone staires leadinge upp unto the
Leades or Roufe . . . and also all the greate stone walls and other
walls which do enclose devide and belonge to the same seaven great
upper romes, And also that great paire of wynding stairs with the
staircase thereto belonging which leadeth upp into the same seaven
great upper romes out of the greate yard there which doth lie next
unto the Pipe Office which saide seven great upper roomes were
late in the tenure or occupacion of William de Lawne Dr of Phisicke
or of his assignes, and are scituate lyeinge and beinge within the pre-
cincte of the late Blackfryers Preachers near Ludgate . . . (and all
appurtenances) Together with the easiament and comodite of a
vaulte being under some part of the said seaven great upper romes,
or under the entry or voide rome lyinge betwene those seaven
great upper romes and the saide Pipe Office by a stoole (*sic*) and
Tonnell to be made into the same vaulte in and oute of the greate

stone wall in the ynner side thereof nexte and adioininge to the said entry or voide rome being towards the south. And also all those romes and lodgings with the Kitchen thereunto adjoining called the Midle Romes or midle stories late being in the tenure or occupacion of Rocco Bonnetto and nowe beinge in the tenure and occupation of Thomas Bruskett, gentleman, or of his assignes, conteyning in length fiftie and two foote of assize more or lesse and in bredith Thirty and Seaven foote of Assize more or lesse, lyeinge and beinge directly under parte of those of the saide Seaven great upper romes which lye westwarde, which saide midle romes or midle stories do extende in length southward to a part of the house of Sir George Cary, Knight . . . together with the dore and entry which do lye nexte unto the gate enteringe into the house of the said Sir George Cary, and used to and from the said midle roomes or midle storyes oute of a Lane or waye leadinge unto the house of ye said Sir George Cary, with free waye ingres egres and regres, into and from the said Midle romes or midle stories in by and thorough the wayes nowe used to the saide house of the saide Sir George Cary, And also all those two vaults or Cellers late beinge in thoccupacion of the saide Rocco Bonetto, lyeing under parte of the said midle romes at the north end thereof, as they are now divided and are nowe in the tenure or occupacon of the saide Thomas Bruskett, and of John Favor and are adjoyning to the two little yards nowe in thoccupacions of Peter Johnson and of the saide John Favor, Together also with the staires leading into the same vaulte or cellers oute of thaforesaid kitchen in thoccupacion of Thomas Bruskett, And also all those two upper Romes or Chambers with a little Buttery att the north ende of the saide seaven greate upper Romes and on the west side thereof nowe beinge in thoccupacion of Charles Bradshawe, Together with the voide rome waye and passage, nowe thereunto used from the saide seaven greate upper romes. And also all those two romes or Loftes nowe in thoccupacion of Edward Merry, thone of them lyeinge and beinge above or over the saide two upper romes or chambers in thoccupacion of Charles Bradshawe and on the est and Northe parte thereof, and having a chymney in it, And thother of them lyinge over parte of the forsaide Entry or voide rome next the forsaid Pipe Office, Together with the staires leading from the roomes in thoccupacion of Charles Bradshawe up unto the two roomes in thoccupacion of the said Edwarde Merry. And also

all that little Rome nowe used to laye wood and coles in being aboute
the midle of the saide staires, westwarde which saide little Rome is
over the foresaide buttery nowe in thoccupacion of Charles Bradshaw
and is in thoccupacion of the said Charles Bradshaw, And also all
that Rome or garrett lyeing and beinge over the said two romes or
loftes last before mencioned in thoccupacion of Edward Merry together with the dore entry void ground waye and passage and
staires leadinge or used to with or from the said romes in thoccupa-
cioo of the said Edward Merry up unto the said Rome or garrett
over the said two roomes in thoccupation of Edward Merry And
also those two lower Romes nowe in thoccupation of the saide Peter
Johnson Lyeinge directlie under parte of the saide seaven greate
upper Romes And also all those two other lower romes or chambers
nowe being also in the tenure of Peter Johnson beinge under the
forsaide Romes or chambers in thoccupacion of the saide Charles
Bradshawe, And also the dore entry way voide grounde and passage
leadinge and used to and from the said great yarde nexte the saide
Pipe Office into and from the saide fowre lower romes or chambers
And also all that little yarde adioininge to the said Lower romes as the
same is nowe enclosed with a bricke wall and nowe being in thoccupacion of the said Peter Johnson which said fower Lower Romes
and little yarde, do lie between the saide great yarde nexte the saide
Pipe Office on the north parte, and an entry leading into the Messuage
which Margaret Pooley, Wydowe, holdeth for terme of her life,
nowe in thoccupacion of the said John Favor on the west parte, and
a wall devidinge the said yarde now in thoccupacion of the said
Peter Johnson, and the yarde nowe in thoccupacion of the said
John Favor on the South parte, And also the staires and stairecase
leading from the said little yarde in thoccupacion of Peter Johnson, up to the romes in thoccupacion of Charles Bradshawe, And
also all that little yarde or peice of voide grounde with the bricke
wall thereunto belonginge lyinge next the Queen's highwaye leading
unto the River of Thames, wherein an olde pryvie nowe standeth,
as the same is now enclosed with the same brick wall and with a
pale, next adioyning to the house of Sir William More nowe in
thoccupacion of the Rt. Hon. Lord Cobham on the este parte, and
the strete leading to the Thames there on the west parte, and the
saide yarde next the said Pipe Office on the southe part, and the
house of the said Lord Cobham on the north parte, All which pre-

mises before in theis presentes mencioned to be hereby bargayned
and solde . . . Together with all Liberties, priviledges, Lightes,
watercourses, easiamentes, comodities and appurtenance. . . And
also the said Sir William More hath confirmed unto the saide
James Burbage his heirs and assigns free and quiet ingres egres
and regres from the strete leading from Ludgate over uppon
and through the said great yard next the Pipe Office by the
waies nowe thereunto used into and from the said seaven great
upper romes and all other the premyses . . . together with libertie
for James Burbage and his heires to discharge his and their wood
cole and all other carriage necessaries and provisions in the same
greate yarde . . . for convenient tyme . . . until the same may
be carried unto the premysses . . . and at all tymes hereafter
the said James Burbage, his heirs, . . . leaving convenient waies
to and from the gardeyn and other houses and romes of Sir William
More . . . so that the wood and cole be voided within three dayes
next after it shall be brought. . . . And Sir William More grants
the reversions and remaynders of all and singular the premises by
theis presents mencioned . . . except and reserved to Sir William
More and his heires one Rome or stole as the same is now made in
and oute of the foresaid wall next the saide entry adjoyning the
Pipe Office into the foresaid vault. . . . All which . . . premises
Sir Thomas Cawarden, Knt., deceased late had to him and his
heirs . . . of the gift of Edward Sixth . . . as by his letters patent
. . . Westminster (12th March, 4th Ed. VI . . . and in his last will
and testament . . . bearing date on the day of St. Bartholomew
thapostle 1559 . . . his executors should have full power to alyen
for the performance of his last will and testament . . . and made
Dame Elizabeth his wife and the said Sir William More, of Loseley
. . . Executors . . . and Thomas Blagrave and Thomas Hawe
Overseers . . . and they bargained and sold unto John Birch,
gentleman, John Austen, and Richard Chapman and their heirs
forever . . . on 20th Dec. 2 Eliz. . . . enrolled in Court of Chancery . . . all which premises the said John Birch John Austin and
Richard Chapman did on the 22nd Dec. 2 Eliz. sell to the said Dame
Elizabeth Cawarden and Sir William More and their heirs for ever.
. . . The said Dame Elizabeth Cawarden is long sythens deceased
. . . the premises have accrued to Sir William More and his heir by
right of survivorshippe . . . and he has bargained and sold, with

the exception aforementioned . . . to the onelie use and behoufe of the said James Burbage and his heirs for evermore . . . Sir William More standeth . . . lawfullie and absolutely seased of all the premises . . . in fee simple . . . and the said James Burbage and his heirs shall be saved and kept harmless . . . from all former bargains, chardge, arreradge . . . fees, fines, amerciaments . . . and from all other chardges, titles, trobles, and incombrances whatsoever . . . and may from henceforthe forever peaceablie and quietlye have hold occupie and enioye all the said roomes . . . (excepte above excepted) without any lett troble vexacion, interruption or contradiction . . . of Sir William More . . . or any other person . . . and within three years . . . to execute all and every such further acte . . . assurance in the Lawe whatsoever . . . Be it by deed indented or inrolled. . . George Austin gent, and Henry Smyth, Marchantaylor his deputies.

In witness whereof the parties firste above-named to theis Indentures sounderly have sett their seales the daye and yeare above written.   JAMES BURBADGE.

(From original in Loseley Papers only a few phrases cut out and a few words worn off.)

His seal is a griffen.

(Endorsed).

" Sealed and delivered in the presence of the persons whose names been (sic) hereunder subscribed.   George Austin.
                                    William Serche Scryvener."

The other part of this indenture was sealed by Sir William More before a M^r in Chancery same day. No bond for performance of the covenants within mentioned."   See p. 63.

NOTE X.—PETITION OF THE INHABITANTS OF THE BLACKFRIARS.

To the right Honble. the Lords and others of her Majesties most honorable Privy Councell, 1596.

Humbly shewing and beseeching your honors, the inhabitants of the precinct of the Blackfryers London, That whereas one Burbage has lately bought certaine roomes in the same precinct neere adioyning unto the dwelling-houses of the Rt. Honorable The Lord Chamberlain and the Lord of Hunsdon, which roomes the said Burbage is now altering and meaneth very shortly to convert and turn the same into a common playhouse which will grow to be a very great

annoyance and trouble, not only to all the noblemen and gentlemen
thereabout inhabiting but allso a generall inconvenience to all the
inhabitants of the same Precinct both by reason of the great resort
and gathering together of all manner of vagrant and lewde persons,
that under cullor of resorting to the Playes will come thither and
worke all manner of mischeefe and allso to the greate pestering and
filling up of the same precinct, yf it should please God to send any
visitation of sicknesse as heretofore hath been, for that the same
Precinct is allready growne very populous And besides that the same
Playhouse is so neere the Church that the noyse of the Drumms
and Trumpets will greatly disturbe and hinder both the Ministers
and parishioners in tyme of devine service and sermons.   In tender
consideracion whereof As allso for that there hath not at any tyme
heretofore been used any comon Playhouse within the same Precinct
But that now all Players being banished by the Lord Mayor from
playing within the Cittie, by reason of the great inconviences and
ill rule that followeth them they now thincke to plant themselves
in Liberties.   That therefore it would please your honors to take
order that the same Roomes may be converted to some other
use and that no Playhouse may be used or kept there.   And
your suppliants as most bounden shall and will dayly pray for your
Lordships in all honor and happiness long to live.

Elizabeth Russell, Dowager	John Robbinson
[1] Hunsdon	Thomas Homes
Henry Bowes	[2] Ric. Field
Thomas Browne	Will. Watts
John Crooke	Henry Boice
Will Meredith	Edward Ley
Stephen Egerton	John Clarke
Richard Lee	Will Bispham
—— Smith	Robert Baheire
William Paddy	Ezechiell Major
William de Lavine	Harman Buckholt
Francis Hinson	John le Mere.
John Edwards	John Dollin
Andrew Lyons	Ascanio de Renialmire
Thomas Nayle	John Wharton.
Owen Lochard	Dom. Ser. State Papers, Eliz. cclx. 11 6, (*in extenso.*)

[1] Burbage's Master, afterwards Lord Chamberlain, died 9th Sept., 1603.
[2] Shakespeare's fellow-townsman and publisher.

By papers in the year 1619 and in those of 1631 undated, vol. 205, No. 32, iv., reference is made to this petition as presented in *November*, 1596.

Following this is an opposing petition of the Players, certified by all authorities but Mr. Lemon to be a forgery. Any one may be satisfied that it is so, by the list given of the players, and by their reference to their " ordinary place of playing at the Globe," which was not FOUNDED until two years after. Also the players speak of *their* expense, whereas, at the time of the petition, the building and all *expenses* concerning alterations referred to James Burbage alone, and afterwards to his sons.

BLACKFRIARS.

Guildhall MSS. (Repertory 34, f. 38b.) 21st Die Jan., 1618–9.

Item this day was exhibited to the Council the petition by the Constables and other officers and inhabitants within the precinct of Blackfryers, London, therein declaring that in Nov. 1596 divers honorable persons and others then inhabiting in the said precinct made knowne to the Lordes and others of the Privy Councell what inconveniences were likely to fall uppon them by a comon Playhouse then preparing to be erected there, and that their Honors then forbad the use of the said howse for playes. And in June 1600 made certaine orders by which for many weightie reasons therein expressed it is limited there should be only two playhowses tolerated whereof the one to be on the Banckside, and the other in or near Golding Lane, exempting thereby the Blackfryers. And that the Letter was then directed from their Lordships to the Lord Maior and Justices strictly requiring of them to see these orders put in execucion and so to be continued. And nowe, for as much as the said Inhabitants of the Blackfryers have in their said peticion complayned to this court that, contrarie to the said Lordes orders, the owner of the said Playhouse within Blackfryers, under the name of a private howse hath converted the same to a publique Playhowse unto which there is daily soe great resorte of people and so great multitudes of coaches, whereof many are hackney coaches bringing people of all sortes, that sometimes all their streets cannot conteyn them that they endanger one the other, breake downe stalls, throwe downe men's goods from their shoppes, hinder the passage of the inhabitants there to and from their howses, lett the bringing in of their necessary provisions that the Tradesmen and Shopkeepers cannot utter their ware, nor the passengers go to the common water staires, without danger of their lives and lyms, whereby many times quarells and effusion of blood hath followed and the minister and people disturbed at the administracion of the Sacrament of baptisme and publique prayers in the afternoones, wheruppon and after reading the said order and letter of the Lordes showed forth in this court by the aforesaid inhabitants, and consideracion thereof taken, this court doth thinke fitt and soe order that the said playhowse be suppressed and that the players shall from thence forth forbear and desist from playing in that howse in respecte of the manifolde abuses and disorders complayned of aforesaid. (Copy.) See p. 65.

NOTE XI.—ROSE AND SWAN. (*Full abstract* in " The Stage " Jan· 6, 1910.)

COURT OF REQUESTS, ELIZABETH, UNCALENDARED PAPERS. S. 2. To the Queen.

Robert Shae, Richard Johns, Gabriell Spenser, William Birde alias Bourne, and Thomas Dounton, servants to the Rt. Honorable the Earle of Pembroke, complaining, That whereas your Highness' subjects, together with others their accomplices and associates, have of a long tyme used and professed the arte of Stage-playing, being lawfully allowed and authorized thereunto, during which tyme, your Highness' said Subjects being familiar and acquainted with one Francis Langley, citizen and gouldsmith of London, about February last in this 39 yeare of your Highness' reygne, fell into conferences and communications with the said Langley about the hiring and taking a playhouse of the said Langley situated in the old Parris Garden in the parish of St. Saviour, in the County of Surry, commonly called and known by the name of the signe of the Swanne, which said speeches took such effect, in respecte of the said Langley his forwardness as they fully concluded and agreed together and among divers other agreements between them in and about the same, the said Langley craftily and cunningly intending and going about to circumvent and overreache your said subjects in Law, about the taking of the said house, moved and required that your said subjects would become bound to him the said Langley in some great penalltie with the condicion that they should not absent themselves nor playe elsewhere, but in the said place now called the Swanne as aforesaid, wheruppon your Highness said subject, never suspecting the said Langley, his purpose and dishonest dealing, and craftie complot, which nowe appeare soe verie palpable, soe accordingly did concede to that his request, in or about the monthe of February last in this said 39th yeare of her Majesties reigne, became bound accordingly by himself and for himself and others in five severall obligacions in one hundred poundes a piece with conditions hereupon indorsed, among the other things to this or the like effect, that yf yor Highness said subject Robert Shaa one of the said obligors should, until the 20th day of February now next ensuing, in good sorte and manner, and from tyme to tyme continewe and attende as one of the Companie of players which then were agreed to plaie in the said playhouse of him the said Langley, in oulde Parris Garden, aforesaid, called the Swann, without absenting himself at any tyme from the companie when they shoulde plaie there, unles the said Robert Shaa your Majesties subject, should in his place and stead bring in or procure a sufficient person such as he the said Langlie or his assignes should like of, whiche, as one of the saide companie, should plaie there until the said twentieth daie of February now next ensuing as beforesaid, and further it was conteined in the said conditions, among diverse other things therein conteined, that yf your said subject Robert Shaa or this other sufficient person so by him to be procured and appointed should from tyme to tyme until the said 20th February, plaie in the said plaie house, as one of the said companie, and not in any other place or places within fyve miles distant from the city of London, except private places only, or then the companie of players should not in the mean tyme plaie within the citie of London and so allwaies should plaie in the said plaiehouse in manner and forme aforesaid without fraude or covin, that then the said obligacion to be voyd. And so consequentlie eache of your highness' subjects became solue ? and severally bounde by a like obligacion in the some of one hundred pounds, which condicion was to the effect before mentioned.

But nowe soe yt ys most gracious Sovereign, that sithence that tyme, as well your Highness' said subjects, as all other the Companies of Plaiers in and about your Highness' said Citie of London, have been prohibited and restrained from their libertye of playing for some time together, and allso the said Francis Langlie, being of a greedy ? desire and dishonest disposicion indevouring and seeking by all underhand and indirect meanes to bringe your said subjects into the danger and forfeiture of everie said severall obligacions by seaveringe of their Companie he, the said Langlie, by meanes as aforesaid hathe procured from your said subjects two of their Companie, so as they cannot continue there to play and exercise as they should nor as the condition of the severall obligacions require, whereby the same are become forfeyted, and now the said Langlie, shewing his lewdity and dishonestie to procure your said subjects to incurre the penaltie of their said severall obligacions, and effect all thinges to his owne mischievous mind, hathe of late published and given oute, and still doth threaten to commence suit at the common lawe against your Majesties subjects, meaning by the rigor and strict course thereof to recover the penaltie of £500 of one and all of your said subjects against all right, equity and good conscience. In tender consideracion whereof, and forasmuch as by reason of the restraint lately published, as well against your said subjects, as against all others, as also by the cunning and craftie complotting of the said Francis Langley, thereby causing some seavering of your subjects' Company to be sequestered from the rest, whereby they could not continue in the condition their several bonds requireth, by means whereof the same are become forfeyted by course of the Common Law and no remedy or relief given, (may it please your Majesty to make the said Francis Langley to appear in this court and answer this complaint).

REYNOLDS.

24th Nov. 40 Eliz.

The answer of Francis Langley defendant, unto the bill of complaint of Robert Shawe and others complainants.

The bill is insufficient and untrue. The said Shaw and the rest of the complainants his complices and playfellows, about the time stated in the bill were earnest suitors to the defendant, to have his house to plaie in, whereuppon it was agreed they should play for a year in defendant's house, and he was to allow such benefits as are usually given, and the defendant giving credence unto their faithful promises disbursed and laid out £300 and upwards, in making the playhouse ready, and in preparing rich apparel fit and necessary for playing, and they became bound to play there for a year, but Shaw and the others, not regarding their said promises, but being resolute to defraud the defendant, and make him lose most of the charges, they have departed and so severed themselves from the rest of their company without any just cause, and so have ever since absented themselves from his house, and now, since their libertye to pleye they have played in the house of one Phillipp Henslow commonly called by the name of The Rose on the Bankside.

True it is, there was a restraint upon players for a tyme, but the defendant saith that the players were at liberty, ever since the feast of All Saints last, and they might have played if it had so pleased them, in the defendant's house as other of their fellows have done, but they have refused ever since to play in the defendant's house and thereby have wilfully forfeited their said bonds, for and in respect of the great cost and charges he hath laid out at and by their appointment and direction for the furnysshing of the playhouse and such attire as they needed, of which he hath had but little use since being bought and provided for them to play with.   He denied having " craftily and cunningly, intending to circumvent the company, or that by greedy and dishonest disposition, he sought to bring them into the danger of the forfeyture, or that he severed the company from their companions, or that he had procured two of their companions from them."   He denied that he had lewdly and dishonestly procured the company to incurre the penaltie of their forfeiture, or that he hath of late published and given out that he doth threten to commence suite at Common Lawe or otherwise than is lawful to doe, as they have wilfully come into danger, in withdrawing and absenting themselves from his house, and continuing of their playes in other houses the defendant having disbursed for provision of their apparel etc., £300.   True it is that it was concluded and fully agreed between the defendant and the said Shawe and the rest of the complainants, with their fellow-players, that they should playe in the defendant's howse for a year next immediately ensuing, and the defendant was to allow to the complainants and the rest of their fellows such benefits as was then lykewise agreed between them, and the defendant, upon the said agreement, giving creditt unto their faithful promises, disbursed and laid out for the making of the said house ready and providing of apparell fytt and necessarie for their playing, the sum of £300 and upwards, and thereuppon true yt is that they became bounde to the defendant as in the bill ys alledged. But the said Shawe and the Rest of the complainants, not regarding their said promises and agreement but contrariwise being resolute, and as yt seemeth meaning to defraude and deceive the defendant, left his house, and went to play at another. Therefore he prays to be dismissed from this case with his reasonable costs.

5th Feb. 40 Eliz.

The Replicacion of Robert Shaw, Richard Jones, Gabriell Spenser William Byrd, alias Bourne, and Thomas Downton, complainants, to the answer of Francis Langley.

They aver and maintain their said bill and every the matters therein contained. The answer is very untrue, and insufficient in law, and by protestation, they do not acknowledge any material thing contayned in it to be true, otherwise than what is hereby confessed ; they all say that the defendant upon agreement between him and two of the company they were imboldened to depart from the society of these complainants, because they would not continue in the same society or company in the said house of the defendant, and as touching the departure of the complainants from the house, the cause thereof was well known to him as to others, for by Her Majesty's authority and commandment a restraint was publickly made of all companies in any of the playhouses in the city, and the owners of the said howses likewise prohibited to suffer plays, from about the feast day of St. James the apostle, until about All Saints last, whereupon, when the complainants had obtayned licence to play again, they resorted to the said defendant and offered themselves to play again in his house, yf the defendant would bear them out. But he said he had let to them his house, and bade them do what they would. The complainants then replied that they durst not play in his house without lycense, and that it was to their undoing to continue in idleness and that Phillipp Henslowe, (in the sayd answer named,) had obteyned a license for his house, and would beare the complainants out if they would go to him. Then the defendant said the complainants were best to go to him, which the complainants conceived and toke for a lycense of the said defendant, and that he meant well to the company that they should healpe themselves to gett their living. Since which tyme their company have exercised their playing at the howse of Phillip Henslow, as lawfully they might, and these complainants are now persuaded that the said defendant used the said words videlicet that then the said company " might goe play in the house of the said Phillipp Henslow " of policy to drawe them into the penalties and danger of the forfayture of their obligations, and not for any other purpose. They deny that the complainants and their playfellows were earnest suitors to the defendant to play in his house, as the answer untruely alleges, for the said complainants say that the defendant desyred them to play in the house and thereuppon the said agreement was made as in the Bill of Complaint is truly declared.   They also denied that the defendant, giving credit to the faithful promises of the complainants, disbursed and laid out for the making ready of the house and the apparell for them to play in, the sum of £300 and upwards, as is very untruely alledged.   The said complainants say that for the making of the said house ready and fitt for the complainants to play in the defendant was at no cost at all, for the said house was then lately often used to have plaies in it.   And if the defendant were at charge for the providing of the apparel, the complainants say that the same was of his own offer and promise, that he by the agreement was to provide the same and afterwards to acquaint the complainants with the value therof out of the complainants moytie of the gaines for the severall standings in the galleries of the same house, which belonged to them, which the said complainants have faithfully performed from tyme to tyme, and they further say that the said house of the defendant might have been longe or it would have been employed without the gaines, if they, the said complainants had not upon request of the said defendant exercised their playing therein, wherby the defendant hath gained at least a hundred pounds and above out of their company, and hath also received for apparell which he in his answer provided for the complainants a hundred pounds out of their moitie which was due to the complainants and yet he hath all the apparel to himself, part whereof the complainants have truly paid for, and therefore ought to have a consideration for the same.   They deny that Shaw and the other complainants did not regard their promise and agreement and resolved to defraud and deceive the defendant and make him lose most of the charges of disbursement about making ready the house and providing apparel as the answer untruely alledges.   These complainants desired to let the defendant have his money he had disbursed as agreed, which he refused, and took the apparell, and converted it to his best profit, by lending the same for hire whereby he hath receaved great gaynes ; or that the complainants have departed and severed themselves from the rest of their company without any just cause unto them by the defendant given, in such manner and form as in the said answer is untruely alledged. And without that the defendant hath sustained any losse by reason of the complainants, for he, the said defendant hathe ever since had the said house continually from tyme to tyme exercised with other players to his great gains. They denied that the complainants have ever since refused to playe in the defendant's house, and thereby have wilfully forfeited their bonds, as the answer untruely alledges, for as they before have truly declared, the cause was for that the said defendant did advise them to goe to the said Henslowe's house, and also because the defendant, in very subtle sort procured some of their company to be separated from them. They denied that the defendant in law, equity or conscience may lawfully sue and implead them upon their bonds in respect of the great costs and charges he hath disbursed and laid out by their appointment, for the supposed making ready of the playhouse and furnishing such attire for them to playe in, or that he had little use of it, being bought and provided for them, for the defendant hath from tyme to tyme, let out the apparel to his great advantage and the complainants ought to have had part, for that they had truely paid for part and the defendant made no little gaines through them, and therefore the complainants pray this honourable court to take some order whereby the defendant may be compelled to deliver some of the said apparell to the complainants, or to have their said obligacions delivered up. They can aver and prove that the defendant of a greedy disposition, did endeavour, by indirect or undewe means to bring the complainants into danger of forfeyting their bonds. The defendant hath procured their companions to continue their playe, and they were bound by several obligacions to continue their playing in his house and did not. But they deny that they have wilfully forfeyted them but by the cunning policy of the defendant by procuring some of their company from them whereby they could not play. They deny that the defendant hath disbursed the full sum of £300 and all that they have stated in their complaint is true. p. 72.

NOTE XII.—*What Meres said of Burbage's Play-writer.*

The History of Literature published in 1598, by Francis Meres, Professor of Rhetoric in Oxford, shews how the cultured literary man of the period looked at Shakespeare's works. In his " Wit's Treasury," second part of " Wit's Commonwealth," he says :—

" As the Greeke tongue is made famous and eloquent by Homer,

Hesiod, etc., and the Latine tongue by Virgil, Ovid, Horace, etc., so the English tongue is gorgeously invested in rare ornaments and resplendent habiliments by Sydney, Spenser, Daniell, Drayton, Warner, Shakespeare, Marlowe, Chapman.

" As the soul of Euphorbus was thought to live in Pythagoras, so the sweet wittie soule of Ovid lives in mellifluous and hony-tongued Shakespeare.   Witness his Venus and Adonis, his Lucrece, his sugred Sonnets among his private friends, etc."   " As Plautus and Seneca are accounted the best for Comedy and Tragedy among the Latins, so Shakespeare among ye Englishe is the most excellent in both kinds for the Stage, for Comedy witness his Gentlemen of Verona, his Errors, his Love's Labour Lost, his Love's Labour Wonne, his Midsummer's Night's Dream, and his Merchant of Venice ; for tragedy his Richard II, Richard III, Henry IV, King John, Titus Andronicus, and his Romeo and Juliet, As Epius Stolo said that the Muses would speak with Plautus' tongue if they would speak Latine ; so I say that the Muses would speak with Shakespeare's fine-filed phrase if they would speak English."

This list alone must somewhat discount the judgment of the railers at the *Theatre*, and its contents shew the advance made in the tone of Dramatic Literature since Shakespeare entered the field.

NOTE XIII.—*Cuthbert Burbage's suit for Alleyn.*

Coram Rege Rolls, Hil. Term, 41 Eliz., f. 320.

Cuthbert Burbage *v.* Roger Ames and others.

Memorandum that in Trinity Term 38 Eliz. Cuthbert Burbage presented Roger Ames, John Powell, Richard Robinson, all in the custody of the marshal, saying by his attorney John Tanner, in a plea of trespass that the said Roger John and Richard, entered upon the Close in the tenure of Cuthbert between the parcel of land belonging to the dissolved priory of Holywell and the great barne formerly called the Oatbarn, in the occupation of John and Richard Walker *Vi et armis* on the 1st of May 38 Eliz., while the grass was growing, and trampled and consumed it to the loss of the said Cuthbert of 40s. ; and from the 1st of May they took and kept the close, until the 27th of June of the same year, in their own custody, and committed other enormities, the damage of which in all was £20. The case had been postponed until this day, Tuesday in the Octaves of Hil. ; these defendants or their attorney having power to answer to Cuthbert's plea. They deny the force and injury, and say they are not guilty of trespass, and put themselves on the country, and request a jury.

(It is not appointed, so this does not give the end of it, being interrupted by the Earl of Rutland's case. See p. 68.)

NOTE XIV.—THE EARL OF RUTLAND AGAINST ALLEYN AND BURBAGE. Mich. 42 Eliz., 1599.

EXCHEQUER BILLS AND ANSWERS, Elizabeth, 369.

In Michaelmas, 41 Eliz., Roger now Earl of Rutland complained to Lord Buckhurst, Lord High Treasurer, etc., pleading that his father Edward, Earl of Rutland, was lawfully possessed by lawful conveyance of and in the capital Mansion House of the late dissolved priory of St. John the Baptist in Holiwell in the Countie of Middlesex, and of one garden and divers buildings, yards, courtes and waste and void ground and all their appurtenances, for divers years, yet enduring by lease, from the Queen's most excellent Majestie, whereupon there is a yearly rent of £9 6s. 4d., payable to her Majesty the reversion thereof being to her Majesty, her heirs and successors in the right of the crown. But so it is that of late to the great hindrance of the said Earl, and disinheritance of the Queen one Cuthbert Burbage hath wrongfullie entered into one piece of voide grounde or yarde, parcel of the said House, adjoining a certain building now in the occupation of John Powell, Richard Robinson, two undertenants of the said Earl, and not so satisfied, but also by the procurement and abetment of one Richard Allen, hath pursued severall actions of Eiectione fermi against John Powell, Richard Robinson, and one Roger Amyes in the Queen's Bench, not onlie to the great vexacion trouble and molestacion of the said pore tenants, but also the great hindrance and damage of the said Earle now complainant and also to the disinheriting of the Queen's most excellent Majesty's and her inheritance and that without all right and equity the recordes whereof remaineth in this honourable court and thereby the Queen's Majesties title may best appeare, to graunte unto your said complainant the Queen's Majesties writ of Subpoena to be directed to the said Richard Allen and Cuthbert Burbage commanding them on a certain paine and at a certaine daie therein to be limited to appeare personallie before your Good Lordship, in the Court of Exchequer Chamber, as well to answer the premises and to abide to such further order as shall stand with right and equity and also to grant her Majestie's most gracious injunction to be directed to them for stay of proceedings in the Court of the King's Bench.

(At foot is written)—

Let Subpoena and Injunction be granted as is sought.

JAMES SAVILLE, 1599.

22nd Oct., 42 Eliz.

The answer of Gyles Allen gent, defendant to Roger Earl of Rutland.

He thinks the bill exhibited by the procurement of Thomas Scriven, servant to the said Earl of Rutland, uppon a fained colour of title, which Thomas Scriven hath untruely surmised on behalf of the Earl of Rutland to delaie the just and lawful suites which the said Cuthbert Burbage in the said Bill named under the title of the defendant hath commenced against Powell, Ames and Robinson. It is utterly insufficient in law, not being set forth on any matter of equity and he demurs.   Nevertheless he answers that under a covenant made between Sir Edmund Peckham, Knight, deceased and Henry Webbe, Esq., gent porter of the King's Majesties Tower of London, in consideration of a marriage to be solemnized between Sir George, then Mr. Peckham, younger son of the said Sir Edmond and Susan Webbe, daughter of Henry Webbe, who promised he would make to certain persons, named by Sir Edmund, a good sufficient estate in the premises to have and to hold for the use of Henry Webbe during his natural life, and after his decease, and the marriage between George and Susan to them, and to their heirs, and in default of her heirs to his heirs, and Henry Webbe by another deed dated the last of February, 6th Ed. VI, did grant the premises to Thomas Mynd and Francis Darell gents appointed by Sir Edward Peckham, to have and to hold for the uses above ; by force whereof, and of the act of Parliament made 4th Feb. 27–28, Hen. VIII for the transference of uses, Henry Webbe was seized, with remainder to George and Susan, who, being so seized by their deed dated 6th of Aug. 2 & 3 Ph. & M., made between Sir George Peckham and Susan Peckham and Christopher Bumpstead, citizen and Mercer of London, that in consideration of £533 6s. 8d., paid by Christopher Bumpstead, they did sell in law to him and to his heirs, and he, by deed indented 1st Nov. 2 and 3 Ph. & M., and enrolled in the court of

Chancery, in consideration of £600 paid him by Christopher Allen deceased and Gyles Allen his son, the now defendant, the said Christopher Bumpstead sold and assured the demesne to the said Christopher and the defendant, and they were lawfully seized of it, as of fee. Christopher Allen long since died, and the defendant was seized as of fee and held the premises by right of survivorship, and he and his undertenants received the rents peaceably and without disturbance until of late, namely, about the 1st of Maie, 38 Eliz., the said Powell, Robinson and Amys, by command of Thomas Scriven, did wrongfullie enter into the said piece of ground, and thence did eiecte the said Cuthbert Burbage, then the defendant's farmer thereof, and enclosed the same with a mudd wall, and hath so kept the defendants from occupying it and from its profits, which piece of ground was never inclosed but lay always open to the inner court, as being a part and angle thereof, for the which wrongful entry and eiectment of the said Cuthbert Burbage, and against the trespass under the title of this defendant, the said Cuthbert Burbage did sue and commence an action of trespass against the said John Powell, Richard Robinson and Roger Amys in her Majesties Bench, as he supposeth he had a good and just cause to doe, which action being then depending Thomas Scriven in the Trinity Term following without the knowledge of the said Earl of Rutland (he then being beyond the seas) caused an information to be exhibited in her Majesties Court of Wards and Liveries in the behalf of the said Earl, being then in Ward to her Majesty against the said Cuthbert Burbage, the defendant's farmer and against the defendant, by the name of Richard Allen, misnaming him of purpose, as it seemeth, that the defendant should not theare make his answer for the setting forth both of the defendant's title and of the injurious dealings of the said Thomas Scriven, in whose informacion it was wrongfullie surmised that the said Cuthbert Burbage had wrongfullie entered into a piece of voyd ground or yard, parcell of the Capitall House of the said Priory, wherein it was supposed the said Earl was interested by virtue of a lease made by her Majestie, and that by procurement of the defendant, the said Cuthbert Burbage had pursued several actions against the said Roger Amys, Richard Robinson and John Powell, the undertenants of the said Earl in her Majestys Bench to the prejudice of the said Earl and disinheritance of her Majesty, and thereupon, before an answer made or injunction awarded to stay the suit commenced by the said Cuthbert Burbage against the said Ames, Robinson and Powell, commenced this countersuit in this court against the now defendants which suit depended in her said Majesty's Court of Wards about two years, at which time the said Earl being come to his full age and having sued his livery the power of that court ceased further to hould plea thereof, whereupon the said Cuthbert Burbage, after such long delay proceeded in that suit which he had formerly commenced in the Queen's Bench against Ames, Robinson and Powell, who only acted by the direction of Thomas Scriven, who managed the said proceedings, and paid all the charges thereof and procured many delays praying in aid of her Majestys inheritance, whereby the defendant, to his great trouble and cost, was enforced oftentimes to move the Judges of her Majestie's Bench, and to show them the great delays which had been used, and the great wrongs and vexacion which the unjust and indirect dealings of the said Thomas Scriven had made him sustain, wherupon in Hilary Term, 41 Eliz., they ordered that Ames, Robinson and Powell should forthwith plead to the action of the said Cuthbert Burbage and in the same term, Ames, Robinson and Powell pleaded not guiltie, wheruppon issue being joynd between them, and the matter ready to be tried in Easter term, it was then, by means of the said Thomas Scriven, delayed and put off until Michaelmas, the now defendant expecting trial and being then to his great charges prepared, having retained his Counsel for trial, and the attorney being ready.

The said Thomas Scriven a day or two before the matter should have been tried, exhibited his said Bill of Complaint to your Lordship in this honorable court, in the name of the Earl of Rutland, without his Lordship's privity and consent, as the Earl hath himself confessed unto the defendants, all which wrongs and injuries, offered to the said defendants he prays to be taken into consideration. The defendant Gyles Allen denied that the late Earl was possessed of the capital Mansion House of the dissolved priorie, or that any estate in it has come to the present Earl, and denying everything else material in the complaint, is ready to aver and prove all that he has stated.

The Replicacion of the Rt. Hon. Roger, Earl of Rutlande, complainant (undated further than Michaelmas, 42 Eliz.)

The Earl said that the answer is all frivolous, uncertain, insufficient, and untrue, and that his complaint is sufficient, just and true. The said piece of void ground which Cuthbert Burbage entered, was for this 50 or 60 years used with the part of the site of Holywell mentioned in the Bill, and denied everything, even that Giles Allen and his undertenants since the death of the said Christopher Allen had taken the proceeds to his own use, till 1st May, 38 Eliz.

Giles Alleyn's " Rejoynder." Michaelmas, 42 Eliz.

He said he can bring his grants and indentures and support all his points concerning the capital messuage. The piece of void ground did belong to the capital messuage but the House of the Earl of Rutland was not the Capital Messuage, but it was a smaller house, which had been enlarged by the late possessors. He denied that the piece of void ground had been used by the Earl of Rutland, during the last 50 or 60 years, and he traversed every point in the complaint, the land does not belong to the Earl of Rutland at all, and there is no reversion of it to the Queen.

EXCHEQUER DECREES AND ORDERS, Vol. 27, p. 110, Midd., Hil. 43 Eliz., 30th January.

Whereas in the matter depending in this court by English Bill and answer betweene the Rt. Hon. Earl of Rutland, plaintiff, and Giles Allen, gent and others defendants, it was ordered the 19th November that the said Earle should forthwith reply to the answer of the said Allen and proceede to examynacion of their witnesses this last Vacacion, as by the said orders at lardge it doth and may appeare. Nowe the Courte being this daye informed on behalf of the said defendant that the said Earle hath not ioyned in commission for examinacion of witnesses according to the said order and therefore prayed that the matter might be dismissed this court. It is this daie ordered by the Court, that if the said Earle doe not ioyne in commission with the defendants for examynacion of their witnesses before the end of this present Hillary term, that the said matter shall be dismissed out of this court.

EXCHEQUER DEPOSITIONS, 44–45 Eliz., No. 18.

A Royal Commission appointed to hear witnesses, dated 23rd June, 44 Eliz.

The Interrogatories appointed to be put are undated. The chief interrogatories are—

1 and 2. How long have you known the site, part of the monastery of Holywell, formerly in the tenure of the late Earls of Rutland,

Thomas, Henry, Edward, John and now in the tenure of complainant Roger, Earl of Rutland?

3. Do you know John Powell and Richard Robinson, undertenants of the void ground?

8. Do you know another barn among the new buildings of Giles Alleyn? When was the old one pulled down?

9. Whether were they in the said great yeard, and neare and along the late great Howse called The Theatre?

10. Whether the said Allen, his servants and tenants, before the Theatre was builded had their ordinary way of going to the Fields; only against the place, where late the Theatre stood?

11. Do you know that the Lane from the Great Street of Shoreditch along before the Gate of the late dissolved monastery was chained by the late Earl Thomas or Henry or their assigns?

Depositions of Witnesses taken at Shoreditch co. Middlesex at the Church House there the twelveth daie of October in the 44th year of Elizabeth, etc. before Francis Goston and Richard Thekesdon, Esq., by virtue of a commission out of her Majestie's Court of Exchequer at Westminster unto them and others directed for the examining of witnesses as well on the parte and behalf of the right Hon. Roger Erle of Rutland complainant, as on the part and behalf of Gyles Allen and Cuthbert Burbage defendants.

The name of the first deponent is worn off, but it is evidently Mrs. Farrar, aged 57.

1. She knows the whole site of the monastery, and hath known it for 42 years, and the part that the late Earls had occupied, for her husband Robert Farrar deceased was Steward, and secretary and survayor to Henrie late Earl, and the only dealer for him in such business, and dwelt within a part of the monastery as tenant for the most part of 42 years and there remaineth. The house in which the Earles used to dwell is let to divers persons whose names she doth not know. She knew the piece of void ground by the Stable and Barn, part of the monastery. She did not know Thomas late Earl, but she knew Henry late Earl, and that he did inhabit and keep house there, and he held the said farm and the plot of ground for his necessary service, sometimes for his own horses, sometimes for the horses of his son Edward Lord Roos, and their servants, and she knew a great ponde near unto the stable, where they watered and washed the horses of the Earl when they inhabited the mansion.

Those who had occupation of the Stable and farm had the piece of void ground, she had known it 40 years. She had heard that one Robinson who held the barn held also the piece of void ground as tenant to the now Earl of Rutland compl. She knows it had been the same piece of ground as the Late Earl had who had horses in the stable and the use of the yard ; and one Roger Woode, having the use of the barne as tenant had the use of the void ground, to carry his hay to the barne. She never knew it used for a slaughter-house. She did not know at whose costs and charges the new houses built in the great yarde near and along the great house called the Theatre, nor whether those other new builded houses that were on the other side of the great yard and against the former mentioned great House, were erected by Giles Allen by his direction or at his cost, or any other, and she doth not remember how long it is since they were built. But before the building of the House she remembers there was standing in the same place a Brew House, occupied by one Wood, which was afterwards converted to an oaten meal mill.

She cannot remember that Allen and his servants and tenants had before the new buildings or before the Theatre was builded their ordinary way of going and coming through that place where the Theatre stood into the Fields. But she hath heard that since the Theatre was builded there is a way made into the fields, and that Allen and his tenants for a long time hath held another way out of the site of the Priory to the High Street of Shoreditch.

She knows that the Earls and their assigns have heretofore at their pleasure, chayned and barred the lane called Holywell Lane leading from the great Street of Shoreditch all along before the great gate of the Monastery towards the Fields, and kept the same chained and a private way and would suffer no cart or caryage or wain to pass that way but for their licence.

Anne Thornes, of Shoreditch, aged 74, supports her evidence.

Nicholas Sutton of Haggerston co. Midd.—

1. Aged 61, said that he knew the site.

2. But he did not know how much belonged to the Earl.

4. He knew the void ground, parcel of the house adjacent to the barn, in possession of Roger Wood, tenant of the Earl, but he knew no more personally. He said he had heard it credibly reported that the piece of void ground hath been used by the Earls and their tenants, and he heard that, because he was to have hired the barn, and

the neighbours told him that the piece of void ground did belong to the said barn.

7. One of the Earls 40 years since did keep house there. He does not remember whether he used the barn, but heard it credibly reported he used it for a slaughter-house.

Mary Hobblethwayte, of Shoreditch, 76. She hath known the site for 54 years. She knew that one of the Earls held the Monastery, but does not remember how much.

One of the Earls of Rutland kept house in Holywell, she does not remember the uses of the barn, but she remembers that one Sir Henry Capell, Knight, did use a stable and barn near to a great pond which she well knew and the Earl's servants washed their horses there, and so did many of their neighbours, and the barn and the stable belonged to the priory and lay on the left hand and south-west side.

8. She did know another barn standing in the great yard of the new building of Gyles Allen, in the west part of the yard, which stands still, and has been converted into tenements within 30 years, by whom she knows not.

9. She does not know whether the new houses in the great yard along by the great House called the Theatre, and those on the other side were built by Gyles Allen or at his direction, but they were built about 26 years past and where they were built was a brew-house converted into an oatmeal mill.

10. That Allen and his servants and tenants before the new buildings, and before the Theatre was builded had their ordinary way of going and coming only by a way directly towards the north, enclosed on both sydes with a brick wall, leading to a crosse neere unto the well called Dame Agnes a Cleere's Well, and that the way made into the field from the Priory was made since the Theatre was builded, as she remembers. And that the said Allen his servants and tenants had not any other way leading to the High Street at Shoreditch.

John Rowse, of Shoreditch, 55, says the same as the above. He hath known the place for 44 years and hath known many tenants. He remembers John Powell and John Robinson two late undertenants of the Earl for 2 or 3 years. He knew that John Robinson and Powell held the piece of void ground between the stables, and occupied it and the barn and that Robinson made in the barn saltpetre and had no other way to carry it but over the void ground. For all his remembrance of 44 years he knew the stable and the void ground held by Earl and tenants.

7. He knew that the Earl Henry inhabited it, and kept the barn, and stable and ground for his own service (and confirmed the depositions of the others). He never knew the barn used for slaughter, but knew that the pond was used to wash horses, and generally called the Earl's horsepond. He knew the other barn of Giles Allen. It was occupied and the west end used by Robt. Stoughton, a butcher, for a slaughterhouse, and the east end by the Innholder of the Blew Bell in Coleman Street to lay in hay, and it stands east and west by the common sewer. It stands unpulled down, but altered into tenements by one James Burbage, but he does not know the names of the inhabitants. He does not know whether the new houses were built at the cost of Giles Allen or one Burbage.

8th. The said Allen his servants and tenants, before the new buildings were set up, took their ordinary way against where the Theatre stood into the fields, and none of them came out by the great gate, and he remembers this to be true, because Allen now and then coming from Holliwell did give the examinate's father (he being appointed Porter of the House of the said Earl) for his pains sometimes 3s. and sometimes 4s., and he hath known Allen use another way through his long orchard into Shoreditch Street some 30 years since. He knew that Henry Earl of Rutland did ordinarily chayne and barre at his pleasure the Lane leading from the High Street of Shoreditch, all along the gate of the Late Priory into the fields, and kept it barred, not suffering any horse or cart that way to pass but by his licence.

Leonard Jackson of Shoreditch, 80.

He has known all these parts for 54 years. He knew that Powell and Robinson hired the Barn, not to inhabit but to make salt-petre.

He knew the piece of void ground.

The new houses were not built by Giles Allen, but by James Burbage about 28 years agoe. Allen had an exit into the Fields, near the Theatre and he and his tenants had also another way through his great orchard into the High Street at Shoreditch, and that he hath used that way 30 or 35 years.

(*Note at the end.*) " Delivered in Court by the hand of Richard Theckston gent., one of the Commissioners 18th October, 44 Eliz.

EXCHEQUER DECREES AND ORDERS, Vol. 28, p. 270.
18th Oct. Mich., 44 Eliz. Midd.

Whereas a commission hath been heretofore awarded out of this Court for the Examinacion of witnesses in a matter depending in this court by English Bill between the Right Honorable Roger Earl of Rutland and Gyles Allen and others defts., for as much as the Courte was this daye enformed by Mr. Chibborne of Counsell with the defts. that the said Commission hath beene executed on the parte of the said Earle, and that the Plaintiff hath not examined any witnesses by reason he could not have his commission readie at the tyme appoynted for the executinge of the said commission, and therefore moved the Courte that he might be at libertye to examine his witnesses in this courte and that the deposicions of witnesses retourned might in the meantyme staye unpublisht. It is this day ordered by this Court that each partie shall be at libertie to examine such witnesses as they have in that matter, before one of the Barons of this court before All Souls day next and ymediately after they shall have examined their witnesses then each parties to deliver to the others attorney the names of such witnesses as shalle be soe examined to the ende thay maye be now examined, and then all deposicons taken in that matter to be published ; And whereas it is alleadged that the plaintiff by vertue of the said commission hath examined witnesses upon matters not concerned in the bill and Answer ; It is further ordered by the courte, that, if upon hearing of the said cause it shall appear to the court that the plaintiff hath examined witnesses upon matters not contayned in the said Bill and answer, then such deposycons to be suppressed.

NOTE XV.—SUBSIDY ROLLS, 23 Ed. VI, $\frac{142}{167}$

Hadley.	Thomas Hemming, Esq.	.	£50	*assessed*	50s.
Hendon.	Richard Allen *in goods*	. .	£14	,,	14s.
	Thomas Allen	. .	£13	,,	13s.
Popler.	John Gardiner	. .	£16	,,	16s.
Hackney.	Robert Hyde	. .	£20	,,	20s.
	John Smith of Clopton .	.	£20	,,	20s.
Hoxton.	My Lady Seamer .	.	£80	,,	£4
Whitechapel.	Humfrey Aleyn . .	.	£10	,,	10s.

SUBSIDY ROLL, Ed. VI, $\frac{142}{179}$

Hoxton.	My Lady Seamer	. .	£60 *assessed*	£3
	Richard Haddon	. .	£30 ,,	30s.
Church-end.	John Hall Junior	. .	£25 ,,	25s.
Holywell Strete.	Thomas Page	. . .	£60 ,,	£3
	Humphrey Underhill .	.	£60 ,,	£3
	John Hall the Younger	.	£30 ,,	30s.

SUBSIDY ROLL, Edward VI, $\frac{142}{177}$

Holywell Street.	Thomas Price. . . .	£60 *assessed*	£3
	Humfrey Underhill . .	£60 ,,	£3

SUBSIDY ROLLS, MIDDLESEX, 12th Jan., 5 Eliz., $\frac{142}{123}$

Shorediche *in Land.*	Giles Allen, gen.	£67 *assessed* £8	16s.–8d.
Whitechapell.	Robert Alleyn .	£3 ,,	6s.–8d.
Bromley	George Allen .	£5 ,,	8s.–4d.

SUBSIDY ROLLS, Eliz., $\frac{142}{223}$, 29 Eliz.

Shorediche.	Thomas Tressam	. .	£90 *assessed* £4	10s.
	Edward Bassano	. .	£20 ,,	20s.
	Jeronymy Bassano	. .	£20 ,,	20s.
	Andrew Bassano	. .	£20 ,,	20s.
	Thomas Haddon, Sen.	.	£20 ,,	20s.

$\frac{142}{234}$, 39 Eliz.

East Smithfield.	Marmaduke Dorrall, gent. £20 *assessed*		£4
Whitechappell.	*Goods*, Robert Miles .	£3 ,,	8s.
Ratcliffe.	George Street. . .	£4 ,,	10s. 8d.
Holywell Street.	Cuthbert Burbage .	£4 ,,	10s. 8d.
	Richard Burbage .	£3 ,,	8s. 0d.
Shorediche *Land.*	Sir Thomas Tresham £100 ,,		£20
rent.	Edward Bassano, The Queen's		
	Man . . . . £20 ,,		53s. 4d.
	Jeronymo Bassano, The Queen's Man £20 ,,		53s. 4d.
	— Brown, The Queen's Man. . £5 ,,		13s. 4d.

SUBSIDY ROLL, MIDDLESEX, 39 Eliz., $\frac{142}{239}$

Whitechapel.	John Gardiner	. . £4 *assessed*	10s. 8d.
	Robert Myles	. . £3 ,,	8s.

Ratcliffe.	John Gardiner	.	.	£10	*assessed*	26s. 8d.
Mile End.	Edward Hemming		.	£10	,,	26s. 8d.
Holywell Street.	Cuthbert Burbage		.	£4	,,	10s. 8d.

SUBSIDY ROLL, $\frac{142}{236}$, 39–40 Eliz.

Holywell Street.	*Goods*, Richard Burbage	£3	,,	8s.
	Lionel Field	.	.	£4	,,	10s. 8d.
Shoredich *Lands*.	Sir Thomas Tresham	.	£100	,,	£20
	Mr. Humble	.	.	£10	,,	40s.
Ratcliffe.	Robert Pope, Esq.	.	£40	,,	£8
Hackney.	John Street Monyer	.	£3	,,	8s.

NOTE XVI.—SITE OF THE GLOBE.

The site of the Globe is evidently that given by comparing old maps and papers, opening upon Globe Alley, a passage rectangularly leading from Dead Man's Place on the East to Maiden Lane on the North. It is true that Professor Wallace (*Times*, 2nd Oct., 1909) places it to the north of Maiden Lane and south of the Park, on the strength of a Coram Rege description of the extent of the property sold to the Burbages and others for the Globe. The whole consensus of opinion and of proof is against this. The *Park* certainly lay to the south as given in Sir Matthew Brend's lease to Memprise (11th Dec., 2 Car. I). There was not space for it on the north, beside the rows of houses and gardens proved to have been there.

The land brought by the daughter of Thomas Brend to Timothy Cason, lay at this point, where a Workhouse was later built, referred to in later title deeds as all within the site of Barclay's brewery.

The whole depends upon the Clerk's rendering of " abutting on " or " adjoining to," and whether he is thinking of the site or its boundaries when he talks of North and South. Dr. Martin has written a pamphlet on " The Site of the Globe " which preserves many deeds and maps illustrative of its position.

ENROLMENT 3 CHARLES I. Part 23, No. 22. No. 2,713. CLOSE ROLLS. An indenture inrolled. (Contracted.)

Brend mil et Memprise This indenture 11th Dec. 2 Car. I between Sir Matthew Brend of West Moulsey co. Surrey and Hilary Memprise citizen and Haberdasher of London in consideracion of £633 paid by the said Memprise exonerates and discharges Mem-

prise for the purchase of " All that tenement and garden, or little
plott of ground thereto belonging, divided into three tenements
in the occupation of Widow Lugg, John Gates and John Holdges,
as it was, or lately was divided into the 2 severall tenures of Joane
Garret Widow and Roger Asbourne, and also that other tenement
and other gardens devised by John Godly, Esq., to Francis Carter
20th Feb. 1615, for 31 years, and the tenement called The Gunne, the
tenement called The Blew Bore, and that called The Gatehouse, etc."

The premises are bounded by the King's High way called Dead
Man's Place on the east, and upon the south, by the brook or
Common Shewer, deviding them from the parke of the Lord Bp. of
Winchester on the south, and the garden commonly called The
Lumbard's Garden on the west, and the Alley or way leading to
the Gloabe Playhouse, commonly called Gloabe Alley on the north,
and containing in length from the King's High way called Deadman's
place, on the East, to Lumbardes garden on the west 317 foot or
thereabout and in breadth from the path called Gloabe Alley on the
north, to the Common Sewer on the south, 124 feet.   See p. 77.

NOTE XVII.—*The players at the Globe and the Essex conspiracy.*

" The Examinacion of Augustine Phillipps, servant unto the
Lord Chamberlayne and one of his players, taken the 18th of February, 1600–1, upon his othe.

" He seyeth that on Fryday last was sennyght, or Thursday Sir
Charles Percy, Sir Jostlyn Percy, and the Lord Montegle with some
three more spake to some of the players in the presence of this
examinate, to have the play of the deposing and killyng of Kyng
Rychard the Second to be played the Saturday next, promising to
give them 40s. more then their ordynary to play yt, wher this
examinate and his fellows were determyned to have played some
other play, holding that play of King Richard to be so old and so
long out of use, as that they shold have small or no company at yt.

" But at their request this examinate and hys fellowes were content
to play yt the Saterday, and hadd their 40s. more than their ordinary
for yt and so played yt accordingly.

by ye   "AUGUSTINE PHILLIPPS."
J. POPHAM,   (a good signature).
EDWARD FENNER.

Dom. Ser. St. Pap. Eliz. 278 (85).   (See p. 88.)

NOTE XVIII.—GILES ALLEYN AGAINST PETER STREET.

CORAM REGE ROLL. Trinity Term, 42 Eliz., 1362, R. 587, Middlesex,
Before C. J. Popham.

Memorandum that in Easter Term, 41 Eliz., in the Court of the
Queen at Westminster, Gyles Alleyn, Armiger, brought in a bill of
complaint, by his attorney, John Tanner against Peter Street,[1] who
was brought up in the charge of the Marshal, by Thomas Petre his
attorney, on a plea of trespass, it was put off until Friday the next
after Trinity and is now heard.

Gyles Alleyn, by his attorney John Tanner affirmed that on the
20th day of Jan., 41 Eliz.,[2] the said Peter Street *Vi et armis* broke
the Close of the said Gyles called The Inner Courtyard, parcell and
formerly part of the disused Monastery of Holywell in the county
aforesaid, entered it, trod down and consumed the Herbage belonging to the said Gyles, and did other enormities, and pulled to pieces,
destroyed, took, and carried off a structure belonging to the said
Gyles Alleyn called " the Theatre," which was of the value of £700,
and committed other enormities against the peace, and committed
damages, to the amount of £800 in all.

Peter Street, by Thomas Petre his attorney, appeared this day
and defended his case against the said complainant. He denied
the use of force and arms, or any wrong-doing except treading down
the grass. He acknowledged having taken away and removed the
Theatre. But he is not to blame for he acted only as the servant of
Cuthbert Burbage, and Gyles Allen ought not to have brought the
action against him. Because long before Giles Alleyn and Sara his
wife were seized as of fee in this land of the disused Priory of Holywell, and on the 13th day of April, 18 Eliz., the said Giles and Sara
had demised granted and let it to James Burbage, the father of
Cuthbert, for a term of years to have and to hold. They had entered
into an indenture with him the said James Burbage, one part of
which was signed and sealed by the said Giles and Sara, and the
other part signed and sealed by the said James Burbage, was by
mutual consent produced in court. The Indenture gave the extent
of the property, on which there was no dispute ; and the conditions.
James Burbage was to pay £14 a year rent on the four quarter days,

---

[1] Mich. 41 & 42 Eliz. Coram Rege Roll, a case in which Peter Street is
entitled carpenter.

[2] Evidently wrong date, see pp. 74–76.

and £20 on the sealing in the nature of a fine ; to hold the lease for 21 years, and if he had, before the end of the first ten years, in consideration of the value of the wood, stone, tile, and stuff of the old houses on the property, he had spent the sum of £200 in repairing and rebuilding the other tenements on the estate he was to be enabled to take down and carry away the Theatre to his own use. Further he was then at his own expense, to be allowed to draw up a new lease for an extended term of 21 years, i.e. thirty-one years in all (therefore due to end in 1607). James Burbage had so entered, had fulfilled the conditions, had spent £200 on the repairs and rebuilding of the tenements, and on the 1st Nov. 27 Eliz., before the ten years had expired James Burbage had retained William Daniell now Sergeant at Law, and he had drawn up the new Indenture. It was in English and is recited in full following the old Latin one, with the exception that it had no clause for the extension of lease.

The said Giles Alleyn was always to have a free seat in the house for himself and his wife and family, on condition that he came in time, and took them before they were otherwise taken up. But this the said Giles had refused to sign. And further the said Peter Street says that on the 1st Nov. 21 Eliz. aforesaid, the said James Burbage so possessed, before the time of the trespass, assigned the Theatre to John Hyde, citizen and grocer of London, who on 7th June 31st Eliz., assigned the same to Cuthbert Burbage. Wherefore the same Peter as servant of Cuthbert and at his command, did enter into the close, took down the tenement, called the Theatre, as was lawful for him to do, as in the aforesaid Indenture, and in the indenture drawn up by William Daniell, having spent the £200 in repairs, it was lawful for him to do. He therefore seeks judgment, that Giles Allen should have no plea.

Giles Allen says that for all Peter Street alleges, he should have his plea, because Peter Street's defence is insufficient in law, nor is it necessary for him to answer, when the plea is insufficient in law.

He therefore seeks judgment in his cause, for damages and costs.

Peter Street says that his plea is good and sufficient in law to preclude Giles Allen from any action, and he is prepared to verify his statements.

Giles Allen does not answer, nor deny, therefore Peter Street prays that Giles may be precluded from continuing his action.

Because the Court of our Lady the Queen is not yet fully informed of the cause, a day is given therein to both parties, on Thursday next before the Octaves of Michaelmas.

Let a jury be summoned for that day.

(The Jury is not summoned because meanwhile the case in the Court of Requests came on, a Royal Commission was appointed, and a decision given that Alleyn was not to continue his suit.)

(A free translation, and much curtailed, of the Latin abstract.)

NOTE XIX.—Burbage *v*. Allen, COURT OF REQUESTS. 87/74. 26th January, 42 Eliz.

To THE QUEEN.

In all humbleness complayninge, sheweth unto your most excellent Majesty your Highness' faithful and obedient subject Cuthbert Burbage of the city of London, gent, that whereas one Gyles Alleyn of Haseley in the Countie of Essex, gent, was lawfullie seized in his domain as of fee in certein garden growndes lying and being near Hallewell in the parishe of St. Leonard's in Shoreditch, in the Countie of Middlesex and being so seized, together with Sara his wife, did by their Indenture of Lease bearing date 13th day of April (18 Eliz.) for good consideracions therein expressed, amongst other things demised, and to fearme lette the said gardein growndes, and all profitts and commodities thereto belonging unto one James Burbage, father of your saide subject, to have and to hould to him the said James Burbage, his heirs, assigns and executors, from the feast of the Annunciation of our Ladie then last past, before the date of the said Indenture, for the term of 21 years from thence, yealding and paying therefore yearelie during the said tearme unto the saide Gyles Alleyn and Sara his wife, their heirs and assignes, £14 of lawful money of England. Among other agreements, the said James for him and his heirs granted to the said Gyles and Sara and their heirs that in consideracion of the said lease and of certain bricks, tyles, lead, and other stuffe coming of other tenements, mentioned in the said indenture, should and would at his own costes and charges within tenne yeares next ensuing the date of the saide Indenture imploie and bestowe upon the said buildings, altering and amending of certain houses and buildings on and upon the premises the some of £200, the value of soe much of the said old Stuffe and tymber, as should be imploied thereabout to be accounted part of the said £200, and the said Gyles and Sara did covenant with the said James

that the saide Gyles and Sara should and would anie tyme within
ten years next after the date of the agreement upon the lawfull
request of the said James or his executors at their costes in law,
make, or cause to be made to the said James and his heirs,
etc., a newe lease or grant like to these same presents of all
the foresaide gardens—growndes and soile, and of all other thinges
graunted by the said Indenture for the term of one and twentie
years more, to begin from the date of making the said lease
yielding therefore the rent reserved in the former indenture, and
under such like covenauntes expressed, (excepte this said Covenant
for making a new lease within 10 yeares), and the foresaid covenant
for employing the some of £200. And further, the said Gyles and
Sara, and their heirs, etc., did thereby covenant to James Burbage
that it should be lawful to the said James that in consideracion of
employing and bestowing of the foresaid £200 in forme aforesaid,
at anie time before the end of the first terme of 21 yeares, granted by
the said Indenture or before the end of the said 21 years after by vertue of the covenant to be granted, to have, take downe, and carrie
away to their own proper use for ever, all such buildings as should
be built or set upp upon the gardeins and voide grounds by the said
Indenture granted, or any part of them by the said James, etc.,
either for a Theatre or playing place or for anie other lawfull use for
his commodities, without anie stoppe, clayme, lett, trouble, or
interruption of the said Gyles and Sara, or anie other person in their
behalf. By vertue of which lease the said James did enter into the
premises and was thereof possessed accordingly and did performe
all the covenants on his part to be performed, and did also, to his
great charge erect and builde a playing House called The Theatre in
and upon the premises. Afterwards the said first tearme of 10 years
drawing to an end the said James did oftentymes in a gentle manner,
solicit and require the said Gyles Alleyn for making a new lease of
the premises according to the purporte of the first indenture, and
tendered unto the said Alleyn a new lease, devised by his cownsell
readie written and engrossed with labels and waxe thereto affixed,
agreeable to the covenant before recited, which the said Allen made
shew that he would deliver, yet by subtill devices and practices did
from tyme to tyme shift off the fynyshinge thereof. After which and
before the terme of 21 yeares were expired the interest of the said
terme, and all benefit and profit that might growe by the said inden-

ture of lease, came by good conveyance of the same to your said subject by virtue whereof your saide subject was thereof possessed or
demised and being possessed your said subject did often require the
said Allen and Sara his wife to make unto him the said new lease of
the premises, according to agreement in the first indenture, which the
saide Gyles Allen woulde not denie, but for some causes which he
feigned, did differe the same from tyme to tyme but yet gave hope
to your subject and affirmed that he would make him such a lease.
By reason whereof your subject did forbear to pull downe and carie
awaie the tymber and stuffe ymploied for the said Theatre and playing house at the end of the said first terme of 21 yeares as by the direct
covenant expressed he might have done.   But after the said first
tearme of 21 years ended, the said Allen hath suffered your subject to
continue in possession of the premises for divers years, and hath accepted the rent reserved by the said Indenture from your subject.
Whereuppon your said subject having occasion to use certain tymber
and other stuff which were ymploied in makinge and errecting the
said Theatre, uppon the premises (being the chiefest profitt that your
subject hoped for in the bargaine thereof did to that purpose), by
the consent and appointment of Ellen Burbage, Administratrix of
the goodes and Chattells of the said James Burbage, take downe and
carie away parte of the saide new building, as by the true meaning of
the said Indentures and Covenants was lawful for him to doe, and
the same did emploie to other uses.

But nowe soe it is, may it please your Majestie, that the said
Gyles Alleyne minding to take advantage of his own wrongfull and
unconscionable dealing in not making the said new lease, finding
the wordes of the said covenant to be that the said James, etc.,
might *before* the end of the said terme of 21 years, of the first indenture, or before the end of the said 21 years *to be granted* by new lease,
take down and carrie away the said tymber and stuffe used for the
making of the said Theatre, that therefore (in regard that your subject, trusting his promises to have a new lease, did not take the same
away at the end of the first term granted, and that noe newe tearme
being granted by the said Alleyne to the said James, etc., by the
wordes of the said covenant) he hath not libertie to take the same
away afterwards in strictness of law.   Thereuppon he; the said
Gyles Alleyn, hath brought an accion of Trespass in your Highness'
Court at Westminster, called the Queen's Bench, against Peter

Street, your subject's servante, who, by your subject's direction and commandment, did enter upon the premises, and take down the said building, mynding most unconscionablie to recover the value of the building in damages (which must in the ende light uppon your said subject if he should therein prevayle), and there doth prosecute the same with all rigour and extremitie which will tende to your subject's great losse and hinderance excepte your Majesties favour and ayde in such cases used be to him herein extended. In tender regard whereof, for as much as it is against all equitie and conscience that the said Giles Alleyne shoulde, contrarie to his covenant and agreement aforesayde through his owne wronge and breache of covenant hinder your subject, to take the benefit of the said agreement in the foresaid Indenture expressed to take awaye the said Tymber and buildings before the end of the saide 21 yeares, and for that your said subject or his servants can mynyster noe perfect plea at the Common Lawe in barre of the saide accion, And yet in all equitie and conscience ought to be releeved according to the true meaning, And the sayd Gyles Alleyn ought to be stayed of his saide suite. Maye it therefore please your most excellent Majestie, the premises considered to grant unto your said subject your Highness' writ of Privie Seale to be directed to the said Gyles Alleyne, commanding him thereby, at a certaine daye, and under a certain payne, therein to be lymytted to be and personallie to appeare before your Majestie in your Highness' Court of Whitehall at Westminster, then and there to answer to these premises and to abide such further order and direction therein as to the Masters of the said Courte shall be thought meet and convenient, And also to grant your Majesty's subject most graciously a writte of Injunction to be directed to all the Councillors, Attorneys, Sollicitors, and factors of the saide Alleyn, commanding them to cease all proceedings in the said Accion untill the matter in Equitie (wherein your poor subject humblie prayeth to be releeved) be first heard before the Masters of your Highness' said Courte, And your poor subject will, according to his bounden duty, daylie pray to God for the preservacion of your Royal Majestie in all health and happinesse longe to reigne over us. WALTER.

Endorsed 26th Jan., 42 Eliz.

Burbage *versus* Allen, gent.

The answer of Giles Allen, gent, 6th February, 42 Eliz.

That the Bill in the material part is very untrue and uncertaine in law, for divers faults and imperfections, and exhibited to this honorable Court of malice and evil will, without any just cause, and to the intent unjustly to vexe and molest the defendant with tedious travell, being an aged man, and to putt him to great trouble and chardges, Yet if it should appeare to this hon. Court that the defendant shall be compelled to make any further answer to the untrue and insuffycent Bill, then he claims the advantage of exception now and at all future time for further answer.   The said defendant saith that it is true that he and Sara his wife did by their indenture of lease bearing date 13th April 18 Eliz. ( ) 1576, for and in consideration of the some of £20 in hand to be paid by James Burbage for, and in the name of a fine, let and lease all the following property in Holywell—the 2 houses and tenements with appurtenances then being in the tenure of Joan Harrison, widow, and John Draggon ; and the tenement and garden, lying behind them, in the tenure of William Garnett, gardener, and the howse called, or knowne by name of The Mill-House and the garden lying behind, in the tenure of Ewin Colefoxe, weaver, and the three upper rooms with appurtenances next adjoyning the Mill House, in the tenure of Thomas Doncaster, shoemaker.   And also all the nether rooms with appurtenances, lying under the same upper rooms next adjoining to the Mill Howse then in the possession of Alice Dotridge widdow, and Richard Brakenburye and the garden and also one great Barne with appurtenances, then in the occupation of Hugh Richards Innholder and Robert Stoughton Butcher (except the defendant or his wife or assignes should inhabit the capital messuage there, late in the occupation of the defendant, and to and for the tenants of the said defendant if he should dwell in Hollowell, free libertie to fetch and drawe water from the well there from time to time during the said terme), to have and to hold by James Burbage, his heirs or executors, from the feast of our Lady last past before the date of the Indentures to the full end of 21 years to be fully completed, yielding to the defendant or his wife Sara, or their heirs or assignes £14 by the year at the 4 terms of the year within 28 dayes of the feasts in even porcions, and James Burbage agreed at his own proper cost to keep up reparacions, repair, susteyn and amend the buildings as required till the end of 21 years, and so leave them repaired ; that it should be lawful for James Burbage or his heirs at any time within the first ten yeares of the lease to alter, change, take down or remove anie of the houses,

barnes or walles or Buildings and the same to alter and frame into
whatever houses seemed good to the said James Burbage or his heirs
for bettering thereof, in what form he pleased, and that the new buildings should be sett at more value and greater rent, and that it should
be lawful for James Burbage or his heirs to take to his proper use,
all the timber, tile, brick, and stuff whatsoever of said ould houses
and Burbage agreed that in consideration of the lease and the grant
of the timber and stuff coming from the old tenements, he would at
his proper cost, within the ten years next ensuing the date of the
indentures, employ on the buildings altering and mending of houses
and bettering thereof the sum of £200 for the value of so much old
timber and stuff that should be employed in making the said new
buildings during the term repaired and that they should be left and
yielded up at the end. It was further agreed that if the rent of
£14 be left unpaid and noe sufficient distress be in the premises by
which rent might be found, or if £200 should not be employed on the
buildings the defendant should be empowered to re-enter. It was
further covenanted that at any time within the first ten years, upon
lawful request of James Burbage and at his own costs, a new lease like
the former one might be drawn up for 21 years to begin and take
commencement from the date of making the new lease, yielding £14
for the rent thereof, and it should be lawful for James Burbage, if he
had spent £200 before during the term, at the end of the 21 years to
take down and carry away to his own use all such buildings as had been
set up on the gardens and voide ground by him either for a Theatre or
playing place, or for any other lawful use for his and their commodity.
It is true that James Burbage asked him to make a new lease, and
did tender a draught written and engrossed, which he the defendant
did not seal nor promise that he would deliver it, nor by subtle
devices in the delaying thereof, as the complainant most untruly
alledged, but contrariwise, the defendant did, upon manie and very
just and reasonable causes, utterlie refuse to seale and deliver to the
complainant for the plaine and true declaracion whereof, that, as
he taketh it, the lease so tendered by James Burbage, differed in
many material points from the first and therefore in respect that
the second lease should be made like to the former, he did not think
he was bound by law to seale the same and for the further manifest-
ation of which variance the defendant referreth to the Indenture
and the draught of the new Lease. But if soe it were that the defend-

ant had acted contrary to his covenant, yet had the complainant noe cause to seeke relief in this Honorable Court, for the Complainant hath divers times said unto the defendant, that he the said defendant was bound unto him the said James Burbage by the some of £200 for the performances of covenants and that he would sue him at the Common Law ; and the Defendant saith that by the bad dealing of the said James, there is nothing in favour of the said James. He hath been a troublesome tenant unto the defendant, and did not perform his covenants further than by the law he was [1] compelled to do, for whereas the said James Burbage was bound to pay £20 for a fine for the lease, he neglected the payment thereof at the time appointed and long after, and hardly could the defendant, after much delaie and trouble by sute-in-lawe, obtaine the same. And further the said James continually failed in the payment of his rent, and never duelie paid the same, whereby the defendant was often driven to his great trouble, to go about to distraine for the same, and yet could not the defendant manage that way to help himself, for either the dores and gates were kept shut so that he could not enter to take any distresse, or otherwise, the matter soe handled that the defendant could not finde sufficient distress to satisfie him for the arrerages, and at the time of the said new lease tendered, he the said James, did then owe £30 for rent for the houses and gardens which as yet remayne unpaid, notwithstanding the said James in his life time, and the complainant hath, before divers credible persons as the defendant can prove, oftentymes confessed the same to be due. And further touching the repairs which the said James ought to have done, he neglected, for one great barne of fourscore feet of assize in length, and 24 in breath very substantially built, for which defendant formerly had a rent of good value, the said James did divide it into eleven several tenements and did let out the same to poor persons for the severall rentes of twenty shillings by the year to be paid by every tenant, who were unable to do any reparacions uppon them, for such is their poverty they usually begg in the fields and in the streets to get money for the paiement of their rent, whereof the defendant hath been much blamed and censured by the parishioners that he should be the cause of bringing so many beggars among them and annoyance to others. This proceeded not from any fault of the defendant, but from the covetous humour of

---

[1] The writing is much worn off in this passage.

the said James, who respected more his own commoditie, than the
good report and credit of the defendant or himself, and the like
evill disposition is in the complainant who, since his father's death,
hath continued the poor people there and doth continue, and doth
not repair their tenements, where in they are growen in great decay,
and are almost utterly ruinated, and are now by the complainant,
underpropped with stones to keepe them from falling down, instead
of repairing them as by the covenant he ought to have done, and
regards not credit, but seeking to enrich himself only by the rents
and other profits, which he unconscionablie receaveth for the same,
and they have placed other poore people in other tenements, which
still continue there, and the tenements decay so that the deferdant
seeth he will not be answered of the old rent of £14, by the tenants
as are able to pay ; so that however the complainant hath surmised
that the said £200 came to be bestowed by his father, and that the
tenements were greatly amended and bettered, as they ought to have
been, the defendant will make it appear that they are rather impaired
and in worse plight than they were when the said James first took
them. At the time of the second lease tendered, nor ever after hath he
expended the some of £200 or more than that in bettering the tenements, the said second lease being tendered a very short time before
the tenure of 10 years, therefore the defendant did refuse to seal the
said lease with just cause, both in law and conscience, and afterwards, a little before the death of James Burbage through great
labour and entreatie of the said James, and the complainant and
" other their frendes, who often moved the defendant in their
behalf," and the saide James Burbage pretending and making
shewe to the defendant with many faire speeches and protestacions
that he would duly pay his rente and repaire the houses and perform
his covenant, as a good and honest tenant ought to do, and that he
would pay the arrears of £30, and there grew a new agreement that
he would have a new lease of the premises contained in the former
lease, for the terme of 21 years to begin after thend of the former
lease, for the yearly rent of £24, for the said James Burbage in
respecte of the great profit and commoditie which he had made,
and in time to come was further likely to make of the Theatre and the
other buildings and grounds and was very willing to pay the £10
yearly more than formerlie and it was agreed further between them
that as he the said defendant hopes he will sufficiently prove the said

Theatre should continue as a playing place for the space of 5 yeares only after the expiration of the first lease and no longer, by reason that the defendant saw that many inconveniences and abuses did growe thereby, and that after the said 5 years it should be converted by the said James Burbage and the complainant to some other use, and be employed upon the grounds demised, whereby the benefit and profit should after the term be unto the defendant.

But before that agreement was perfected, because the said James had not obtained such security for the performance of his covenants which the defendant required, James dyed, After whose death the complainant did often move and entreate the defendant that he might have a new lease of the premises like the former one, and he would put in good security for payment of rent and repairing, etc. There were often communications between the complainant and defendant, who was contented to have made the same lease with the complainant who seemed very willing to have it, under the same agreement as were formerly agreed on by the said James Burbage, and the matter was at last concluded. The complainant drew it up, yet found means by colorable shiftes and delays to deferre the execution thereof. The defendant, hoping the complainant had honestly and faithfully meant to have taken the lease whereby defendant would have received the arrearages of £30, and had the houses repaired, and that he should have had security, and not such disquietude and trouble as formerlie, wherupon the defendant was contented to suffer the complainant to enjoye the premises after the first lease expired for the space of a year or two paying onelie the old rente of £14, which the defendant did the rather because the said James and the complainant had placed soe many poor people there, who were not able to paie their rent, that yf the defendant had taken the same, he would have through pitty and compassion have forborne their rente to his great losse, and would have been forced to have turned them out because the buildings were so decayed, he must pull them down and erect new.

But now by the dealing of the complainant, it appeareth that he never in truth meant to take the lease as he pretended, but onlie sought to take occasion when he might privilie, and for his best advantage pull down the said Theatre which, about the feast of the nativitie of our blessed Lord in the fortieth year of Eliz. he caused to be done, without the privity or consent of the defendant, he being

then in the countrie, for the which the said defendant hath brought
an action of trespass in her Majesty's Bench against him, who by the
commandment of the complainant performed the work, for which
action the defendant thinketh he had verie good and just cause in
law and conscience, for that the libertie which the said James had
by the same lease to pull down the said Theatre at anie time of his
lease was granted only in consideration that £200 had been spent on
the houses and buildings which summe not having been spent on
them, there was no Colour to take away the same, and further the
defendant could not see by what means he should receive satisfaction for the £30 due unto him and for the losse by lack of repairs, a
very great losse, which amounteth to a very greate value not onelie
by the said Theatre which the defendant intended to convert to his
own use, and thereby to be recompensed, seeing himself otherwise
lost without remedie by reason that the wife of the said James, whom
the said complainant supposeth to be administratrix, is neither willing nor able for aught the defendant can prove, to yield him any satisfaction at all, for the complainant (so the defendant is informed)
having gotten the greatest part of the goods and substance of the
said James into his hands, and the said Ellen Burbage the wife of
James being a poore woman, " the defendant " (sic) " very subtillie
caused her to take the administration of the goods of the said James "
so that they might be able to trouble and molest the defendant,
and avoid paiment of the debts of the said James and performance
of his covenants, and further whereas the complainant supposeth
that the said James did to his greate charges erect the said Theatre
and thereby pretended that there should be greater cause in equitie
to relieve him, The defendant says in return, that considering the
great profit and benefit which the said James and the complainant
in their lives have made, which the defendant is crediblie informed
doth amount to the sum of £2,000 at the least, the defendant taketh
it they have been very sufficiently recompensed for their chardges
which they have bestowed upon the Theatre, or upon any other
building had they been much greater than they were.

And further the defendant hath crediblie heard that the said
Theatre was not built at the alone chardges of the said James, and
that one John Braynes did defray the greater part of the chardges,
and was therein defrauded by the said James Burbage, as the defendant hath heard, that there was an agreement that the said John

Braynes should have the moyetie of the lease, and the profitts, which the said John Braynes did not enjoy, according to the covenant, but was therein defrauded by the said James, as the defendant hath heard one Robert Myles executor to the executors of the said John Braines, did exhibite in a bill into her Majesty's High Court of Chancery, against the complainant and the said James, and the defendant saith that the said complainant, subtillie intending to defraude both the said Robert Miles and this defendant, hath pulled down the said Theatre, in great contempt of the said Honorable Court, and to the great wrong and injury of the said defendant, he saith that the said complainant nor the said Ellen Burbage, having no colour in law and conscience, unless he the said James had performed the covenants in manner and form, and did to his great chardges erect the Theatre. And without that all benefit of the interest of the said tenure, and all benefit and profits by lease and good conveyance came unto the complainant, or that he was lawfullie possessed thereof and without that the complainant did often require the defendant and Sara his wife to make him the said new lease, and that the defendant on any fained cause defferred from time to time, as the complainant most untruely hath alledged, and without that the said Ellen is the lawful administratrix, and did consent and appoint that the said complainant should pull down the said Theatre, or that, in virtue of the lease, the Complainant might lawfullie pull down the same, and without that the defendant intendeth to take advantage of his own wrongfull and unconscionable dealing as the complainant hath untruelie surmised, &c.

The defendant hopes this honourable Court will see the defendant's just and honest claims and thinks the complainant's bill is sufficiently answered, and prayeth to be dismissed with reasonable costs.

Burbage v. Allen, 27th April, 42 Eliz.

The replicacion of Cuthbert Burbage. Reserving to himself all future advantage of the uncertain and insufficient answer of the defendant, the complainant will aver and prove all and every matter contained in the said Bill to be just and true, that the said new Lease tendered by James Burbage to the defendant, was the same as the old one, and he did not behave badly nor was the said James such a troublesome tenant to the said defendant as he says ; that there was no cause in conscience to move the said defendant to yeald to anything in favour of the said James, except by law he might be compelled as in the said answer is most untruely alleged ; nor that he failed in paying his rent duely, nor that the defendant had to go about to distraine for the same, nor that the doors and gates of the said James Burbage were kept shut that the defendant could not enter in any distress ; nor that the defendant could not find sufficient distress to satisfy him for the arrearages of the rent (if any were) as in the said answer is alleged. There was much variance between the defendant and one Edmund Peckham through the title of the premises in the said answer mentioned. James Burbage, the plaintiff's father, was very much troubled, and often chardged to provide men to kepe the possession of the said premises from the said Edmund Peckham, neither could the plaintiff's said father enjoy the lease of the said premises to him made by the said defendant, for which cause it was that part of the rent was left unpaid. It may be that the said plaintiff's father detained the rent in his own handes, and did not paie the same at the daies lymitted for payment thereof, the certainty whereof the complainant does not know, but that the said James Burbage, at the time of the said new lease tendered, owed the defendant £30 for rent, or that the complainant, since the death of the said James Burbage did confess the sum to be due to the defendant, as in the said answer untruely is alleged ; the complainant doth not acknowledge, nor the debt. Howbeit the complainant had said to the defendant that if he would use him kindly and deale justly with him, that he for quietness and friendship to be had would satisfie the defendant of all such rent as the said defendant could reasonably demand ; and whereas the said defendant said that James Burbage had neglected to do reparacions in the house and buildings, or that the said James did divide the said barne into eleven separate tenements and did let the same to poor persons, and did take severall rents of 20s. by the year. It is true that he divided the barne, which laye empty then at his own great charge. He was not restrayned by the said lease to build or convert any of the premises to his immediate use, and he can prove that he disbursed for and spent a great sum in reparacions.

Without that the said tenants are so poore that they usually begge in the fields and streetes for money to pay their rents, or that there were any cause the said defendant should be much blamed or hardly censured by the parishioners or that the said james re-

spected more his own commoditie than the good repute and credit
of the defendant as in the answer is slanderously alleged ; without
that the complaynant since the death of his father hath not repaired
the tenements, or that they are grown in great decay and ruin, or
that the said tenants should complain that they were ready to fall,
as in the said answer is untruely surmised, as the complainant can
prove that he hath disbursed this very last year the some of 20 markes
and better ; without that the said James Burbage had not at the time
of the second lease expended two hundred pounds or more for the
bettering of the houses and buildings, or that there was not anie like-
lihood that the said James Burbage should perform the same during
the limited time. He can prove that the said James Burbage did
so by the evidence of divers good workmen who performed the work,
and others, that the said James, before tendering the second lease did
disburse for the bettering of the said houses above £200, and therefore the defendant had no just cause to refuse to seal the second
lease and dischardge the new agreements. And the complainant
saith that true it is, that the said James was very willing to have a new
lease for 21 years from the defendant, under such rent and reasonable
covenants as in the former lease were conteyned and that therefore
speeches and communications were often had between the defendant
and the said James, but the defendant according to his own will and
discretion did cause a draughte of a lease to be drawn wherein were
inserted many unreasonable covenants on the part of the said James
for the performance thereof, that the said James utterlie refused to
proceed any further in the said bargain. And the said James within a short time after died. Without that the said James was willing to pay the said defendant £10 more rent than he had formerly
done, or that it was agreed that the said Theatre should continue for a
playing place for the space of five years only after the first term of 21
years, no longer, or that the same, after 5 years should be converted
by the said James to some other use and bee emploied upon the
ground demised, whereby the benefit and profit thereof, after the
terme, should remain to the defendant, as in the answer is alledged,
without that the complainant did often move and intreate the said
defendant that he might have a new lease, according to the former
one, or that the complainant did promise to pay the defendant £30
or that the complainant seemed very willing to have the lease in such
manner as the defendant proposed, or a new lease should be drawn

up for the sum of £24 rent, or that the matter was so concluded or that there was a new lease drawn accordingly by this complainant, or that the defendant was content to suffer this complaynant to enjoy the premises after the first lease expired for the space of a yere or two, paying onelie the old rent of £14, for such reasons as in the answer is most untruely suggested ; without also that the complainant never meant to take the lease of the premises, but merely sought occasion when he might privilie and for his best advantage pull downe the Theatre, for the complainant said he was very willing to have had a new lease of the said premises from the defendant, so as the same lease might have been made reasonable and according to the former lease made by the defendant and his wife to this complainant's father. He doth not denie that he hath pulled down the said Theatre, which he thinks it was lawful for him to do, being covenanted in the former lease to the complainant's father ; without that the complainant hath gotten most part of the substance and goods of the said James Burbage into his owne hands, or hath subtilly caused the said Ellen Burbage to take the administration of the goods of the said James Burbage thereby to trouble and molest the said defendant, and themselves to avoide payment of the debts of the sayd James, and the performance of his covenants and other duties, as the said James, his executors and administrators ought, both in law and conscience, unto the said defendant ; or that the said James or this complainant hath made £2,000 profitt and benefit by the said Theatre, as in the said answer is also alleadged ; and without that any other clause in the said answer contained material or effectual in lawe to be replied unto by this complainant, or not sufficientlie replied to and traversed, is true. All which matters the complainant will be readie to aver and prove as this honorable Court shall award, and prayeth as before in his said bill of complaint he prayed.

Burbage *v.* Allen, Privy Seal Mandate. 5th June 42 Eliz.
" By the Queen,—

" Trustie and well beloved we greet you well ; " and send on articles on behalf of Gyles Allen defendant against Cuthbert Burbage Complainant " whereuppon, in your approved wisdoms, learning and indifference, will and desire you by Authoritie calling before you such witnesses as shall be nominated by said defendant, and duly and sufficiently examine them by their oaths in form of law, not only uppon the content of the said articles here enclosed, but upon all such other articles which shall be exhibited," that you endeavouring by all means possible to search and try out the verytie of the premises and thereupon to certifie us and our Counsell by your writing, at our Court of Whitehall in Westminster, in the Octaves of St. Michael the Archangel next coming ; and of the true depositions of the witnesses, that we by thadvice of our said courte, may further therein deale as the case shall require. " As you do tender our pleasure and thadvancement of justice." Privy Seal, Greenwich, 5th June, 42 Eliz.

(*Endorsed.*)   " The execution of the commission appeareth by the schedule annexed."

Interrogatories on behalf of Giles Allen, 5th June.

I. Do you know both the parties ?

II. " Whether was there not an agreement made between complainant and defendant that the defendant should make a new lease of the houses and grounds demised to James Burbage, father of complainant, from 21 years from and after the expiration of former lease, and that the Complainant should pay £24 yearly and whether it was then agreed that the Theatre there erected, should continue for a playing place, by the space of 5 years only, and that it should be converted to some other use for the benefit of the complainant during his terme, and afterwards, for the benefit of the defendant, and whether did not the complainant, upon that agreement, promise the defendant to pay him the sum of £30, which was due the defendant as arrearages for rent, and to put the houses and buildings in good reparacion, and how long is it sithence such agreement was made ?

III. Whether was it agreed that the complainant should take a new lease of the said houses and grounds for the term of 10 years, and that the plaintiff should give £100 for the said lease, and £24 rent yearly and whether there was any such agreement made between the defendant and James Burbage, and at what time was it made, and how do you know ?

To Robert Sandford, Arthur Breather and John Sammes.   (The names of those on the Commission written on the back signed Julius Cæsar, and dated also 5th June 42 Eliz.)

Depositions taken at Kelvedon, Essex, 14th August 42 Eliz., before Arthur Breather, Gent, and John Sammes, gent.

First witness, Robert Vigerous of Langham in Essex, 47 years of age who had known Giles Allen for five years, and Cuthbert Burbage for four years.

He cannot answer the second question.

To the third he says that about four years past the complainant and his father James Burbage were in communication with the defendant about a new lease of the houses and grounds of the Theatre, and it was concluded and agreed that there should be a new lease for ten years for the rent of £24, which was an increase of £10 on the former lease expired, or near to be expired, and that at the conclusion, the plaintiff should pay certain arrearages of rent on the previous lease, amounting to £30.   This deponent was of counsell with them, and was especially named to draw up and write the lease and he wrote the draught of the lease, and he gave it to the plaintiff when he came to the deponent's chamber to see it, and paid him his fees, with promises of further rewarde for his paynes about the effecting of the lease, which should be a satin doublett.   Howbeit he never had it.   But whether the complainant should give £100 for the lease, he knew not, by reason of his discontinuance from the Temple.   But he saith that he hath seen a draft purporting to be a lease of the same premises, wherein the £100 are mentioned, made by complainant, and brought by him to defendant's house in the country.   He did not remember for what consideration, but that the defendant had said that the said James had not spent £200 in the buildings or reparation of the said houses according to the contract mentioned in the former deed, nor half so much, or words like that, and whether the £100 was inserted in that consideration he could not tell.

Deposition of Thomas Neville of Bricklesea, gent, in the County of Essex, 35 years of age.

I. He knew both of the parties.

II. There was an agreement between plaintiff and defendant for the houses and grounds, with the Theatre, formerly demised to the said James Burbage, with rent increased from £14 to £24 which should begin at the expiration of the old lease, and continue 21 years ; and the defendant was at first very unwilling that the said Theatre should continue one day longer for a playing place, yet nevertheless he yealded that it should continue as a playing place for certayne years, and that the complainant after these years should convert the said Theatre to his own benefitt for the residue of the term, and that afterwards it should remain to the sole use of the defendant.   Further the said James Burbage did acknowledge the sum of £30 mentioned to be due to defendant for rent behind, and the said complainant Cuthbert Burbage did often since promise the paying of the same, at the sealing of the new lease.   And this agreement was made 2 years since or thereabouts at Michaelmas terme now next coming.   And further he cannot depose.

III To the third he cannot depose.

(*This case little contracted.*)

(The depositions on behalf of Burbage have been lost.)

From the uncalendared proceedings of the Court of Requests, Elizabeth, Bundle 372, I secured a fragment of a volume (Decrees and Orders), 11th June 42 Eliz.

Seeing Giles Allen contemned the order of Council made in the cause between Cuthbert Burbage gent, plaintiff, and the said Giles Allen, defendant, bearing date 31 May ult. past.   It is therefore decreede now, that letters of Attachment be made, directed to the Sheriff of the County of Essex, and also to Hugh Barbon [1] gent, to attach the body of the said Giles to return immediately, etc.

JUL. CÆSAR.

Allen *v.* Burbage, COURT OF REQUESTS, Witness Book, Easter 42 Eliz., 9th April.

Giles Allen def. (1)	Philip Baker, Gent.
Cuthbert Burbage plaintiff.	Henry Johnson. John Gobourne.
Cuthbert Burbage pl. (2)	William Smyth, gen. Richard Hudson.
Giles Allen def.	Thomas Osborne. Thomas Brymefield.

Trinity Term, 42 Eliz., 23rd May.

Cuthbert Burbage gent., pl.	Oliver Lilt. Randall Maye.
Giles Allen gent., def.	John Goborne. Henry Johnson.

[1] From another case I find that Hugh Barbon is proved to be one of the Messengers of her Majesty's Chamber, sent on a similar Mission.

Giles Allen
gent., def.
Cuthbert Burbage
gent, pl.

}

Robert Myles, gent.
Raff Myles, gent. See pp. 78–84.

NOTE XX.—*Giles Alleyn against Cuthbert Burbage.*
Coram Rege Roll, Easter, 44 Eliz., No. 1,373. R. 257. Midd.
Breach of Covenant.

" Memorandum that in the Hilary term previous, 43 Eliz., there came Giles Alleyn and Sara his wife by John Tanner their attorney, in the court of the Queen's Bench at Westminster, before J. Popham versus Cuthbert Burbage in the custody of the marshal in a plea of broken agreement. Giles and Sara on the 13th day of April 18 Eliz. drew up an indenture and signed it at Holywell in the parish of St. Leonard's, Shoreditch, with James Burbage, Joiner. The other part, sealed, dated and signed and sealed by the said James was produced in court by their mutual consent, wherein it was shewn that for a rent of £14 a year, paid quarterly and the sum of £20 at the sealing of the Indenture, by the name of a fine they should let and lease certain lands in Holywell for a period of 21 years. These included two houses and tenements ; another house or tenement with appurtenances and the garden ground behind, which extended from the great stone wall there which enclosed it, to the garden tenanted by Ewin Colefox, and from the house in Colefox's garden to the brick wall next unto Finsbury Fields, the house or tenement called the Mill-house and its garden extending to the brick-wall by the said fields. Three upper rooms adjoining the mill-house and the nether roomes in the same tenement and the garden ground extending in length from these rooms to the brickwall, and the ground from the outward part of the houses to the pond next the barn or stable then in occupacion of the Rt.Hon. Earl of Rutland, in breadth from the millhouse to the midst of the well before the said tenements ; and also all that great barne with the appurtenances once in occupation of Hugh Richards, Innholder ; and also a little piece of ground there inclosed with a pale next the barne ; with the ground from the nether rooms and the great barn and the pond, to a ditch beyond the brick wall next the fields. And the said Giles and Sara let demised and granted to James Burbage and to farm let all their right and title in all the grounde and soil lying between the said great barne and the barn of the Earl of Rutland—extending in length from the pond and stable or barne of the Earl of Rutland down to the brick wall next the fields and all the void ground lying betwixt the ditch and the brick wall, extending in length from the brick wall which enclosed the garden then in the occupation of Gyles and Sara, unto the barn of the Earl of Rutland, with all the liberties to other free persons coming to the said James Burbage by any ways made or that were to be made through the brick wall during the term of years, without hindrance by the said Gyles and Sara, except for their right of drawing water, and of all the other tenants the liberty of drawing water from the aforesaid well or fountain, upon lawful requeste and to pay one moitie in and about the repairs to the said fountain, with free egress and ingress to the said Gyles and Sara, to and for the Rev. Father John Scory the Bishop of Hereford, his wife, and servants, with ingress and egress from the garden into the fields by the bridge and way. To have and to hold from the Feast of the annunciation, March 25th, before the date of the Indenture, paying £14 yearly at the 4 terms of the year or 28 days after. The repairs to be done by the said James Burbage when needed, and everything to be handed over at the end of 21 years to the said Giles Alleyn.

James Burbage on this agreement entered the premises, and afterwards, on the 17th Sept. 21 Eliz., at Holywell, he assigned all his interest therein to a certain John Hyde, citizen and grocer of London, by virtue of which, John Hyde entered on the premises, and afterwards, on the 7th June 31 Eliz., handed them back to Cuthbert Burbage, son of James Burbage who became thereof possessed. And Gyles and Sara say that they well and truly performed their covenant and all agreements, till the end of the 21 years, protesting that James Burbage during the time when he was so possessed, and the time when John Hyde was possessed, by the assignment of the said James and when Cuthbert Burbage was so assigned did not hold, keep, nor perform any of the before mentioned agreements made to be observed ; and Gyles and Sara say that before the expiration of the said term of 21 years, i.e. on 1st Oct. 36 Eliz., the great Barne, and all the houses mentioned as assigned to them had become greatly ruinous, were deficient in covering and roofing, tiling as well as daubing, and that the barn remained thus ruinous from the 1st of Oct. 36 Eliz., till the end of the

term of 21 years, by which was caused gross damage of the barn
and houses, by reason of rain and tempest falling upon them, so
that the great timber thereof became entirely decayed, and rotten,
and so Gyles and Sara say he and they did not keep their agreement ;
and after the assignment by Hyde to Cuthbert at his and their
proper cost and charges, they should have repaired the houses, and
should have relinquished the same, cleaned and repaired. This
they were often required to do, and entirely broke their covenant
to do so and have refused to pay the damage of £200 ; and they join
suit to be heard on Wednesday next after the Quindene of Easter
this same term, till which day Cuthbert has been given time to
imparle the Bill and answer.

The said Cuthbert defends the case and says that Gyles Allen
and Sara his wife ought not to maintain this case, because the said
House, barn, and edifices in tenure, leased to James, were well and
sufficiently repaired, and being so repaired, were handed over not
ruinous. He is also prepared to seek judgment whether the said
Gyles and Sara should have brought their case in this court
seeing judgment had been found against them. The said Giles and
Sara say that for all the said Cuthbert Burbage alleges, they
should not be precluded from bringing their case, and they seek to
have it enquired into, and throw themselves upon the country,
demanding a jury.

Jury not fixed, see pages 76–83.

(The information given above, a rough translation from the Latin,
is repeated so often it need not be quite full.)

Immediately after the latter case Coram Rege Roll., Easter 44
Eliz. f. 257 comes another f, 260.

Giles Alleyne *v.* John Knapp.

Memorandum. That in Hilary Term last came Giles Allen by his
attorney John Tanner, who said that the said John Knapp had
broken the close on the Inner great Court pertaining to the said Giles
Allen on 28th Jan. 44 Elizabeth, and fixed and erected a door, by
which Giles Allen and his dependents could not use some of their
property, and trampled and crushed the grass of the said close to the
loss of 40s., and committed other enormities, to the damage and
cost of £10.

NOTE XXI.—*Star Chamber Case Alleyn v. Burbage.*

XII. 35.   *Endorsed 23rd Nov.*, 44 *Eliz.* 1601.

To the Queen's most excellent Majestie.

In most humble wise complaining sheweth unto your most excellent Majestie, your Highness' obedient and faithful Subject, Gyles Alleyn of Haseleigh in co. Essex, gent, that your subject, with Sara his wife by Indenture 13th April 18 of your M. reign &c., demised to James Burbage, late of London, Joiner, " certain housing and void groundes lying in Hallywell " at the rent of £14 by the year, and it was covenanted by your said subjects to make a new lease if at any time within the first ten years, the said James Burbage or his assigns should bestow £200 in building and repairing the old tenements in the property, which £200 was to include the value of the old stuff, bricks, tiles, etc.   In the new lease it would be granted him to take down and take away the said new Building Theatre or Playing Place, which he had built on the void ground, at the end of the first lease, or at the end of the added term.   A Theatre being then and there erected at the cost not of Burbage, but of Braynes to the value of 1,000 marks Burbage tendered a new lease, which he the said Alleyn refused to sign because it was different from the first, and also because Burbage had assigned the Theatre to John Hyde, and had also been a very badd and troublesome tenant to your orator, who was therefore in noe wise bound to sign it.   Hyde conveyed the lease to Cuthbert son of James, who, desirous still to make gayne, suffered the same to remain till after the expiry of the lease, whereby the right and interest of the said Theatre was vested in your said orator, who, seeing great and grievous abuses grew by that said Theatre intended to pull it down, to convert the wood and Timber thereof to some better use for his own benefit, whereby he might be relieved from the £30 arrearages of rent, which the said James Burbage, in his lifetime did owe him, and also for the breach of divers covenants in not repairing the houses on the property, and for that the said James had made in his life time, a deed of gift of all his goods to the sayd Cuthbert and Richard, who, after the death of James, procured Ellen, his widow, a very poor woman to take the administration upon her to the intent, to defraud your said subject and other creditors.   But the said Cuthbert, having intelligence of your said subject's purpose, and unlawfully combining and confederating himself with Richard Burbage, Peter Street, William Smith, and divers others to the number of twelve to your subject unknown, in and about the 28th day of December 41 Eliz., and sythence your Highness last and general pardon, did riotouslie take downe and carry away the said Theatre by confederacy with others armed with unlawfull and offensive weapons, as namely swords, daggers, bills, axes, and such like, and soe armed did enter, and in very riotous and outragious manner did attempt to pull down and carry away the said Theatre, divers of your said subjects servants and farmers, peaceably going about to procure them to desist, they violently resisted, to the great disturbing of the peace, and terrifying of your said subject's servants.

Whereupon your subject in Hilary term following did commence an action of trespass in the King's Bench, for wrongfull entry into your subject's land, and taking away the Theatre, but Cuthbert Burbage, maliciously intending to vex and molest your subject, in the Easter term following, exhibited a bill in the Court of Requests for stay of your subject's suit at Common Law, and he appeared, and made answer. And afterwards in Trinity term afterwards, 42 Eliz., an order was published that your subject's suit should stay till the cause in Equity were heard, which was appointed to be in Michaelmas Term 42 Eliz. Your subject's demurrer was made up, which was formerly joined in the said suit between your subject and Peter Street, which was expressly granted, whereuppon your subject gave orders to his attorney to cause the demurrer to be made up. But Cuthbert Burbage, further to entrap your subject, did very maliciously and fraudulently combine and practise, with one John Maddoxe, then his attorney, and one Richard Lane the Registrar [1] of the Court of Requests who, by confederating together, got John Maddox to draw up an order which did not appertayne to him to do, directly contrary to that which was delivered by your Highness' Counsel that your subject should not proceed to the making of the demurrer, therein abusing your Highness' Court, and injuring your Subject. However, being ignorant of this fraudulent confederacy, and sinister practice, he gave orders to make a demurrer and repaired home to the country, thinking everything should rest till the hearing of the cause. But Cuthbert Burbage pursuing his former wicked and ungodlie devices, and seeking to plunge your Subject in very grievous trouble and in mischief, did, on the last

[1] He was the Deputy Registrar ; Henry Allington was Registrar then.

day of Trinity Term, by practise and confederacy with the said John Maddox make oathe in the Court of Requests that your subject had broken order by making that demurrer, wheruppon your subject, for supposed contempt, was in the Vacation tyme then next following, by privity of Cuthbert, and by the confederacy aforesaid,[1] fetched up to London by a pursevant, to his great vexation and annoyance, a man very aged, and unfitt to travell, to his excessive chardges in journey, and otherwise to his great discredit and disgrace in the country.

And your subject being brought by the Pursevant before one of the Masters of the said Court, did by the said Master's order, become bound to Cuthbert Burbage in a bond of £200 to appear in the said Court in Michaelmas following to answer the said contempt, and stand to the order.   And he appeared at the said Court accordingly and was discharged of the supposed contempt and afterwards, on the day appointed, your said subject appeared at the court, and having divers witnesses then present to testifie *viva voce* on his behalf, the said Cuthbert and Richard Burbage, still persisting in their unlawful and malicious courses against your said Subject by the confederacy, did very shamefully and unlawfully revile with many reproachful terms your said subjectes witnesses, and said they had formerly testified untruths, concerning the same lease, and said they would Stab some of your subject's witnesses, because they had testified to the fraudulent deed of gift of James Burbage to the said Cuthbert and Richard.   By which furious and unlawful threats your said subject's witnesses were then soe terrified that they durst not testifie the truth on behalf of your subject.   Further so it is, if it may please your Majestie, Cuthbert very maliciously and corruptly suborned and procured one Richard Hudson of S. Albons in London, Carpenter, and Thomas Osborne of Fanchurch in London, Carpenter, to commit very grievous and wilful perjury in the said suit in your Highness Court of Requests in material points on behalf of Cuthbert.   Hudson said that he was present at an estimate of the Costes bestowed by James Burbage in his life time, upon the houses demised unto him by your Said Subject, on 18th July, 1586, when it was said that James Burbage before that time had spent upon the repairs £240 ; and Osborne said the same, that it appeared that 4 or 5 yeares before that view £240 had been spent on the

[1] See page 87.

houses, Whereas Richard Hudson was not present at any view in that year, but only present at a view taken in 33 Eliz., as by deposition of Richard Hudson himself heretofore made in your Highness Court of Chancery and there remaining of record, it doth evidently appeare, whereas James Burbage had not bestowed anything near that sum at that time, as your subject can make very sufficient proof. "By which unlawful practises of the said Cuthbert Burbage, your subject *did then lose his said cause."* Further, so it is, if it may please your majestie as well the said sute between your subject, and Peter Street, as also the said sute between your subject and Cuthbert Burbage, was prosecuted against your subject by the malicious procurement and unlawful maintenance of the aforesaid William Smith, unlawfully laying out divers sommes of money on behalf of the said Cuthbert . . . wherefore . . . for that the ryot rout, forcible entries confederacies, abuse of justice . . . maynt . . . and other the misdemeanours contrary to your Highness' Lawes and ordinances established for the happy governance . . . arose . . . and example (the gaps here caused by worn holes in membrane) of misdemeanour worthy of condigne punishment, wherefore he prays a subpoena may be directed to Cuthbert Burbage, Richard Burbage, Peter Street, William Smith, Richard Lane, Richard Hudson, and Thomas Osborne to appear in the court of Starchamber to answer to their misdemeanours.

JEFFREYS.

(Put off till Hilary Term, then to Easter.)
28th April, 44 Eliz.

The joynt and several Demurrers of Cuthbert Burbage, Richard Burbage, Peter Street and William Smith *fyve* [1] (*sic*) of the defendants, By protestation, not acknowledging nor confessing any of the matters contained in the complaint. The Bill is insufficient in Law, the defendants are not tied to answer it, for divers and sundry faults and manifest imperfections.

Whereas the said complainant charges them with a riott by them committed in pulling down the said playhouse called The Theatre, and for carrying away the wood and stuff, True itis that the playhouse was built upon the said void ground demised by the complainant to James Burbage, the complainant having for that cause in Hilary Term next following the supposed riot commenced an accion

---

[1] It is probable that John Maddox the attorney was intended as the fifth.

of trespass against Peter Street and Cuthbert Burbage two of the
now defendants in the King's Bench at Westminster, the said
Cuthbert being assignee, and well able in good conscience and equity
to justifie the pulling down though in strictness of law (by the complainant's own wrong and breach of convenant) he had no sufficient
matter to allege in barre of the said accion. Cuthbert Burbage
did for his relief, and stay of the unjust proceedings of the said complainant, exhibit his Bill of Complaint before your Majesties Council
in your Majestie's Honorable Court at Whitehall, at which the now
plaintiff appeared and answered and the said Cuthbert replied and
divers witnesses were heard on both sides and publication granted,
and several days appointed for the hearing of the cause, and upon
the open hearing, and full deliberate debating of the cause it plainly
appeared unto your Majesties Council that the said James Burbage
had well and truly on his part performed and kept all and singular
the covenants contained in the said indentures, and the now complainant in refusing to seal the new lease of the premises tendered
unto him by James Burbage according to covenant on his part to be
performed contrariwise to his own covenant, through his own wrong
and breach of covenant, by not sealing the new lease sought to hinder your subject Cuthbert Burbage in receiving the interest of the
premises, and to take the benefit of the Indentures, in taking away
the said Playhouse erected by James Burbage at his chardge, according to covenant. Therefore it seemed to the Council that there was
a good cause in equitie to staie the complainants action at the Common Law, and it appeared to council that the said Cuthbert Burbage had just cause to be relieved in the premises. It was therefore
by your Majesties Council the 18th day of Oct. 42 Eliz., ordered
and decreed that the now complainant, his councillors, attorneys and
solicitors should from thence surcease and stay, and no further
prosecute at Common Law the trespass, and that the said complainant should not at any tyme after, commence or cause to be commenced by any other any action or suit, against the said Cuthbert
or his servants for the pulling down or carrying away of the timber
of the theatre, and that Cuthbert Burbage should be at Libertie to
take his remedy against Alleyn, the now complainant, at Common
Law, for not agreeing to seal the new Lease according to Covenant
more at large expressed in the said Judicial decree and sentence of
that court, as it doth and may appeare, For which cause, and for

that the complainant if he had suspected, or had shewed any cause of grief for any fraud or indirect practises or dealings by him supposed to be practised, by any of the officers of your Highness' Court, in drawing or entering orders contrarie to those your Counsell had before pronounced or delivered by any of the other defendants, as by the Complainants Bill he falsely and untruly surmises, the said Honorable Court might at any time while the Bill was pending, have been told by complainant and the said Council would have had such faults and misdemeanours redressed and finished and justice ministered in that behalf.

And for the Complainant offers great scandal and abuse to your Majestie's said Councill by càlling the same matter again into question, and to have the said cause, after such judiciall sentence and decree passed against the complainant to bring it again into court to be again examined before your Majesty in this Court, wherefore, and for divers other defects, faults and imperfections the defendants demur in Law, demand the judgment of this court, and pray to be dismissed with their reasonable costs.

Jo. Walter.

28th April 44 Eliz. (same date as above).

The answer of Richard Lane, one of the defendants to the untrue and slaunderous bill of complaint of Giles Alleyn complainant.

This defendant saving to himself hereafter all advantages and exceptions to the uncertainties and insufficiencies of the Bill.

For answer and plain declaration of the truth of so much as concerneth him.

True it is there was a sute in the Court of Requests concerning the stay of Alleyn's suits against Burbage in the King's Bench touching the Playhouse called the Theatre, commenced at Whitehall by Burbage against Alleyn, this defendant then and yet acting as deputy Register in the Court of Requests, did on the hearing of the case, and to the best of his understanding, and with as much knowledge and diligence as he could he did attende and took such brief notes of orders as from tyme to tyme by her Majesties Council were pronounced in the Court, without any affection to either parties.

Amongst which, on the 31st May 42 Eliz. was the matter moved in presence of Mr. Sergeant Harris and Mr. Walter, being severally of Counsel learned in the Law, and agreed to by all. To the best of this defendant's remembrance an order was issued that the matter

Q

should be set over to be heard in the said Court on the 5th day of the next term, and in the meantime the defendant should stay his suit at Common Law, and no further proceed therein, And it was also then further ordered that Alleyn making oath that he was not privie to the said deposicions published and setting down the names of the deponents he intended to examine, should be at liberty to examine them until the 2nd day of the next term, and then the same to be published as by a note to that effect then taken and set down in the Book of Remembrance kept by the defendant appeareth, uppon the copie of which note so conceived and delivered by this defendant, the said John Maddox (being attorney for the said Burbage) or some of his clerks, or some other on behalf of Burbage's cause did draw up an order at large touching the same cause, and brought the same subscribed and confirmed by one of her Majesties Councel of the said Court, and brought the same to be entered into the Register's Office, which was done as by the same is ready to be showed unto this Court.   If Maddox or any other did add or diminish anything material in the words of the said notes it concerned them and their oaths and credit not the defendant, who did nothing therein more than he had good warrant to do as aforesaid.   Further the attorneys being sworne to observe orders, have for the 30 years last past to the knowledge of the defendant (as so long he has served) used to draw their clients' orders sworn to deal indifferently therein, and not the Register as the said Allen in his said Bill hath untruly alledged especially such as doe concern decrees and orders made for the graunting of Injunctions for stay of proceedings at Common Law, dismissions of causes, delivering out of money or delivery of writings for possession . . . are usually confirmed by the hand of one of her Majestie's Counsell of the Court before being entered into the Register. And for thother short order, they are usually entered by the Register or Deputy without any contradiction.   The said Alleyn hath in his Bill untruly alledged concerning the decree which the defendant entered, and slanderously and untruely alleged that the said Burbage combined with his attorney Maddox and the defendant the Deputy Register and by confederacie procured John Maddox for a consideracion to draw an order not appertaining to him to do but unto the Register, and likewise procuring the same to be set down directly contrary to that which was done and procured that the said Allen should not proceed to the making of the demurrer in the

Bill mentioned therein, very highly abusing her Majestie's said Honorable Court, and greatly injuring the said Alleyn now plaintiff.

The said defendant for plea and answer thereunto and to every other matter of misdemeanour confederacie and combynacion laid to his chardge in the said Bill sayeth that he is not guilty, and that every other part of the Complainant's bill is untrue.

" Without that this defendant did at any time directly or indirectly practise, combyne, or confederate with the said Cuthbert Burbage and John Maddox or with any other about the drawing or procuring the order to be entered. But did faithfully and sincerely take the note of the said order as the same was pronounced."

Without that any other matter contained in the Bill concerning the defendant is true All which matters this defendant is ready to aver and prove, as this honorable Courte shall award, And humblie prayeth to be dismissed out of the same with his costs and chardges in this behalf most wrongfully had and susteyned.

> Jur. 12th June 44 Eliz., per Richard Hudson.
> 17th June 44 Eliz., per Thomas Osborne.

The joynte and severall demurrers of Richard Hudson and Thomas Osborne defendants. By protestation not acknowledging nor confessinge anie of the matters conteyned in the said Bill that they are charged with are true.

The Bill of Complaint brought against them and others is very untrue, slanderous and uncertain and insufficient in Lawe to be answered and they are not tied to make any answer for divers faults and namelie for that the matters and supposed perjury in the said Bill, in which they are charged, are so uncertainly layed, these defendants cannot make any answer and the other defendants having been served with a process, and having appeared and demurred " which demurrer being referred by the Orders of the Court to the right worshipful Francis Bacon Esquire, he uppon perusal and consideration had of the said Bill of Complaint hath already reported that the said Bill is very uncertayne and insufficient, and that *no further answer nedeth to be made thereto.*"

For which causes and for divers other matters and defects in the said Bill appearing, they the said defendants do demur in Law upon the said Bill and pray to be dismissed from this honorable court with costs.

NOTE XXII.—*The players' patents*, 1603.

Pro Laurentio Fletcher and William Shakespeare et aliis 1603.
Pat. 1, James 1, p. 2, m. 4.

" James by the grace of God, etc., to all Justices, Maiors, Sheriffs, Constables, Hedboroughs, and other our Officers and loving subjects, greetinge.

Knowe ye that Wee of our speciall grace, certaine knowledge and mere motion, have licensed and authorized and by these presentes doe licence and authorize theise our servaunts Laurence Fletcher, William Shakespeare, Richard Burbadge, Augustyne Phillipps, John Hemings, Henrie Condell, William Sly, Robert Armyn, Richard Cowley, and the rest of their associates, freely to use and exercise the Arte and Faculty of playing Comedies, Tragedies, Histories, Enterludes, Morals, Pastoralls, Stage Plaies, and such others like as theie have alreadie studied or hereafter shall use or studie as well for the Recreation of our lovinge Subjects, as for our solace and pleasure, when Wee shall thincke good to see them, duringe our Pleasure ; and the said Commedies, Tragedies, Histories Enterludes, Moralls, Pastoralls, Stage playes and suche like, to shewe and exercise publiquely to theire best Commoditie when the Infection of the Plague shall decrease, as well within theire now usuell House called the Globe within our Countie of Surrey, as also within anie Toune Halls or Moute Halls, or other convenient Places within the Liberties, and Freedom of anie other Cittie, Universitie Town or Boroughe whatsoever, within our said Realmes and Dominions.

Willing and commanding you and everie of you, as you tender our Pleasure, not onelie to permit and suffer them therein, without anie your Letts, Hindrances or Molestations, during our said Pleasure, but also to be aiding and assistinge to them if anie Wrong be to them offered, and to allow them such former curtesies as hath been given to men of their place and qualitie ; and also what farther Favour you shall shewe to theise our Servaunts for our sake Wee shall take kindlie at your handes.

In witnesse whereof, etc.
Witnesse our selfe at Westminster the nyneteenth daye of May
Per Breve de Privato Sigillo.

The Players' Patent, 1619.

James to all Justices, Mayors, Sheriffs, etc.

Knowe yee that wee of our speciall grace, certaine knowledge and meere mocion, have lycensed and authorized, and by theis presents doe lycense and authoryze theis our welbeloved Servants John Hemmings, Richard Burbadge, Henry Condall, John Lowen, Nicholas Tooley, John Underwood, Nathan Field, Robert Benfield, Robert Gough, William Ecclestone, Richard Robinson, and John Shancks and the rest of their associates, freely to use and exercise the Art and facultie of playing &c.

In witness whereof, etc.   Signed,   PEMBROKE,
27th *March*, 1619.

Endorsed by Windebanck.

Sign. Man., vol. 8, 56, No. 1.

The Confirmation of their patent by Charles is in practically the same words, though some of the names of the " fellows " are new.

" John Hemmings, Henry Condall, John Lowen, Joseph Taylor, Richard Robinson, Robert Benfield, John Shanck, William Rowley, John Rich (or Rice) Elliart Swanston, George Birch, Richard Sharpe, and Thomas Pollard."

Pat. I, Car. I, n. 5. 24th June, 1625.

NOTE XXIII.—*The Actors in Shakespeare's Plays.*

The List of the Chief actors in Shakespeare's Plays taken from the list in first folio, classified and approximately dated. New Shakespeare Society, Transactions, 1886.

Armin Robert, dead by 1615.

Benfield Robert, last heard of 1647.

Bryan George, 1600.

Burbage Richard, bur. 16th March, 1619.

Condell Henry, bur. 29th Sept., 1627.

Cooke Alexander, bur. 25th Feb., 1614.

Cowley Richard, bur. 12th March, 1619.

Crosse Samuell, alive 1612.

Eccleston William, alive 1622, bur. 1652 ?

Field Nathan, bur. 20th Feb., 1633.

Gilburne Samuel, after 1605.

Goughe Robert, bur. 19th Feb., 1625.

Hemings John, bur. 12th Oct., 1630.

Kempe William, d. before 1609.
Lowen John, bur. 18th March, 1659.
Ostler William, d. (1615).
Phillipps Augustine, d. May, 1605.
Pope Thomas, 1603-4.
Rice John, after 1622.
Robinson Richard, 23rd March, 1647.
Shakespeare William, bur. 23rd April, 1616.
Shancke John, bur. 27th Jan., 1635.
Slye William, bur. 16th Aug., 1608.
Taylor Joseph, (?) 1653.
Tooley Nicholas, bur. 5th June, 1623.
Underwood John, 1624-5.

See p. 136.

NOTE XXIV.—THE COMPLAINT OF THE YOUNG PLAYERS AGAINST
THE OLD.

LORD CHAMBERLAIN'S BOOKS, Class V, vol. 94, p. 45.
Petition—

To Ye Right Honourable Philip Earle of Pembroke and Montgomery, Lord Chamberlaine of his Majestie's Houshold.

Robert Benefield, Heliard Swanston, and Thomas Pollard
humbly represent their grievances, ymploring his Lordships noble
favor towards them for their reliefe.

That the petitioners have a long time with much patience, expected to bee admitted Sharers in ye Playhouses of the Globe and
the Blackfriers wherby they might reape some better fruit of their
labours then hitherto they have done, and bee encouraged to proceed
therein with cheerfulness.

That those few, interested in ye Houses have (without any defalca-
cion or abatement at all) a full moyety of the whole gaines arising
therby, except the outer dores.   And such of the said housekeepers
as bee Actors doe likewise equally share with all the rest of the
Actors both in the other moiety and in the sayd outer dores also.

That out of the Actors Moiety, there is notwithstanding, defrayed
all wages to hired men, Apparel, Poetes, lightes, and other charges of
the Houses whatsoever, soe that between the gaynes of the Actors,
and of those few interested as Housekeepers, there is an unreasonable inequality.

That the House of the Globe was formerly divided into 16 partes, whereof Mr. Cutbert Burbidge and his sisters had 8, Mrs. Condell 4, and Mr. Hemings 4.

That Mr. Tailor and Mr. Lowen were long since admitted to purchase 4 partes betwixt them from the rest (viz.), 1 part from Mr. Hemings, 2 partes from Mrs. Condell, and half a part a piece from Mr. Burbidge and his sister.

That the 3 partes remaining to Mr. Hemings were afterwards, by Mr. Shankes, surreptitiously purchased from him, contrary to the petitioners' expectation who hoped that when any partes had beene to bee sold they should have beene admitted to have bought and divided the same amongst themselves for their better livelyhood.

That the petitioners desire not to purchase or diminish any part of Mr. Taylor's or Mr. Lowen's shares (whose deservings they must acknowledge to bee well worthy of their gaines), But in regard the peticioners labours (according to their severall wages and abilityes) are equall to some of the rest, and for that others of the sayd Houskeepers are neither Actors, nor His Majestie's servants, and yet the peticioners profit and meanes of livelyhood soe much inferior and unequall to theirs, as appeares before, They therefore desire that they may be admitted to purchase for theire moneys, at such rates as have beene formerly given, single partes a peece, only from those that have the greatest shares, and may best spare them (vizt.) that Mr. Burbadge and his sister having 3 partes and a halfe a peece may sell them two parts, and reserve two and a halfe a peece to themselves, And that Mr. Shankes having three may sell them one and reserve two, wherin they hope your Lordship will conceave their desires to be just and modest ; the rather for that the peticioners, not doubting of beeing admitted sharers in the sayd house The Globe, suffered lately the sayd Houskeepers, in the name of His Majesty's servants, to sue and obtaine a decree in the Court of Requests against Sir Matthew Brand, for confirmation of a lease paroll for about 9 or 10 years yet to come, which they could otherwise have prevented, until themselves had been made parties.

That for the House in the Blackfriers, it being divided into 8 partes amongst the aforenamed Housekeepers and Mr. Shankes having two partes thereof, Mr. Lowen, Mr. Taylor and each of the rest having but one part a peece which two parts were by the said Mr. Shankes purchased of Mr. Heming together with those 3 of the Globe as before, the peticioners desire and hope that your Lordship will conceave it likewise reasonable, that the sayd Mr. Shanks may assign over one of the sayd parts amongst them three, they yielding him such satisfaccion for the same as that hee bee noe looser thereby.

Lastly, that your Lordship would to that purpose bee nobly pleased, as their onely gracious refuge and protector, to call all the said housekeepers before you and to use your Lordship's power with them to conforme themselves therunto, the rather considering that some of the sayd Housekeepers, who have the greatest shares, are neither Actors nor his Majesty's servantes as aforesaid, and yet reape most, or the chiefest benefitt of the sweat of their browes, and live upon the bread of their labours, without taking any paynes themselves.

For which your peticioners shall have cause to bless your Lordship, as however, they are dayly bound to do with the devotions of most humble obliged Beadsmen.

Shares in The Globe	Burbadge 3½	of a lease of 9 years	**Blackfryers** Shanks 2
	Robinson 3½	from Lady Day last	Burbadge 1
	Condell 2	1635	Robinson 1
	Shankes 3	Not yet confirmed	Taylor 1
	Taylor 2	by Sir Matthew Brand	Lowen 1
	Lowen 2	to be taken to feoffees	Condall 1
			Underwood 1

FROM THE COURT AT THEOBALDS, 12th July, 1635.

Haveing considered this petition and the severall answeres and replyes of ye parties, the merites of the petitioners and the disproportion of their shares, and the interest of his Majestie's service, I have thought fitt and doe accordingly order that the peticioners Robert Benefield, Eyllardt Swanston, and Thomas Pollard bee each of them admitted to ye purchase of the shares desired of the severall persons mentioned in ye petition for the fower yeares remayning of the Lease of the House in Blackfriers, and for five years in that of the Globe, at the usuall and accustomed rates, and according to ye proportion of the time and benefitt they are to injoy, and heereof I desire the Housekeepers and all others whome it may concerne to take notice and to conforme themselves therein accordingley.

The which, if they or any of them, refuse or delay to performe if they are Actors and His Majestie's servants I doe suspend them from the stage, and all the benefitt thereof, and if they are only interested in ye Houses, I desire my Lord Privy Seale to take order that they may bee left out of the Lease, which is to bee made upon the Decree of the Court of Requests.

P. AND M. [*i.e. Pembroke and Montgomery.*]

Robert Benefield, Eyllardt Swanston and Thomas Pollard doe further humbly represent unto your Lordship—

That the Housekeepers being but six in number (vizt.) Mr. Cutbert Burbage, Mrs. Condall, Mr. Shankes, Mr. Taylor, Mr. Lowen and Mr. Robinson (in ye right of his wife) have amongst them the full moiety of all the Galleries and Boxes in both houses, and of the tireing house door at ye Globe.

That the Actors have the other Moyety with the outer dores, but in regard the Actors are halfe as many more (vizt.) nine in number, their shares fall shorter, and are a great deal lesse then the Housekeepers; And yet notwithstanding out of those lesser shares the sayd Actors defray all charges of the House whatsoever (vizt.) wages to hired men and boyes, musicke, lightes, etc., amounting to £900 or £1,000 per annum or thereabouts, being £3 a day one day with another, besides the extraordinary charges which the said Actors are wholly at for apparell and Poetes, etc.

Whereas the said Housekeepers, out of all their gaines have not till our Lady Day last payed above £65 per annum rent for both houses, towards which they rayse between £20 and £30 per annum from the Taphouses and a Tenement and a garden belonging to the premises, etc., and are at noe other charges whatsoever, except the ordinary reparations of the houses.

Soe that upon a medium made of the gaynes of the Housekeepers and those of the Actors, one day with another throughout the yeere, the petitioners will make it apparent that when some of the Housekeepers share 12s. a day at ye Globe, the actors share not above 3s. And then what those gaine that are both Actors and Housekeepers, and have their shares in both, your Lordship will easily iudge and thereby finde the modesty of the petitioners' suite, who desire only to buy for their money one part a peece from such three of the Housekeepers as are fittest to spare them, both in respect of desert and otherwise (vizt.), Mr. Shankes one part of his three, Mr. Robinson and his wife one part of their three and a half, and Mr. Cuthbert

Burbage the like. And for the House of the Blackfriers, that **Mr.** Shankes, who now inioyes two partes there may sell them likewise one, to bee divided amongst them three.

Humbly beseechyng your Lordship to consider their long sufferings and not to permit the said Housekeepers any longer to delay them but to put an end to and settle the sayd business, that yr peticioners may not bee any further troublesome or importunate to your Lordship, but may proceede to doe their duty with cheerfulness and alacrity.

Or otherwise in case of their refusall to conforme themselves that your Lordship would bee pleased to consider whether it bee not reasonable and equitable that the Actors in generall may inioy the benefit of both houses to themselves, paying the sayd Housekeepers such a valuable rent for the same as your Lordship shall think iust and indifferent.

> And ye peticioners shall continue their dayly prayers for your Lordship's prosperity and happiness.

The answere of John Shankes to ye Peticion of Robert Benfield, Eyllardt Swanston and Thomas Pollard lately exhibited to the Right Hon. Philip Earle of Pembroke and Montgomery, Lord Chamberlain of his Majestie's household
Humbly sheweth—

That about almost 2 yeares since your suppliant, upon offer to him made by William Hemings, did buy of him one part that he had in the Blackfriars for about 6 yeares then to come, at the yerely rent of £6 5s., and another part hee then had in ye Globe for about 2 yeares to come, and payd him for the same two parts in ready money £156 ; which sayd partes were offered to your suppliant, and were as free then for any other to buy as for your suppliant.

That about 11 months since, the said William Heming, offering to sell unto your suppliant the remaining parts, hee then had (viz.) one in the Blackfriars, wherein he had then about 5 yeares to come and 2 in the Globe wherein he had but one yere to come.

Your suppliant likewise bought the same and payd for them in ready moneys more £350. All which moneys soe disbursed by your suppliant amount to £506, the greatest part whereof your suppliant was constrayned to take up at interest and your suppliant hath besides disbursed to the said William Hemings diverse other small somes of money since hc was in prison.

That your suppliant did neither fraudulently nor surreptitiously defeat any of the petitioners in their hope of buying the said parts, neither would the said William Hemings have sold the same to any of the petitioners, for that they would not have given him any such price for the same, but would (as now they endeavour to doo) have had the same against his will and at what rates they pleased.

That your suppliant, being an old man in this quality, who in his youth first served your noble father and after that the Queen Elizabeth, then King James, and now his Royal Majesty and having in this long time made noe provision for himself in his old age, nor for his wife, children and grandchild for his and their better livelyhood, having this opportunity, did at deere rates purchase these partes, and hath, for a very small time as yet receaved the profits thereof, and hath but a short time in them, and is without any hope to renew the same, when the termes bee out, hee therefore hopeth hee shall not bee hindred in ye inioying the profitt thereof, especially when as the same are thinges very casuall, and subject to bee discontinued and lost by sickness and diverse other wayes, and to yield no profit at all.

That whereas the petitioners in their complaint say that they have not meanes to subsist, it shall by oath (if need bee) bee made apparent that every one of the three petitioners, for his own particular, hath gotten and receaved this yeare last past of the sum of £180, which, as your suppliant conceaveth, is a very sufficient meanes to satisfie and answere their long and patient expectation, and is more, by above the one half than any of them ever gott, or were capable of elsewhere, besides what Mr. Swanston, one of them who is most violent in this business, who hath further had and receaved this last yeer about £34 for the profit of a third part of one part in the Blackfriers, which hee bought for £20, and yet hath inioyed the same 2 or 3 yeers allready, and both still, as long time in ye same as your suppliant hath in his, who, for soe much as Mr. Swanston bought for £20, your suppliant paid £60.

That when your suppliant purchased his partes he had noe certainty thereof more than for one yeer in the Globe and there was a chargeable suit then depending in the Court of Requestes between Sir Matthew Brend Knt., and the lessees of the Globe and their assignes, for the adding of nine years to their lease, in consideration that they and their predecessors had formerly been at the charge of £1,400 in building of the sayd house upon the burning downe of the former, wherein if they should miscarry, for as yet they have not the assurance perfected by Sir Matthew Brend your suppliant shall lay out his money to such a losse as the peticioners will never be partners with him therein.

That your suppliante and other the lessees in ye Globe, and in the Blackfriers, are chargeable with the payment of £100 yearely rent besides reparacions, which is daily very chargeable unto them, all which they must pay and beare whether they make any proffytt or not, and soe reckoning their charge in building and fitting the sayd houses yeerly and reparations, noe wise man will adventure his estate in such a course, considering their dealing, with whome they have to doe, and the many casualties and dayly troubles therewith that in all the affayres and dealinges in this world between man and man it was and is ever held an inviolable principle that in what thing soe ever any man hath a lawfull interest and property, hee is not to bee compelled to depart with the same against his will, which the complainantes endeavour. And whereas John Hemings, the father of William Hemings, of whom your suppliant made purchase of the sayd parts inioyed the same 30 years without any molestation, being the most of the said yeers both Player and Housekeeper and, after hee gave over playing diverse yeers, and his son William Hemings foure yeeres after, though hee never had anything to doe with the stage, inioyed the same withoutt any trouble, notwithstanding the complainants would violently take from your petitioner the sayd parts who hath still of his owne purse supplyed the Company for the service of his Majestie with boyes, as Thomas Pollard, John Thompson deceased (for whom hee payd £40) your suppliant having payd his part of £200 for other boyes since his coming to ye company, John Honiman, Thomas Holcome, and diverse others, and at this time maintains 3 more for the said service.   Neither lyeth it in ye power of your suppliant to satisfie the unreasonable demandes of the complainants, hee being forced to make over the sayd partes for security of moneys taken up as aforesaid of Robert Morecroft of Lincoln his wife's uncle, for the purchase of the sayd parts, untill hee hath made payment of the sayd moneys which hee is not able to doe unless he be suffered to inioye the sayd parts during the small time of his lease, and is like to bee undone if they are taken from him.

All which, being considered your suppliant hopeth that your Lordship will not inforce your suppliant, against his will to departe with
what is his owne, and what hee hath deerely payd for unto them that
can claime noe lawfull interest thereunto. And your suppliant
(under your Lordship's favour) doth conceave that if the petitioners by those their violent courses may obtaine their desires, your
Lordship will never bee at quiet, for their daily complaints, and it
will be such a president to all young men that shall follow hereafter
that they shall allwayes refuse to doe his Majesty's service, unless
they may have whatsoever they will though it bee other men's
estates, and soe that which they pretend shall tend to the better
government of the Company, and inabling them to doe his Majesty's
service, the same will bee rather to the distruccion of the company
and disabling them to doe service to his Majesty. And besydes the
benefitt and profitt which the petitioners doe yearly make without
any charge at all is soe good, that they may account themselves to
bee well recompensed for their labours and paines, and yet when any
partes are to be sould, they may buy the same if they can gett the
bargaine thereof, paying for the same as others doe.

The humble suite of your suppliant is that your honour will be
pleased that hee may inioy that which hee hath deerly bought and
truly payd for, and your suppliant (as in duty hee is bound) shall
ever pray for your Lordship.

To the Rt. Honorable Philip, **Earle of Pembroke** and Montgomery,
Lord Chamberlaine of **His** Majesties Household.

Right Honourable, and our **singular** good Lord, Wee your humble
suppliants, Cutbert Burbage, and Winifred his brother's wife, and
William his sonne, doe tender to your honorable consideration for
what respectes and good reasons wee ought not in all charity to bee
disabled of our livelyhoode by men soe soone shott up, since it hath
beene the custom that they should come to it by farre more antiquity
and desert, then these can justly attribute to themselves.

And first, humbly shewing to your Honour the infinite charges,
the manifold lawsuites, the lease's expiration, by the restraintes in
sickness times and other accidentes, that did cutt from them the best
part of the gaines that your Honor is informed they have received.

The father of us, Cutbert and Richard Burbage, was the first
builder of Playhouses and was himself in his younger yeres a Player.
The Theater hee built with many hundred pounds taken up at inter-

est ; the Players that lived in these first times had only the profits arising from the dores, but now the players receve also the cominge in at the dores to themselves, and halfe the galleries from the Housekeepers.   Hee built this house upon leased grounds, by which meanes the Landlord and hee had a greate suite in law, and by his death, the like troubles fell on us his sonnes.   We then bethought us of altering from thence, and at like expense built the Globe, with more summes of money taken up at interest, which lay heavy on us many yeares, and to ourselves we joined those deserving men Shake-spere, Hemings, Condall, Phillipps and others, partners in ye profitts of that they call the House, but making the leases for 21 yeares hath been the destruction of ourselves and others, for they dying at the expiration of 3 or 4 yeeres of their lease, the subsequent yeeres be-came dissolved to strangers, as by marrying with their widdowes and the like by their children.

Thus Rt. Honorable, as concerning the Globe, where we ourselves are but lessees.   Now for the Blackfriars, that is our inheritance, our father purchased it at extreame rates, and made it into a playhouse with great charge and troble, which after was leased out to one Evans that first sett up the Boyes, commonly called the Queen's Majesties children of the Chappell.   In processe of time, the boyes growing up to bee men, which were Underwood, Field, Ostler and were taken to strengthen the King's service, and the more to strengthen the service, the boyes daily wearing out, it was considered that house would bee as fitt for ourselves and soe purchased the lease remaining from Evans with our money and placed men players which were Hemings, Condell, Shakespeare, etc.   And Richard Burbage, who for 35 yeares pains, cost and labour, made meanes to leave his wife and children some estate (and out of whose estate soe many of other Players and their families have been mayntained) these new men that were never bred from children in the King's service, would take away with oathes and menaces that wee shall bee forced, and that they will not thank us for it, soe that it seems they would not pay us for what they would have, or wee can spare, which, more to satisfy your honor then their threatening pride we are for ourselves willing to part with a part between us, they paying according as ever hath beene ye customary number of yeeres the lease is made for.

Then to shew Your Honour against their sayinges that wee eat the fruit of their labours, wee referre it to your Honour's judgment to consider their profitts, which wee may safely maintain, for it appeareth by their owne Accomptes for one whole year last past beginning from Whitson Munday 1634 to Whitson Munday 1635, each of these complainants gained severally, as he was a player and noe Housekeeper £180. Besides Mr. Swanston hath receaved from the Blackfriers this yeare as he is there a Housekeeper, above £30, all which accompted together may very well keepe him from starving. Wherefore your honours most humble suppliants intreate they may not further bee trampled upon then their estates can beare, seeing how dearly it hath been purchased by the infinite cost and paynes of the family of the Burbages, and the great desert of Richard Burbage for his quality of playing that his wife should not starve in her old age, submitting ourselves to part with one part to them for valuable consideracion, and let them seeke further satisfaction elsewhere, (that is) of the heires or assigns of Mr. Heming and Mr. Condall, who had theirs of the Blackfriars of us for nothing, it is only wee that suffer continually.

Therefore humbly relying upon your Honour's Charity in dismissing their clamour against us, we shall as we are in duty bound still pray for the dayly increase of yor honor health and happiness.

JOHN SHANKES.

A petition of John Shankes to my Lord Chamberlain shewing that according to his Lordship's order, he did make a proposition to his fellows for satisfaccion upon his assigning of his partes in ye several houses unto them but they not only refuse to give satisfaccion but restrain him from the Stage, that therefore his Lordship would order them to give satisfaction according to his propositions and computation of

M^d. all concerning this and here entered were delivered annexed. } Answered. Vizt., I desire Sir Henry Herbert and Sir John Finett, and my solliciter Daniell Bedingfield to take this petition and the several papers herewith annexed into their various considerations and to speake with the severall parties interested and thereupon and upon the whole matter to sette down a proportionall and equitable summe of money to bee payde unto Shankes for the two parts which he is to passe unto Benfield, Swanston and Pollard, and to cause a finall agreement and conveyance to be settled accordingly and to give mee an account of their whole proceedings in writing, 1st August, 1635. (P. and M.)

(These are published in Halliwell's Outlines, all but the table, but of course without *reference* to the original copy which I give, after having spent many weeks searching for it among the Lord Chamberlain's books, before they were fully catalogued. And this case had *never* been asked for. I print them in the order they occur, which is not, I think, the correct order. See p. 133.

NOTE XXV.—*Unpublished Records from Privy Council Register.*

The register during the reign of Elizabeth has been printed. The succeeding records were destroyed by the fire in Whitehall from the beginning of the reign of James I till 1613.

The earliest reference to the King's players is on 29th March, 1615 : " Warrant to John Sentie Messenger of his Majesties Chamber. . . . Whereas John Hemming, Richard Burbage, . . . with other Stage Players . . . have presumed, notwithstanding the commandment of the Lord Chamberlain, signified unto them by the Master of the Revels, to play this prohibited time of Lent, These are therefore to will and command you to make your repayre unto the persons abovenamed to charge them in his Majesties name to make their appearance here before us of his Majesties Privie Councell on Friday next at 8 of the Clock in the forenoone, without any excuse or delay. And in the meantime, that neither they, nor the rest of their company presume to present any playes or interludes, as they will answer the contrary at their perils."

" 21st August, 1624, To Mr. Secretary Conway.

" According to his Majestie's pleasure signified to this Board by your letter of the 12th of August, touching the suppressing of a scandalous comedie, acted by the King's Players. We have called before us some of the principal actors and demanded of them by what licence and authoritie they have presumed to act the same, in answer whereunto they produced a booke, being an originall and perfect copie thereof (as they affirmed) seene and allowed by Sir Henry Herbert, Knight, M^r. of the Revells, under his own hande subscribed in the last page of the said booke. Wee demanding further whether there were noe other partes or passages represented on the stage then those expressly contained in the booke, they confidently protested they added or varied from the same nothing at all. The poett they tell us is one Middleton who, shifting out of the way, and not attending the board with the rest, as was expected, wee have given Warrant to a Messenger, for the apprehension of him. To those that were before us wee gave a round and sharp reproof, making them sensible of his Majestie's high displeasure therein, giving them straight charge and command, that they presume not to acte the said comedie any more, nor that they suffer anie plaie or enterlude whatsoever to be acted by them, untill his Majesty's pleasure be further known. Wee have caused them likewise to enter into bonds for their attendance upon the board, whensoever they shall be called. As for our certifying to his Majestie (as was intimated by your letter) what passages in the said comedie we should finde to be offensive and scandalous, wee have thought it our duties for his Majestie's clearer informacion to send herewithall the looke itself subscribed as aforesaid by the Master of the Revells, that soe, either yourself or some other whom his Majestie shall appoint to peruse the same may see the passages themselves out of the originall, and calling Sir Henry Herbert before you to know a reason of his licensing thereof, who (as we are now given to understand) is now attending at Court. So having done as much as wee conceived agreeable with our duties in conformitie to his Majestie's Royal Commandments, and that which we hope will give him full satisfaction, wee shall continue our humble prayers, etc."

August 27th, 1624. A warrant directed to Robert Goffe, one of the Messengers of his Majestie's Chamber, to bring one Middleton sonne to Middleton the poett before their Lordships to answer, etc.

" August 30, 1624, This daie Edward Middleton of London, gent, being formerly sent for by warrant from the Board, tendered his appearance, wherefore his indemnity is here entered into the Register of Counsell Causes, nevertheless he is enjoyned to attend the Board till he is discharged by order from their Lordships."

" 17th May, 1626. Letter to the Justices of Peace of the Countie of Surrey, whereas we are informed, that on Thursday next, divers loose and idle persons, some saylors and others, have appointed to meete at *the Playhouse called The Globe* to see a play (as it is pretended) but their end is thereby to disguise some routous and riotous action, we have therefore thought fit to give you notice of the information which wee have received concerning this their purpose, and doe likewise hereby will and require you to take very careful and strict order, that no play be acted on that day, and also to have that strength about you, as you shall think sufficient for the suppressing

R

of any insolencies or other mutinous intencions that you shall per-
ceave, and to take with you the under Sheriff of that County for
the further assisting of you, if there be cause.   And so, not doubting
of your care therein, etc."

(They also write to the Lord Mayor in similar strain.)

" 14th April, 1630. All Stage plays stopped because of the Plague."

" 10th May, 1636, Order.   His Majestie being this day present that
the Lord Chambelain of his Majestie's Household should be hereby
prayed and required to cause all Stage Playes, Enterludes, Showes
and Spectacles whatsoever to be forthwith suppressed until further
notice (because of the Plague)."

" 17th Sept., 1637.   His Majesty's servants ye Players having by
reason of the Infeccion of the Plague in and neare London, been for
a long time restrained, and having now spent what they got in
many years before, and soe not able any longer to subsist and
maintain their families, did by their petition to his Majesty most
humbly desire leave to be now at libertye to use their quality.

It was thereupon ordered, his Majestie present in Councell that
the said Actors should be at libertie to practice at Michaelmas next,
if by that time there be not considerable increase of the sickness, or
that there dye not of the Infeccion in and about London, more than
there dyed last week."

The commencement of the Civil War closes the records of the
Privy Council about 1640.

NOTE XXVI.—*The Censorship of Plays.*

The Privy Council at the Star Chamber, 12th Nov., 1589.

A letter to the Lord Archbishop of Canterbury, that whereas
there hathe growne some inconvenience by comon playes and enterludes in and about the Cittie of London, in that the players take
uppon them to handle in their plaies certen matters of Divinytie
and of State unfitt to be suffered, for redresse whereof their Lordships
have thought good to appointe some persones of judgement and
understanding to viewe and examine their playes before they be
permitted to present them publickly.   His Lordshipp is desired
that some fytt persone, well learned in Divinity be appointed by
him to joyne with the Master of the Revells and one other to be
nominated by the Lord Mayour, and they joyntly with some spede
to viewe and consider of such comedyes and tragedyes as are and

shalbe publickly played by the companies of players in and aboute the Cyttie of London, and they to geve allowance of suche as they shall thincke meete to be plaied and to forbidd the rest.

A Letter to the Lord Mayor with a similar instruction.

A Letter to the Master of the Revels on the same subject, continuing, " and to call before them the severall companies of players (whose servauntes souever they be) and to require them by authorytie hereof to delyver unto them their bookes, that they may consider of the matters of their comedies and tragedyes, and thereuppon to stryke oute or reforme suche partes and matters as they shall fynd unfytt, and undecent to be handled in playes, both for Divinitie and State, comanding the said companies of players, in her Majestie's name, that they forbeare to present and playe publickly anie comedy or tragedy other then suche as they three shall have seene and allowed, which if they shall not observe, they shall then know from their Lordshippes that they shalbe not onely sevearely punished but made (in)capable of the exercise of their profession forever hereafter. See p. 52.

NOTE XXVII.—*Burbageana.*

(1) At the Council Meeting on 16th November, 1576, " a licence was given to one Burbaige to arrest such shippes and goods as should come from Brest and Conquest, for the recompense of such damages as he had sustained by them." I should not have noted this, but that, for the first time, in the accounts of the year before there is the reference to " Burbage and his players " without a Christian name. It is *possible* James had ordered some of his supplies from Brest and Conquest, seeing he was building his theatre that very year. But there were other prosperous Burbages tradesmen in London.

The Privy Council of July 30th, 1581, refers to a Ninion Burbage, Keeper of Northallerton House, a seat of the Bishop of Durham.

(2) Francis Bacon had a case in Chancery against a William Burbage, about property left to his brother Anthony Bacon. See Chancery D. & O., Book 1590, 32–33 Eliz. f. 533, 621, 626, 684, 691.

(3) " Tarlton's news out of Purgatorie," published about 1590, speaks of one " who would needs to The Theatre to a play, where when I came, I found such concourse of unruly people, that I thought

it better solitary to walk in the fields than to intermeddle myself amongst such a great presse."

(4) Sir George More conveyed to James Burbage's sons Cuthbert and Richard, property adjoining the Blackfriars Theatre. Indenture 20th June, 1601. Appendix to 7th Report Hist. Man. Com., p. 597.

(5) The gossip concerning Burbage and Shakespeare preserved in John Manningham's Diary has always been read in an evil sense. This is not necessary, nor probable. It was frequently noted that the rich citizens' wives invited the actors to go home for supper with them, and to rehearse some of their parts. There would not have been the publicity described had there been any evil meaning in the incident. The joke lay in the names of the plays " William the Conqueror came before Richard the Third." Shak. Soc. Publications Manningham's Diary, p. 39. 13th March, 1601.

(6) In regard to the Players and the Royal Procession we may find in MS. 34, 218, Brit. Mus. f. 31b, " A list of the King's Majesties proceedings through London on the 15th March." The " Gentlemen and Esquires, the King's servants " are put first. Would not the Players, as Grooms of the Chamber come then.

(7) There is only one poem which connects Burbage with Shakespeare as an actor, written by their friend John Davies of Hereford, in his " Microcosmos. The discovery of the little World," etc. 1603.

" To W. S. and R. B.

Players, I love you and your quality
As you are men that pass time not abused,
<small>Simonides saith poetry is a speaking painting.</small> And some I love for painting poesy
And say fell Fortune cannot be excused
That hath for better uses you refused ;
Wit, Courage, good shape, good parts and all good,
As long as all these goods are no worse used ;
And though the stage doth stain pure gentle blood,
Yet generous ye are in minde and mood . . .
<small>Stage-plaiers.</small> Some followed her by acting all men's parts.
These on a stage she raised in scorn to fall
And them mirrors by their acting parts
Wherein men saw their faults though ne'er so small,
<small>W.S. and R.B.</small> Yet some she guerdoned not to their deserts,
But other some were but ill action all
Who, while they acted ill, ill stayed behind
By custom of their manners, in their mind.

(From " The Civil Warres of Death and Fortune.")

(8) Chamberlain writes to Carleton : " Lord Coke and his Lady have great wars. At the council table she declaimed so bitterly against him, it was said that *Burbage* could not have acted better." Dom. Ser. St. Pap. James I, 92 (42).

(9) Ben Jonson in " Bartholomew Fair " (v. 3) refers to Richard Burbage as " Your best actor."

(10) And in his " Masque of Christmas," 1616 he introduces Venus as a deaf tirewoman seeking her son Cupid.

" *Venus*. Ay forsooth, he'll say his part, I warrant him, as well as e'er a play-boy of 'em all ; I could ha' had money enough for him, an I would have been tempted, and ha' let h m out by the week, to the King's Players. Master Burbage has been about and about with me, and so has old Master Hemmings too, they ha' need of him."

(11) Sir Thomas Overbury speaks of Burbage in " The character of an excellent actor," 1616.

(12) Webster writes an Induction to Marston's " Malevole," in which he brings on the stage the King's Players by their own names, to explain why they are performing a play that belongs to another company. Therein Richard Burbage hurries off, as he has to take the part of " Malevole " in the play which follows.

(13) When Richard Burbage died the Churchwardens of St. Saviour's recorded in their books, " Mr. Burbage died, 1618."

(14) In Middleton's epitaph upon Burbage there is an allusion to the Comet that " *foretold* " the Queen's death and also in another elegy. The King himself writes the following elegy upon his wife.

UPON QUEENE ANN BY KING JAMES.

Thee to invite ye Great God sent a starr
Whose friends and nearest kinn great princes are.
What though they runne the race of men and dye,
Death seems but to refine their Majesty.
Soe did the Queene her court to heaven remove
And left of earth to bee enthroned above.
Then shee is gone, not dead, noe good Prince dyes
But only with the Day-Starr, shutts their eyes.

" Robert Killegrew's Notebook," Sloane MS., 1792, p. 222.

I have collected many other facts, more than there is space for, concerning Cuthbert's opponent Giles Alleyn of Holywell. But some of them were published in " Notes and Queries," 10 S. XII 341, Oct. 30th, 1909.

I have also found a good many papers about Burbages whom I cannot fit, at present, into any connection with our Burbages.

NOTE XXVIII.—*The Performances of the Burbages' Company at Court for 80 years.*

We collect our information from many different sources, the chief of which are the declared accounts of the Treasurer of the Chamber, which exist in duplicate in the Pipe Office and the Audit Office. These are nearly complete, though there are a few gaps.   In the earlier years of Elizabeth, there are notices of the official Interlude Players.   The most interesting are in the Accounts of the Audit Office Various 1213, among which we find a few preserved in a way that makes us wish there were more.   These are the " particular accounts," which when they are complete give details, and even the names of the plays.   It is from these we glean the names of some of the early performances of Lord Leicester's Company.   There are the gravest doubts however about the reliability of the later lists of plays.   Other papers which give some information are the Privy Council Register, which records the *warrants* they issue during Elizabeth's reign, to the Treasurer of the Chamber to pay many Royal Servants, players included.   The Lord Chamberlain's Books and warrants take their place in James' reign.   Additional information may be gleaned from contemporary correspondence and history.

Dec. Acc. Treas. Chamb. Aud. Off., Bundle 380, Roll 2, 2 to 3 Eliz.   " The Lord Robert Dudeley's Players and to Sebastiane Wescott, M^r· of the Children of Polles by the Councelles Letter dated the 21st January, 1560-, in waye of the Queen's Majesties reward for playing of Enterludes before her Highness at Christmas to eyther of them £6 13s. 4d."   (Also in Pipe Office, 541, R. 29.)

" 380, 3, 3 to 4 Eliz.   " The Lord Robert Dudeleyes playors, and to Sebastian Westcott . . . Warrant 6th Jan., 1561–2 . . . for Interludes at Christmas . . . either of them £6 13s. 4d. (Pipe Office 541, 38.)   A year of this series is awanting here, but there may be found in the Privy Council Register—" A warrant issued 10th Jan., 1562-3 . . . to pay Lord Robert Dudley's playors for playing an Interlude . . . at Christmas £6 13s. 4d."   This is duly entered in Pipe Office, Roll. 541, f. 46b, as " The Players of Lord Robert Duddeley, and the M^r· of the Children of Poles . . . warrant . . . 10th Jan.,

1562-3, . . . for playing before the Queen's Majestie in Christmas, £13 6s. 8d."

Nothing is entered concerning them for ten years, and then they appear again.

Aud. Off., 382, 12, 14 to 15 Eliz. " Therle of Leicesters plaiers, . . . Warrant 1st January, 1572-3, for three severall plaies, in Christmas last . . . for every play £6 13s. 4d., and for a more reward £10 in all £30." (Pipe Office, R. 541, f. 150.) The Revels' accounts shew that they were on St. Stephen's Day and the next two days. (Audit Office Accounts Various, 1213 2).

This is all the more important as the following year, 1573-4, is amissing from the Declared Accounts of this Department. The Revels' Book records, among other expenses, " A Waggon for the first play of my Lord of Leicester's men, 18s.," and " A waggon for cariage to the courte of the second play of my Lord Leicester's men, 18s." The same account gives among " Inventions," " Predor and Lucia, played by Therle of Leicester's servauntes upon Saint Stevens Day at night at Whitehall. . . . " Mamillia, played by Therle of Leicester's servauntes on Innocents daye at nighte there . . . all fitted and furnished from the store of this Office." These performances, evidently of unusual interest, were recorded in the Pipe Off. Roll. 541, f. 166 (15 to 16 Eliz.). " To Therle of Leicester's players . . . Warrant 9th Jan., 1573-4 . . . for two severall playes . . . in the Christmas hollydays last past £13 6s. 8d., and by waye of especiall rewarde for their chardge, cunnynge[1] and skyll shewed therein £6 13s. 4d., in all £20."

The same Roll enters another, " To Therle of Leicester his plaiers . . . warrant 22nd February, 1573-4 . . . for presenting of a playe before her Majestie the 21st February anno predicto, £6 13s. 4d., rewarde 66s. 8d. in thole £10."

The revels book tells us its name was Philemon and Philecia, and that it was " fitted from the Office " during the Shrovetide season.

Aud. Off. 382, 13, 16 to 17 Eliz., has for the following year, " To Therle of Leicester's players . . . warrant . . . 9th Jan., 1574-5 . . . for playe uppon St. Stephen's daie then laste paste the some of £10.

---

[1] Dr. Wallace in his list of the period, makes a queer blunder here, reading this word as " Cumynge."

"To the said Erle of Leicester's players, Warrant 9th January, 1574–5, for a playe upon Newyeres daie at night then laste paste £6 13s. 4d."

The second was evidently a less popular play than the first, which from the Revels Book we know to have been " Panecia." There is no list of that year's " inventions " ; but under date 18th December for " peruzing and reforming of playes," Blagrave gives, " The expenses and charges wheare my Lord of Leicester's menne showed their matter of Panecia, 10s." and 27th December, " Gloves for my Lord of Lesters boyes yt played at the coorte 2s. ; for cariage of their stuff and for the carter's attendance that night, 16d. Rewards to the carpenters and painters, 2s. 6d." Under the expenses of 1st Jan., 1574–5, there is : " Long poles with brushes for chymney sweepers in my Lord of Leycester's Mennes playe and for Mosse and styckes and other implementes for them."

These accounts are not available for the following year, but Audit Office 382, 14, 17 to 18 Eliz., has, " The Erle of Leicester's players . . . upon Warrant . . . 30th Dec., 1575 . . . a play . . . uppon St. Innocente's day at night *anno xix Eliz* (*sic*), £10.[1]

" To —— Burbage and his companye, Servauntes to Therle of Leicester . . . warrant 14th March, 1575–6 for play . . . uppon Sondaie before Shrovetyde last, £10." Pipe Office, 541, 197.

382, 15, 18 to 19 Eliz. " To the Erle of Leycester's servaunts . . . warrant . . . 20th Jan., 1576–7, play presented before her Majestie in Christmas holidayes last past, £6 13s. 4d. and further by way of especiall reward . . . £10 in all the some of £16 13s. 4d."

This is a rather surprising account of " Reward," and I believe the entry must have given rise to heart-burnings and heart-searchings among many officers involved.

Because the warrant was loosely and carelessly drawn up in the Council Chamber just in head lines, and though it could bear this meaning, I do not think it was intended to do so, but just to involve the treasurer in the usual £10 each. The warrant in the Register reads, " Hampton Courte, 20th Jan., 1576–7, Fower warrants to the Treasurer of the Chamber for 4 plaies represented before her Majestie in the Christmas holidaes last past, by the players of thearle of Warwicke, thearle of Leicester, the Children of the Chapell and of

---

[1] This evident slip may have referred to the date of *payment*.

Powles, to pay to each of them £6 13s. 4d. for the playe, and by waye of reward £10 more."

The Revels Book for that year mentions the " Histories and Inventions shewn within the time "—and gives, " The Historie of the Collyer " shown at Hampton Court, on the Sunday following St. John's daie by therle of Leicester's menne."

Aud. Off., 383, 16, 19 to 20 Eliz. " To the Erle of Leicester's Servants . . . warrant 9th January, 1577-8 . . . playe upon St. Stephen's daye dicto Anno, £6 13s. 4d. by her Majestie's special reward, 5 marks—in all £10." (Pipe Office, 541, f. 210.)

" The Earle of Leicester's Players . . . Warrant 18th Feb., 1577-8, for making their repair to the courte, with theire whole Companie and furniture to present a play before her Majestie upon Shrove Tewsdaie at night, in Consideracion of their Chardges for that purpose, although the plaie by her Majesties commandment was supplyed by others, £6 13s. 4d." (Pipe Office, 541, 210.) (This year is omitted from Revels Books.)

" 383, 17, 20 to 21 Eliz. " To therle of Leicester's players . . . warrant 16th Jan., 1578-9 . . . play on Sunday, 4th January, 1578-9, £6 13s. 4d., . . . especiall reward, 66s. 8d., £10." (Pipe Office, 541, 223.)

The Revels Book, among " Histories and Inventions shewen " includes, " A pastorall or history of a Greeke Maide, shewen at Richmond on the Sondaie after New Yeares daie enacted by the Earl of Leicester his servantes,[1] furnished with some thinges in this office." And among expenses, " Three yardes of gray cloth to make my Lord of Leicester's men a fisherman's coat, 5s."

" 4th of January, 1578-9, for the hier of a horse 2 daies to the courte to furnishe my Lord of Leicester's players, the frost being so great no bote could goe and come back againe at 12d. the daie, 3s. 4d. For his meate those two daies, 2s. 8d. ; for holly and Ivie for my Lord of Leicester's servaunts, 12d."

Aud. Off., 383, 18, 21 to 22 Eliz. " To the Players of the Lord of Leicester . . . warrant . . . 25th January, 1579-80 . . . playe before her Majestie on Twelfe Daie laste paste, £6 13s. 4d. more by way of rewarde, 66s. 8d., in all, £10." (Pipe Office, 542, 9.)

The Revels Accounts give us a special note of another day fixed this year before this date, seeing the charges were as great " to the

---

[1] It has struck me, this might be an early draught of " Pericles."

Office " as if it had been played, " A Historye of —— provided to have been shewed at Whitehall on Innocents' Daie at nighte by the Earl of Leicester's servauntes, being in Readynes in the place to have enacted the same, wholly furnyshed with sondry thinges in this Offyce. But the Queenes Maiestie coulde not come forth to heare the same therefore put of." As the men are paid nothing by the Treasurer of the Chamber, it is to be supposed that the same play was produced later that season for the entry follows, " The history of —— shewen at Whitehall on Twelve daye at night by the Earle of Leicester's servauntes furnished in this offyce with many garmentes, utensells and properties, some made newe, some translated and made fitt, whereon was ymployed for Head Attyers scarfes and garters ——ells of Sarcenett, A citie, a Countrie House, and 7 paire of gloves."

Aud. Off., 383 19, 22 to 23 Eliz. " To Therle of Leicester's players warrant 14th January, 1580–1 . . . a playe . . . on Shrove Tewsdaye laste paste, £6 13s. 4d., by waie of especiall rewarde, 66s. 8d. in all £10. (Pipe Office, 542, f. 21.) To them more . . . warrant 14th Januarie, 1580–1 playe on Stephen's day at night last paste, £6 13s. 4d. . . . rewarde, 66s. 8d. in all, £10."

The Revels Book gives " The Earle of Leicester's men. A comedie called delighte . . . St. Stephen's daye at nighte whereon was ymploied newe, one cittie, one battlement, and 12 paire of gloves."

" A Storie of . . . shewed on Shrove Tuesday at night in the Hall whereon was ymploied one great citty, and 12 paire of gloves."

During the following year, 23 to 24 Eliz., the Earl of Leicester's servants were not called on to play, but during the following year they played, and also the Lord Hunsdon's servants (the *first time* they are mentioned).

Aud. Off., 384, 21, 24 to 25 Eliz. " To the servauntes of the Earl of Leicester . . . warrant . . . 17th Februarij, 1582–3. play. . . uppon Shrove Sunday last . . . £6 13s. 4d. and by way of Rewarde towardes the chardge of theare preparacion and attendaunce in that behalf, 66s. 8d. in all £10. To the Servauntes of the Lord of Hunsdon . . . warrant . . . 17th Februarij, 1582–3, play, on St. John's Day . . . £6 13s. 4d., rewarde, 66s. 8d., £10." (Pipe Off., 542, f. 45.)

The Revels Book adds, " A Comodye of Bewtie and Huswyfery . . . St. John's Daie at night by the Lorde of Hundesdon's servauntes for which was prepared newe one Cloth and one Battlement of canvas, 3 Ells of Sarcenet and eight paire of gloves, with sondry other things out of this office.

"A historie of Telomo on Shrovesondaie at night enacted by the Earle of Leicester's servauntes, for which was prepared and imployed one Citty, one Battlement of Canvas, 3 Ells of Sarcenet and 8 paire of gloves. And furnished with sondrey other garments of the store of the office." Then comes the note, " Edmond Tylney Esquire Master of the Office being sente for to the Courte by Letter from Mr. Secretary dated 10th Marche, 1582–3. To choose out A companie of players for her Majestie " (his travelling expenses came to 20s.).

The following year no plays were put forth by Leicester's men.

Aud. Off., 384, 22, 25 to 26 Eliz. " To divers plaiers . . . warrant 12th March, 1583–4 . . . her maiesties servants 3 plaies . . . Mr. of the Children of the Chapel two plays ; . . . the Erle of Oxford's servants two plaies in all £55." In the Revels Book their names are given. There is no mention of Burbage's players the following year.

Pipe Office, 542 f. 79. In 27–28 Eliz. there is an entry " To the Servants of the Lord Admiral and the Lord Chamberlaine, Warr. January, 1585 . . . plaie . . . Twelfe day laste paste, £6 13s. 4d., . . . rewarde, 66s. 8d. . . . in all £10."

Pipe Office, 542, f. 94, 28 to 29 Eliz. " To the Erle of Leicester's players, warrant, last of Marche, 1587, for a play . . . on St. John's day at nighte, £6 13s. 4d., 66s. 8d., in all £10."

There is a gap in the Revels Book here, indeed it records no future *names* of the plays, by Leicester's company.

During a period of silence and seclusion from court of Burbage's men, a period during which Leicester died, and a new distribution of his new company took place, William Shakespeare came to town and joined Burbage's Company, then the Lord Chamberlain's. (Lord Hunsdon was appointed 1584). And the first notice of him records his being in the prominent position of one of the payees. It was in the account drawn up after date by Mary Countess of Southampton, after the decease of her second husband, Sir Thomas Henneage who had left his accounts rather in a muddle. But this entry is clear enough, and means much.

Pipe Off., 542, f. 208, 36 to 38 Eliz. " To William Kempe, William Shakespeare, and Richard Burbage, Servants of the Lord

Chamberlain, Upon the Councells warrant dated at Whitehall 15th March, 1594-5, for two several comedies or Interludes shewed by them before her Majestie in Christmas tyme last past on St. Stephen's Daie and on Innocent's daie . . . in all £20."

(Note that both are *Day*, not night performances.)

The next entry following, in the account of 38 to 39 Eliz. " To John Hemynge and George Bryan, servants to the late Lord Chamberlain, and now servants to Lord Hunsdon . . . Warrant at Whitehall on 21st Dec., 1596, For five Interludes or playes, viz., on St. Stephen's daie at night last, the Sondaye following, Twelfthe Daye at night, on St. John's Day, and on Shrove Sonday at night . . . in all £50." Shortly afterwards Lord Hunsdon became Lord Chamberlain and Burbage's Company by the help of William Shakespeare and Richard Burbage, at last became more popular than the Lord Admiral's Company, who had so long preceded them.

In the same Roll, 542, at the end of 1597–8 a warrant was issued for payments evidently long overdue.

" To Thomas Pope and John Hemynges, Servants of the Lord Chamberlain . . . warrant 27th November, 1597, for six Interludes or playes . . . on St. Stephen's day at night, St. John's Day at night, New Year's Night, Twelfe Night, Shrove Sonday at night, Shrove Monday at night . . . in all £60.

Aud. Off. Bundle, 387, R. 38, 41 to 42 Eliz.

" To John Hemming and Thomas Pope, servaunts to the Lord Chamberlain, . . . warrant 2nd Oct., 1599, for three Enterludes or playes . . . upon St. Steven's day at night, New Yeare's Daye at night, and Shrove Tuesday at night last past, in all £30. . . . To John Hemyng, servant to the Lord Chamberlain . . . Warrant, 17th February, 1599, for three interludes or playes, on St. Stephen's daye at night, Twelfth day at night, Shrove Sunday at night last past . . . in all £30."

Aud. Off. Bdle., 387, R. 39, 42 to 43 Eliz.

" To Richard Brackenbury, for making ready Westminster Hall, against the arraignment of the Erles of Essex and Southampton, February, 1600-1."

" To John Hemmings and Richard Cowley, servants to the Lord Chamberlain . . . warrant, 31st March, 1601 . . . for three plays . . . St. Stephen's day at night, Twelfth day at night and Shrove Tuesday at night—in all, £30." (A year is then missed.)

Bundle 387, R. 40, 44 Eliz. to 1 James I. " To John Hemming and the servants of the Lord Chamberlain . . . warrant dated 20th April, 1603 . . . for presenting before the late Queen . . . 2 plaies on St. Stephen's daye at night, and the other upon Candlemas day at night . . . £20."

Bundle 388, Roll 41, 1603–4.

" To John Hemming one of his Majesties Players, Warrant at Wilton, 3rd Dec., 1603, for the paines and expenses of himself and the rest of his Company in cominge from Mortlake in Co. Surrie unto the Court aforesaide and there presenting before his Majestie one play on 2nd Dec. last £30.

To John Hemmings one of his Majestys players, warrant, 18th Jan., 1603–4 . . . 6 severall plays on St. Stephen's day at night, St. John's day at night, Innocents day, and New Year's day at night, in all £53.

To Richard Burbage, one of his Majesties Comedians, warrant 8th Feb., 1603–4, for the maintenance and Reliefe of himself and the rest of his company being prohibited to present anie plaies publiquely in or near London, by reason of the great peril that might grow through the extraordinary concourse and assemblie of people to a newe increase of the plague till it shall please God to settle the cyttie in a more perfect health by way of his Majesties free gift, £30.

To John Hemmings one of his Majestys Players . . . warrant 28th Feb., 1603–4, for 2 plays performed before his Majesty, the one on Candlemas daye at night, the other on Shrovesundy at night, in all £20.

Bundle 388, Roll 42, 1604–5. " To John Hemmings warrant 21st Jan., 1604, for 6 interludes or plays on All Saints day at night, the Sonday at night following being 4th Nov., 1604, St. Stephen's day at night, Innocent's day at night and the 7th and 8th day of Januarie, for everie play 20 nobles, and for his majesties reward 5 nobles, in all £60.

To John Hemmings one of his Majesties players warrant 24th February, 1604–5, for 4 Interludes on Candlemas day at night, Shrove Sunday at night, Shrove Monday at night. Shrove Tuesday at night, £40.

To the said John Hemmings one of his M. Players . . . warrant dated 28th day of April, 1605 . . . for an enterlude or play . . . 3rd Feb., 1604 . . . in all £10.

Bundle 388, 43, 1605–1606.

To John Hemyngs one of his Majesties players warrant 24th March, 1605 . . . tenne several plays in Christmas last and since uppon a schedule annexed, in all £100.

Bundle 388, R. 44. To John Hemmyngs one of his Majesties players warrant 14th Oct., 1606 for three plays presented before his Majestie and the King of Denmark in all £30.

To John Hemynges one of his Majestie's players . . . Warrant 30th March, 1607, for nyne plays presented 26th and 29th December, 1606, the 4th, 6th and 8th of January, the 2nd, 5th, 15th and 27th of February, in all £90.

Bundle 388, Roll 45, 5 to 6 James I, 1607–8.

To John Hemynges one of his Majesties Players on the Counsells Warrant dated 8th Feb., 1607, for 13 plays . . . viz., on St. Stephen's day at night, St. John's day at night, Childermas day at night, 2nd January at night 2 plaies, 7th January, 9th January, 17th January (2 plaies) 26th January, Candlemas night and Shrove Sunday at night . . . in all £130.

Bundle 389, Roll 46, 1608–09.

To John Hemmings one of his Majesties Players upon the Counsels Warrant dated 5th April, 1609, for 12 plaies . . . at severall times in Christmas 1608 . . . £120.

To John Hemynges one of his Majesties players warrant 26th April, 1609 in the behalfe of himself and the rest of his Majesty's players by way of his Majesties reward for their private practise in the time of infeccion that thereby they myghte be inhabled to perform their serveice in the Christmas hollidays, 1609, £40.

Bundle 389, R. 47, 1609–1610. To John Hemyngs . . . warrant 10th March, 1609, for himself and the rest of his companie being restrained from public playing within the Citty of London in the tyme of infection, during the space of six weeks, in which time they practised privately for his Majestie's service, £30.

To John Hemmings one of the King's Majesties players, upon the warrant 2nd March, 1609, for performing 13 plaies before the King, etc., before Christmas of the previous year 1609, and in the tyme of the holidaies afterwards on severall nights, £130.

Bdle. 389, R. 48, 1610–11. To John Hemynges, one of the King's Majesties players . . . warrant 12th Feb., 1610 . . . for 15 plays . . . in all, £150.

Bdle 389, R. 49, 1611–12.   To John Hemmings for himself and his fellows, the King's Majesties servants . . . warrant . . . 1st June, 1612, for 6 several playes, one on the last October, one on the first of November, one on the 5th of November, one on the 26th Dec., and one on the 5th of January, and one on Shrove Sunday at night being the 23rd February at 20 nobles for every play, and 5 marks for a reward for every play, in all £60.

To the said John Hemmings . . . Warrant 1st of June, 1612, for himself and his fellows for 12 several plays before the Prince and the Duke of York, one on the 9th November last, one on the 19th of the same, one on 16th December, one on the last daie of the same month, one on 7th January, one on 13th of same, one on 19th Feb., one on 20th of the same, one on 28th February, one on 3rd April, and another upon 16th of the same at 20 nobles a play . . . £80.

To the said John Hemmings . . . Warrant 1st June, 1612, for himself and his fellows for 4 severall playes before the Prince and the Duke of York, one on 9th Feb., one on 20th of the same, one on 28th March, and one on 26th April, alter the said rate, £26 13s. 4d.

Bdle. 389, 50, 1612–13.   To John Hemmings.   Warrant . . . 9th July, 1613, for himself and his fellows the King's players . . . play before the Duke of Savoy's Ambassador, 8th June, 1613, £6 13s. 4d.

To him more, warrant 20th May, 1613, for presenting 14 several plays before the Prince, the Lady Elizabeth, and the Prince Palatyne, £93 6s. 8d.[1]   To the said John Hemmings on a warrant dated 20th May, 1613, for 6 several plays before his Majesty, £40, reward £20— in all £60.

Bdle. 390, R. 51.   To John Hemynges, and his fellows his Majesty's servants, Warrant 21st June, 1614 . . . 7 severall playes before the Prince . . . on 4th November, 16th November, 10th January, 4th Feb., the 8th, the 10th, and the 18th of the same month, £46 13s.

To the said John Hemings and his fellows, Warrant 21st June, 1614 . . . 9 severall playes before the King, on the 1st, 5th, and 15th Nov., 1614, the 27th December, the 1st and 4th January, the 2nd February following, and the 5th and 8th March, £90.

[1] See Rawlinson MS., A. 239, Bodleian Library, the same as above expanded, naming the plays.

Bdle. 390, R. 52.

To John Hemmings for himself and his fellows the King's players, upon the Lord Chamberlain's Warrant 19th March, 1615, for 8 several plays before the King . . . £80.

Bdle. 390, R. 54, 1616, 1617. To John Hemmings and the rest of his Majesties players warrant 29th April, 1616, for 14 severall playes from the feast of All Saints', 1615, to the 1st of April, 1616, £140.

To John Hemmings . . . warrant 11th March, 1616, for himselfe and his fellows the King's Majesty's players for 13 severall plays . . . from 1st Nov., 1616, to the 2nd February following, £130.

Bdle. 390, R. 55, 1617–18. To John Hemmings, for himself and the rest of the K. M. Players for 15 several plays . . . warrant 24th Feb., 1617 . . . £150.

To John Hemmings for himself and fellows K. M. Players . . . warrant . . . 20th April, 1618, for 2 plays on Easter Monday, and Monday Twelfe Night the playe so called, and on Easter Tuesday the Winter's Tale. . . . £20.

To the said John Hemmings for himself and fellows. . . Warrant 15th May, 1618, for presenting before his Majesty the 3rd of May the Merry Divell of Edmonton, £10.

Bdle 391, R. 56, is a Roll about Progresses.

Bdle. 391, R. 57, 1618–19. To John Hemmings in behalf of himself and the rest . . . Warrant 19th Aprill, 1619 . . . 8 playes, at Allhallowtide and Christmas, 1618, £73 6s. 8d.

Bdle. 391, R. 58, 1619–1620. To John Hemynge for himself and the rest . . . for 10 severall plays . . . the time of this account, warrant 23rd March, 1619 . . . £100. To him more in the behalf of himself and his fellows, for one other play . . . 30th April, 1620, warrant 20th May, 1620. £10.

Bdle 391, R. 59, 1620–1621.

To John Hemmyng for himself and fellows . . . Warrant 17th March, 1620 . . . for 9 playes . . . £90."

Bdle. 391, R. 60, 1621–2. To John Heminge, in the behalfe of himself and the rest, for 6 severall playes . . . Warrant 27th March, 1622, £60.

Bdle. 392, R. 61, 1622, 1623.

To John Hemynges in the behalf of himself and his fellows, a warrant, 14th March, 1622, for 9 severall plays . . . £90.

To John Hemmings one of his Majesties players, a warrant, 17th Feb., 1623 . . . ten plays . . . in all, £100.

Bdle. 392, R. 62, 1623-4. To John Hemming one of his Majesties players, Warrant 17th Feb., 1623 . . . 10 severall plaies, £100.

To John Hemmings one of his Majesties players, warrant 22nd March, 1624, for himself and the rest of his fellows for presenting five several plaies . . . £50.

Bdle. 392, R. 63, 1623-4. Duplicate of last.

Bdle. 392, R. 64, 1624-5. To John Hemmings, Warrant 20th Feb., 1624, play 12th Jan., 1624 . . . £10.

Bdle. 392, R. 65, 1625, 1626. To John Hemmings one of his Majesty's players, warrant 30th May, 1626, for 10 plaies, £100.

Bdle. 393, R. 66, 1627, 1628 (year evidently lost). To John Hemmings one of his Majesties players; warrant 10th Aprill, 1628, 10 playes, between Michaelmas, 1627, and the last of Jan. following £100.

To him more upon like warrant 20th April, 1628, for one play . . . Easter Tuesday at night, 1628, in all £110. (No other players mentioned.)

This series goes on further but at this date we may turn to the Lord Chamberlain's Books.

The volumes of the Lord Chamberlain's Warrants supply much information concerning plays and players. Unfortunately they are missing for the most important years in Shakespearean History. The only exception is the volume which records the preparation for the Royal Progress through the City of London on March 15th, 1603-4. In view of the fact that many writers think that the Players would not attend the Royal procession it may be noted, that after the greater officers are dealt with, there follow pages of the names of the dealers entitled to be paid for " Red clothe bought of sundrie persons and given by his Majestie to divers persons against his Majesty's said royall proceeding through ye cittie of London." Among the persons to whom that red cloth was given, were the players, beginning as I noted in the text with " William Shakespeare, 4½ yards." [1] (L. C., II, 4, 5.)

The earliest volume of Warrants preserved for that period is V., 93, 1628-1634. The first special entry is one granting to " John [2]

[1] See my " Shakespeare of the Court," "Athenæum," March 12, 1910.

[2] I published the series in full in the "Shakespeare Jahrbuch" under the title of " Shakespeare's Fellows and Followers," 1910.

Hemmings, John Lowen, and Joseph Taylor, on behalf of their fellows the King's Servants the Players . . . the sum of £100, being at the rate of £10 a play, viz., twenty nobles for their charges, and 5 marks by way of reward for tenne playes by them acted before his Majestie at several times between Michaelmas last 1627 and the last of January following, the names whereof particularly appear by this annexed Schedule, 10th April, 1628." (Unfortunately the schedule is lost.)

" A warrant for payment of £160 to John Hemings, etc., for 16 plays acted before his Majesty between Christmas and Candlemas, 1628, 27th Feb., 1628–9."

" A Warrant for payment of £10 unto John Hemings, etc., for a play called *ye Love-Sicke Maid* acted before his Majesty on Easter Monday, May 6th, 1629."

" A warrant for Players Liveries . . . to be delivered to John Hemings, John Lowen, Joseph Taylor, Richard Robinson, John Shank, Robert Benfield, Richard Sharp, Eillard Swanson, Thomas Pollard, Anthony Smith, Thomas Hobbes, William Pen, George Vernon, and James Horne, to each the several allowance of 4 yards of Bastard Scarlet for a Cloak, and a quarter of a yard of crimson Velvet for a cap, their usual allowance every second year.   May 6th, 1629."

" A warrant for payment of £120 to John Hemings for 12 plays played before his Majesty at Christmas 1629.   April 3rd, 1630."
" A warrant for suppressing stage plays and Bear and Bull-baiting on account of the plague, April 17, 1630."

" A warrant to pay to John Lowen for himself and the rest of the King's Company £260 that is to say Twenty pounds a piece for foure playes acted at Hampton Court, in respect of the travail and expenses of the whole company in Dyet and Lodging during the time of their attendance there And the like sum of £20 for one play which was acted at Whitehall in the daytime, whereby the players lost the benefitt of their house for that day. . . .   And £10 a piece for 16 other plays acted before the King at Whitehall . . . between the 30th Sept. and 21st Feb. last past. . . .   As it may appear by Schedule (also lost).   March 17, 1630–1."

" A warrant to deliver to Joseph Taylor and 13 others his Majesty's players, 4 yards bastard Scarlet and a quarter of a yard of Velvet for liveries (as above).   April 27, 1631."

" A warrant to pay £120 to John Lowing, Joseph Taylor and Eilliard Swanston for themselves and the rest of their fellows his Majestie's Comedians for 11 plays (one whereof was at Hampton Court) by them acted before his Majesty at Christmas, 1631. Feb. 22nd, 1631–2."

" A warrant to pay £270 to John Lowen, Joseph Taylor and Eillard Swanston, his Majesty's Comedians for playes by them acted before his Majesty viz—£20 for the rehearsal of one at the Cockpitt by which means they lost their afternoon at the House, and £20 a piece for two at Hampton Court. . . . And £10 for 21 more at Whitehall and Denmark House acted between 3rd May, 1632, and 3rd of March following. March 16th, 1632–33."

" A warrant, Whereas the late decease, infirmity, and sickness of divers principal Actors of his Majesty's company of players, hath much decayed and weakened them, so that they are disabled to do his Majesty's service in their quality, unless there be some speedy order to furnish them with new Actors, his Majesty having signified his royal pleasure . . . to you to choose, take, and receive into your company any actor belonging to the licensed companies in or about London, as you shall think fit or able to do his Majesty service, etc. To John Lowen and Joseph Taylor. May 6th, 1633."

Vol. 95 of the same series runs from 1634–1641. It begins with " A warrant for payment of £220 to John Lowen, Joseph Taylor, and Eillard Swanston for 22 plays by them acted . . . within a whole year ending 27th April, 1634."

" A warrant for liveries to be delivered to John Lowen and 14 others of his Majesty's players as usual. April 3rd, 1635." This is the year in which the Lord Chamberlain gave the decision in favour of Eillard Swanston, see page 232.

" A Warrant to pay £250 to John Lowen for himself and the rest of the King's players, for 20 plays whereof 5 at £20 a piece being at Hampton Court by them acted between 13th May, 1634, and 30th March, 1635, signed May 24th, 1635."

" A warrant for paying £80 unto the King's players for plays acted before his Majesty in 1635." May 10th, 1636.

" Players passes, William Pen, Thomas Hobbes, William Tregg, William Patrick, Richard Baxter, Alexander Gough, William Hart, Richard Hanly, and ten of their fellows ' his Majesty's Comedians of the peculiar company of Players in the Blackfryars, London, are commanded to attend his Majesty and be nigh about the Court this somer progresse in readiness when they shall be called on to act before his Majesty,' that either in going or coming they can go to any town they please, and perform in ' any common halls, moothalls, schoolhouses ' or other convenient places, and act plays, ' without lett or hindrance,' and they are to be ' treated and enterteyned with such due respect and curtesie, as may become his Majesty's loving and loyal subjects towards his servants.' To all Mayors, Sheriffs, Bailiffs, Justices of the Peace, Constables and Headboroughs, etc.' May 17th, 1636."

" A ticket of privilege was also granted to the attendants of the players, Richard Bagstare, Richard Halley, William Hart, William Patrick, Henry Pettington, Richard Bowers, Rowland Dowle, John Bacon, Edward Collins, John Allingham and William Soyles, ' employed by his Majesty's servants the players of the Blackfriars, and of special use to them both on the stage and otherwise for his Majesty's disport and service.' They are to ' be freed from all molestacion or arrest whereby they may be withdrawn from their Company.' If any man had anything against them, due consideration would be had of his complaint in this office. 12th Jan., 1636."

" Warrant to pay £240 to his Majesty's Players, viz. £210 for 21 plays acted by them at £10 a play, and £30 more for the New Play called the Royall Slave. March 16th, 1636."

This is the payment on which some one has exercised his ingenuity in contriving a list of the plays and names and dates of their performance preserved by Cunningham among his " Extracts from the Books of the Master of the Revels." *See* "Athenaeum," July 22nd, 29th, Oct. 7th, 1911 ; April 27th, August 10th, 1912.

" Warrant to swear Mr. Christopher Beeston his Majestie's servant in ye place of Governor of the new Company of the Kings and Queenes boyes. Feb. 21, 1636."

" Warrant to King's Players. Whereas ye charge of ye alterations, reparations and additions which were made unto ye scene, apparell, and propertyes that were employed for ye setting forth of ye new play called *The Royall Slave* . . . at Hampton Court . . . together with the charge of Dancers, and composers of Musique . . . amounteth to £154 appearing by the bills of the several persons imployed therein . . . £50 to the property maker, £50 to the painter, and to Estienne, Nau, and Sebastian La Pierre for them-

selves and twelve dancers the sum of £54.   April 4th, 1637."
"Warrant for liveries of the King's Players, to John Lowen,
Joseph Taylor and Eillard Swanston, (as above).   April 22nd, 1637."
The printing of plays restrained.   Philip, Earl of Pembroke
and Montgomery, Lord Chamberlain, refers to a complaint made
"to his dear brother and predecessor, by his Majesty's Servants
the players, that some of the company of Printers and Stationers
had procured published and printed diverse of their books of
Comedyes, Tragedies, Cronicle-Historyes and the like . . . which
they had bought and provided at very deare and high rates.   By
meanes whereof not only they themselves had much prejudice
but the books much corruption, to the injury and disgrace of the
authors."   Thereupon " The Masters and Wardens of the Company of Stationers were advised by my brother to take notice
thereof and to stay any further impression of any of the playes or
Interludes of his Majesty's servants without their consents. . . .
Notwithstanding which I am informed that some coppyes of plays
belonging to the King's and Queen's servants the players, and
purchased by them at deare rates, having been stolen or gotten
from them by indirect means are now attempted to be printed
. . . which would directly tend to their apparent detriment, and
great prejudice, and to the disenabling of them to do their Majestie's
service."   The Lord Chamberlain desires the Master and Wardens
of the Stationer's Company to inquire if any such play has been
entered and to let the Players know, so that it may be proved to whom
they belong, and that none may be printed, except such as the
players assent to " by some certificate in writing under the hands
of John Lowen and Joseph Taylor for the King's Company and of
Christopher Beeston for the King's and Queen's young company
. . . which is a course which can be hurtful to none but such as
goe about unjustly to prevayle themselves of others' goods without
respect of order or good government.   June 10th, 1637."
" A warrant to pay £150 to John Lowen, Joseph Taylor, and
Eillard Swanston for themselves and the rest of his Majesty's
players for 14 plays acted before his Majesty between the 30th of
September and the 3rd of February follcwing 1637–8, whereof
one was at Hampton Court, for which £20 is allowed.   March 15th,
1637–8."
" A warrant to Players on the King's side for £300.   His Majesty's

servants the Company at the Blackfriars have by special command at divers times within this year 1638 acted 24 plays, six whereof have been performed at Hampton Court and Richmond by means whereof they were not only at ye losse of their day at home but at extraordinary charges. . .   Wherefore they are to have £20 a piece for those plays . . . and £10 a piece for the other 18 acted at Whitehall. . . .   These are to pray you to pay to John Lowen, Joseph Taylor, and Eillard Swanston for themselves and the rest of the Company of £300." March 12th, 1638. (Same page, same date, grant of liveries as usual.)

William Beeston, now governor of the King's and Queen's young company, claims many plays among which are "The Spanish Gipsie," " The Rape of Lucrece." Aug. 10th, 1639.

" A warrant to swear Mr. Joseph Taylor yeoman of the Revells to his Majesty in ordinary in ye place of William Hunt deceased Sept. 29, 1639." Hunt had succeeded Edward Kirkham. Patent follows, 2nd Dec., 1639.

" A warrant for payment of £230 to John Lowen, Joseph Taylor, and Eillard Swanston, and the rest of the King's players for 21 plays acted before their Majesties. Whereof two were at Richmond, for which they were allowed £20 a piece, for the rest £10 a piece, all these being acted between the 6th of August, 1639, and the 11th February following.   April 4th, 1640."

" A Warrant for swearing six persons as ' Grooms ' of his Majestie's Chamber in ordinary without fee to attend his Majesty in the quality of players, and to be of the company of his Majestie's servants at ye Blackfriars, viz. Michael Bowyere, William Robins, William Allen, Hugh Clarke, Theophilus Bird, Steven Hamerton, Jan. 22nd, 1640."

" Tickets of privilege " are issued to all these men " Whereof I advise all such as it may concern to take notice, and to be very cautious how they do any act to the prejudice of the said Theophilus Bird," etc.

" A Warrant for payment of £160 to the King's Players, for plays acted before his Majesty . . . between 10th Nov., 1640, and 22nd Feb., 1640, to be paid to John Lowen, Joseph Taylor, and Eillard Swanston," etc.   March 20th, 1640.

Same date warrant for liveries to the same.

Vol. 96, 1641. The Earl of Essex, now Lord Chamberlain,

writes, To my very loving friends the Master and Wardens of Stationers' Company : " The players which are his Majesty's servants have addressed themselves to me, as formerly to my predecessors in office complaining that some printers are about to print and publish some of their plays, which hitherto they have been usually restrained from by the authority of the Lord Chamberlain. Their Request seems both just and reasonable as only tending to preserve them masters of their proper goods, which in justice ought not to be made common for another man's profitt to their disadvantage. Upon this ground therefore I am induced to require your care, that no playes belonging to them be putt in print without their knowledge and Consent. The particulars to which they now lay claime are contained in a list enclosed, and if any of those playes shall bee offered to ye presse under another name than is in the list expressed I desire your care that they may not be defrauded by that meanes, but that they may be made acquainted with it, before they bee recorded in your Hall, and soe have opportunity to show their right unto them etc. Essex. Aug. 7th, 1641." I have noted this, as illustrative of what would probably have appeared in the lost Lord Chamberlain's Books. They throw light on the views of the players in relation to the publication of their poet's plays. They add a long list which I printed in the "Jahr buch," but omit here. There were none of the old favourites when Shakespeare lived, and Richard Burbage was in his prime. This closes the Records. The Earl of Essex broke his staff and left the King's service and went over to the Parliament.

INDEX

A

Aberdeen, 90
Adams, John, 36
Agamemnon and Ulysses, 44
Alarum against Usurers, 32
Allen of the Cockpit, 137
  John, 51
Alleyn, Christopher, 34, 54, 167
  Edward, 57–61, 85, 123, v.
  Giles, 19, 33, 34, 46, 49, 52,
    64, 65, 67, 68, 73–6, 78–85,
    99, 130, 154, 158, 166–7, 185–
    194, 198, 200–227, xii.
  Sir William, 23
All is true, 111
Ames, Christopher, 45, 141
  Roger, 68, 78, 184, 185
Amadis of Gaul, 21
Anatomie of Abuses, 37
Annes, St., Blackfriars, 64
Anne, Queen, 102, 105, 116, 117.
Apologie for Poetrie, 32
Arden, Edward, 38
Armin, Robert, 27, 100, 229
Art in England, 3, 4, 108
Asbies, 53, 54
Aston, Roger, 89
Authorities—
  Audit Office, acc. various, 247–
    251
  Chamber, Treasurer of the, Dec.
    Acc., Audit Office, 7, 55, 75,
    101, 103, 246–257

Pipe Office, 17–25, 60, 99,
  101, 102, 246–257
Chamberlain's, Lord, Books, 37,
  99, 130, 133, 136, 230, 257
Chancery Proceedings, 49, 51,
  135, 154–9, 164
  Bills and Answers, 106, 107,
    154
  Decrees and Orders, 48, 49,
    50, 51, 129, 159–164
Coram Rege Rolls (King's
  Bench), 54, 75, 77, 78, 79,
  81, 82, 84, 184, 198, 217
Court of Requests, 75, 79, 82,
  83, 107, 129, 130, 200, x.
  Uncalendared, 45, 80, 177, 216
Court of Wards and Liveries,
  34, 52, 166–170
Egerton MSS., Brit. Mus., 61, 116
Exchequer Bills and Answers,
  78, 185–189
  Decrees and Orders, 189, 194
  Depositions, 78, 79, 189–193,
    xii.
Gloucester Records, 8
Guildhall MSS. Journal, 34
  Letter Books, 108
  Remembrancia, 31, 62
  Repertory, 8, 12, 14, 34, 52,
    145, 176
Harl. MS., Brit. Mus., 111, 153
Lansdowne MSS., Brit. Mus.,
  13, 38, 39, 40, 41, 146

Loseley Papers, 170–174, viii, xii
Middlesex Co. Sessions Rolls, 30, 71, 135, 149, 153
Privy Council Register, 17, 24, 25, 35, 47, 103, 114, 115, 126, 127, 128, 240–242
Sloane MSS., Brit. Mus., 12, 70, 118
Star Chamber Proc., 75, 80, 220
State Papers, Dom. Ser, 88, 103, 175, 197
Scotch Series, 89
Subsidy Rolls, 85, 86, 153, 194, vi.

B

Bacon, Francis, 60, 84, 130, 243
Bacon-Shakespeare Question answered, 60, 84, ix.
Baker, Sir Richard, 132, 133
William, 127
Bankside, 21, 22, 57, 61, 62, 69, 74
Bassanos, The, 195
Bath, Marquis of, 10
Beeston, Christopher, 139, 141, 260
William, 262
Benfield, Robert, 125, 136, 230
Biron Tragedy of, 105
Bishop, Nicholas, 51, 164, 165
Blackfriars, 63, 65, 91, 92, 105, 106, 170–177, 230, 262, viii., xii.
Bottom's Play, 5, 60
Brand or Brend, Sir Matthew, 113, 129, 130, 135, 196, 232
Nicholas, 74–6, 113, 129
Brayne, Ellen, 134
John, 18, 21, 28, 29, 30, 45, 47, 48, 80, 81, 154, 156, 209
Margaret, 47–50, 154, 156, 159
Bull, The, 137
Bumpstead, Christopher, 33, 34, 166, 186
Burbage, Alice, 18, 49, 134, 140

Burbage, Anne, 141
Cuthbert, 18, 21, 34, 37, 49, 51, 67, 68, 70, 73–83, 85, 87, 105, 108, 123, 125–7, 129, 130, 134, 140, 151, 154, 164, 195, 200, 227
Ellen or Helen, 18, 47, 67–9, 81, 139, 209 (Mrs. Burbage)
her daughter, 49, 64, 154
Elizabeth, wife of Cuthbert, 124, 126, 134
daughter, 134, 140
Frances, 139, 141
Henry, 135
James, 1, 6–10, 12, 16–21, 23, 25, 27, 29–31, 33–9, 45, 46, 48–52, 54, 56, 59–62, 66, 67, 70, 80, 81, 83, 85, 91, 92, 98, 105, 134, 139, 152, 154, 164, 170, 200, 227, v., vi., xii.
his grandson, 68, 139
his grandson alias Maxey, 134
Joane, 139
John, 6, 18, 152
Julia, 139, 140, 141
Juliet, 139
Richard, 1, 2, 18, 36, 37, 49, 53, 56, 60, 67, 73, 77, 81, 82, 84, 90–7, 99, 100, 104–9, 113, 115–9, 120, 122, 123, 125, 126, 130–5, 139, 140, 151, 154–164, 195, 196, 240, vi.
of Stoke, 134, 135
Robert, 134, 152
Sara, 140–141
William, 115, 127, 134, 135, 141
Winifred, 124, 134, 140, 141
Burleigh, Lord, 57, 58

C

Carleton, 103, 245
Catiline's Conspiracy, 32

Cawarden, Sir Thomas, 173
  Elizabeth, Dame, 173
Cecil, Sir Robert, 83, 88, 102 ;
  Viscount Cranbourne, 102-3
Chambers, E. K., 11, 14, 35, 62, xii
Chapman, 92, 105
Chariclea, 22
Chettle, 96
Child, William, 126, 127
Children of the Chapel, 91, 104,
  ix, x.; of the Revels, 105
Clark, Thomas, 9
Clifton Case, The, 92, 104, 107
Cobham, Lord, 64, 172
Collier, 64, 65, 120, 127, 137
  Lives of the Actors, 137
  Forgeries, 65, 176
  New Particulars, 120, 121
Comedy of Errors, 60
Condell, Henry, 97, 100, 107, 116,
  125, 126,132,133,229, 232, 238
Cooke, Lyonell, 36
Cope, Sir Walter, 102, 103
Corbet, Bishop, 116
Corporation, 2, 4, 25, 38, 52, 56,
  61, 64, 73, 107, 129, 146
Council, Common, 11, 13, 34, 41
  Privy, 11-13, 21-25, 31, 33-35,
  39, 47, 52, 62, 65, 69, 73,
  80, 88, 127, 146, 147
Cox, John, 134
  Elizabeth, daughter, 134
Cowley, Richard, 97-100, 140, 229,
  252
Cunningham's Extracts, 102, 110
Curtain, The, 15, 23, 25-7, 31, 33,
  36, 61, 62, 69, 70, 85, 152

D

Dekker, 73
Dibdin's Hist. Edinburgh Stage, 90
Divers Plots and Devices, 60

Dobson, Austin, 123
Dolphin's Back, 17
Drama, Romantic School of, 111
Dramatic Records from Privy
  Council Register, 114, 240-2
Drayton, 96
Drummond of Hawthornden, 73
Duboys, Davy, 36,
Dudley, Sir Robert, 7, 246
  Earl of Leicester, 9, 12, 16, 17,
  19, 29, 38, 247
Dulwich College, 108
Dutton, John, 36

E

Earthquake, The, 31, 33
Eastward Hoe, 105
Ecclestone, William, 125, 229
Edward VI, 6
Elizabeth, Queen, 11, 14, 16, 17,
  22, 34, 35, 41, 43-5, 52, 59,
  64, 69, 88, 91, 95, 96, 98,
  130, 136 145, x.; Princess, 110
Essex, Earl of, 64, 73, 87, 88,
  90, 95, 96
  Conspiracy, His, 81, 88, 90
Evans, Henry, 91, 92, 104-7, 132
Every Man in his Humour, 110

F

Falstaff, 64
Feake, James, 71, 72, 139
Felix and Philiomena. 45
Field, Nathan, Player, 105, 125,
  132, 229
  Richard, 54, 57, 58, 65, 175
Finsbury Fields, 15, 19, 20, 21,
  26, 27, 42, 70, 191
Five Plays in One, 45
Fleay, Mr., 36, 92, 107, xii.
Flecknoe, Richard, 12

Fleetwood, Recorder of London, 38, 60, 146
Fletcher, Laurence, 88, 89, 90, 96, 97, 100, 107, 228
Fortnightly Review, The, 53
Fortune, The, 136, 153
Furnivall, Dr., 16, 62, 94, 135, x.

G

Gaedertz, Dr., 62
Gardiner, John, 48, 156–9
  Robert, 48, 49, 156
Garland, John, 36
Gascoigne, George, 16
Gentleman's Magazine, The, 120
George, The, Inn, 20, 49, 51, 125, 156, 157
Giles, Nathaniel, 91, 92, 164, 165
Giles, St., Without, Cripplegate, 126
Globe, The, 77, 81, 84, 85, 87, 88, 90, 92, 94, 96, 97, 103–5, 111–3, 123, 129, 132, 135, 137, 196, 197, viii.
" Gorboduc," 37
Gosson, Stephen, 32, 33
Gough, Robert, 125
Gowry, The Tragedy of, 103
Gray's Inn Revels, 60
Green, Robert, 55, 96
  Thomas, 113, 139
Greenstreet, Mr., 92, 107, xii.
Greville, Fulke, 59
Groatsworth of Wit, 55, 56
Graves, Elizabeth, 124
Grosart, Dr., 65
Guilpin, Author of " Skialethia," 76
Gwynn, Matthew, 104

H

Hales, Professor, 86
Halliwell Phillipps, J. O., 49, 81, 85, 101, 112, 240, x., xi.

Hamlet, 92, 94, 95, 103, 104, 118
Harrison's England, 24
Harrys, Mr. Sergeant, 50, 161
Hart, 137
Harvey, Gabriel, 32
  Sir William, 57
Haslewood, 112
Hawkins, Alexander, 104–7; Margaret, 107
Hemmings, John, 77, 97–9, 100, 101, 106, 107, 113, 115, 116, 125, 126, 229, 231, 252–7
  William, 129, 130, 132, 133, 137
Henneage, Sir Thomas, 59
Henry V, 1, 87, vii.; Henry VI, 55; Henry VIII, 6, 111, ix.
Henry, Prince, 108, 110, 115
Henslowe, Philip, 51, 61–6, 72, 73, 85, 177; His Diary, 71, 72
Hilliard, 3
History of the Collier, 22
Holinshed, 84, 104
Holywell Priory, 19, 23, 30, 33, 34, 41, 63, 65, 85, 166, 198
  Lease of, 19, 24, 46, 64, 66, 67, 86, 154, 201–217
Holywell or Halliwell Street, 31, 37, 49, 55, 67, 71, 85, 125, 151
Hope, The, 106
Howe's Cont. Stowe, 36, 111
Hudson, Richard, 83, 84, 227
Hunnis, William, 16, 91, viii., ix., x.
Hunsdon, Lord, Henry Carey, 36, 39, 44, 45, 64, 175
  his son, 64, 65, 66, 68
Hunter, Joseph, Rev., 36, 86
Huntingdon, Henry, Earl of, 135
Hyde, John, 29, 140, 220

I

Imagination, 3, 10
Impresa, 109

J

Jackson, Rev. J. E., 10
  Henry, 124
James, King, 89, 90, 96, 97, 100, 103–5, 113, 136, 228, x.
  His coronation, 99, 100, 244
Jeaffreson, J. Cordy, 30, 72, 73, 149–150
Johnson, William, 9, 12, 36
Jonson, Ben, 72, 73, 92, 96, 110, 111, 123, 136, 245, v.

K

Kempe, William, 60, 77, 90, 91, 251
Kendall Thomas, 104–6
Kenilworth, 16, 59
Kennedy's "Memorials of Aberdeen," 90
Keysar, Robert, 107
Kingsmill, Richard, 52, 156
Kirkham, Edward, 104, 105, 106, 107

L

Lady of the Lake, 16, 17
Lambert, Edmund, 53, 54
  John, 53, 54
Lane, Richard, 82–84, 129, 130
Laneham, John, 9, 12, 16, 36
  Robert's Letter, 16, 17, 59
Langley, Francis, 61–3, 72, 78, 142, 177–183
Law, Mr. Ernest, 101, x.
Lear, King, 51, 118
Legg, Mr. Dr., 51, 162, 163
Leicester, Earl of, 9, 12, 17, 38, 44
Leonards, St., Church, 18, 62, 66, 68, 70, 71, 85, 109, 116, 125, 133
Lodge, Thomas, 32
Lodge's Illustrations, 17

Long, Maurice, 23
Lorkin's Letter, 111
"Love's Labour Lost," 102, 184
Lowen, John, 125, 136, 137, 230–3 258–262

M

Macbeth, 88, 103, 104, 121
Maddox, John, 82, 84, 221
Mamillia, 22
Marlowe, Christopher, 55
Marston, 92, 151, viii.
Martin, 89, 90
Martin Marprelate Controversy, 52
Mary, Queen, 6, 95
Maxey, Amias, 134
Mayor, Lord, 8, 12, 13, 23, 31, 34–36, 38, 40–42, 44, 47, 62, 64, 65, 69, 74, 87, 114, 127, 129, 146, vi.
Meres, Francis, 70, 71, 183–4
Middleton, Thomas, 117
"Midsummer's Night's Dream," 6, 17, 59, 60, 184
Middlesex Authorities, 24, 25, 30, 44, 69
Monasteries, 2, 3
More, Sir William, 63, 66, 170–4
  Gregory, 163
Munday, Anthony, 31, 108, xii.
Myles, Ralph, 51, 164, 165
  Robert, 48–50, 65, 78, 156–165, 195

N

Nash, 55, 64, 65
Neale, Mr. Dr., 100
Neville, Thomas, 80, 215
News from the North, 29
Nicholson, George, 89
Notes and Queries, 10

O

Oberon, 17
Oldcastle, Sir J., 64
Ordish, T. F., 14, xiii.
Orders, 13–15, 17, 20, 26, 33, 40–42, 44, 146–149
Ovid, 57, 184
Osteler, William, 105, 115, 132
Osborne, Thomas, 83, 84, 227

P

Palace of Pleasure, 27
  Petite, ,, ,, 27
Painton, Edward, 106, 107
Panecia, 22
Paris Garden, 13, 15, 35, 41
Payne, 105
  Thomas, 27
  John, 61
Paynter, William, 27
Peckham, Sir Edmund, 33, 34, 186
  Edmund, 34, 52, 166, 186, 211
  Sir George, 33, 166, 186
  George, 34, 52, 166, 186
  Susan, 34, 166–70
Pembroke, William, Earl of, 98, 116, 117, 131
  and Montgomery Philip, 131, 230
Perkinne, John, 9, 12
Pettie, George, 27
Philemon and Philecia, 22
Phillida and Choryn, 44
Phillips, Augustine, 77, 81, 88, 97, 100, 101, 104, 132, 297
Plague Restraints, 24, 29, 34, 35, 42, 43, 47, 51, 57, 90, 98, 105
Play of Playes, 33
Players, 4, 5–8, 10, 11, 25, 45, 64
  as grooms of the Chamber, 101
  In Coronation procession, 99
Plays, 24, 33, Censor of, 242

Objections to them, 6, 7, 10, 13, 16, 24, 25, 26, 29, 31, 32, 38, 41, 42, 69, 154, vi.
  Their patents, 12, 19, 97, 98, 228
  Their petitions, 14, 39, 40–44
  Their profits, 28, 107, 154
  Praises of players, 136, 137, 244
  Their Companies,
    Abergavenny's, Lord, 8
    Admiral's, Lord, 63, 70, 72, vi.
    Arundel's, Lord, 38
    Leicester's, Lord, 13, 16, 25, 29, 33, 36, 44, 89, 247, 249
      His boys, 37, 248
    King's Company, 97, 99, 102, 104, 105, 113, 115, 129, 131, 132, 137, 253–263
    Hunsdon's, Lord, 44, 64, 65, 66, 68, 250, 251, 252, vi.
    Chamberlain's, Lord, 60, 68, 70, 73, 74, 85, 88–90, 91–93, 251, 252, 253, vi.
    Oxford's, Lord, Boys, 44
    Pembroke's, Lord, 63, 72
    Queen Elizabeth's, 35, 38–40, 44, 70, 146, 251
    Queen Anne's Children of Chapel, 132
    Children of Revels, 105, 107
    Sussex's, Lord, 12
  Pollard, Thomas, 137, 230
  Pope, Thomas, 77, 100, 252
  Powell, John, 68, 78, 184
  " Predor and Lucia," 22
  Proclamations, 6, 8, 10, 20

R

Raleigh, Sir Walter, 36, 88
Rape of Lucrece, 58, 65, 184
Rastell, William, 104, 106
Religion and politics, 7, 8
Renaissance, The, 2, 34, vii.

Retainers, Proclamation of, 9
Returne from Pernassus, 90, 91
Revels, Master of, 11, 13, 27, 34, 52, 113
Rice, John, 108, 126
Richard II, 88, 90, 184
Richard III, 116, 184
Robinson, Richard, 68, 78, 124 125, 129, 130, 137, 184
  Mrs. Winifred, 131, 237
"Romeo and Juliet," 120
Romish emissaries, 7, 10
Rose, The, 61, 62, 85, 177
Rosseter, Philip, 114, 115
Rudd, John, 135
Russell, Dowager Lady, 65, 174
Rutland, Roger, Earl of, 68, 73, 76, 78, 87, 109, 185–194
  Francis, 109 ; Henry, 193

S

Sandars, Lady, 114
Saule, Hester, 62, 142
Saviour's, St., Church, 74, 105
Scriven, Thomas, 68, 78, 87, 108, 109, 187, 188
Schoole of Abuse, 32
Scott, Mr. Dr., 50, 160
Shakespeare, John, 16, 109
  Roger, 53
  Thomas, 53
  William, 1, 7, 51, 53–55, 57, 59, 60, 65, 67, 68, 70–73, 77, 85, 88–90, 92, 94–97, 100, 101, 103, 104, 108, 113, 115, 116, 123, 132, 136, 138, 183 228, 230, 251, vi., viii.
  "Aunts and Snitterfield," 57
  his correction of plays, 55
  "his Fellows and Followers," 101, 136
  "of the Court," 101, 257
  his Law, 57

Jahrbuch, 60, 101, 114, 136
" Money interest in Globe," 104
" Official record of his name," 60
Sonnets, 54, 57, 58, 184
  his Warwickshire Contemporaries, 54
" Mr. Shakspeare about Impresa," 109
Shakespeare New Society, 16, 23, 62, 73, 133, v.
Shancks, John, 125, 133, 231, 239
Shaw, or Shae, Robert, 177
Shoreditch, 18, 31, 36, 42, 66, 69, 71, 85, 128, 138, 150, 191–2
Shrewsbury, Earl of, 7
Sidney, Sir Philip, 32, 33
Simon, John, 36
Singer, John 36
Sly, William, 97, 100, 139
Smith, Humphrey, 127
  William, 76, 77, 83, 216
Snug, the Joiner, 60
Somers, Sir George, 110
  William, 139
Southampton, Countess of, 57–9
  Henry, Earl of, 56, 57, 68, 73, 87, 88, 92, 96, 98, 102, 103, 109
Southwark, 61
Spenser, Edmund, 32, 184
  Gabriel, 70, 73, 150, 177, 183
Stanhope, Mr. Dr., 51, 162, 163
Stockwood, John, 26, 28
Stopes, Rev. James, 135
Stow's History, 135, 146 ; Howe's Cont., 36, 111
Stow's Survey, 70 ; Strype's Cont., 133, 134
Stratford-on-Avon, 6, 53, 54, 100
Street, Peter, 26, 74, 75, 77, 78, 83, 85, 142, 198
Stubbes, Philip, 31, 37
Swan, The, 61–3, 177

Swanston, Eillardt, 130–3, 139, 230–3

Symons, 44

T

Tarleton, Richard, 36, 37, 123, 139

Taylor, Joseph, 230, 231

Taylor's Works, 111

"Tempest, The," 110

Tereus, 37

Theatre, The, 15, 20–6, 29–33, 38, 39, 46, 48–52, 54, 56, 62, 64, 68, 69–71, 73, 74, 76, 77, 79–81, 85, 132, 154, 164, 184, 191, viii.

Theseus and Hippolyta, 59

Tilney, Edmund, 34, 52

Tooley, Nicholas, 124, 125

Towne, John, 36

U

Underwood, John, 105, 125, 132

Utrecht Library, 62

V

Vagabonds, 3, 7, 10, 11, 69

Vautrollier, Thomas, 57

"Venus and Adonis," 57, 58, 65, 184

Vernon, Elizabeth, 73, 87

Vigerous, Robert, 79

W

W. T., 24

Walker, Alice, 126

Wallace, Prof., 77, 107, 115, 196, ix., xi., xii.

Walsingham, 32, 35, 36, 38

Ward, Roger, 45, 48

Watermen of London, 62

Webbe, Henry, 33, 166–70, 186

Susan, 33, 34, 166–70, 186

Webster, John, Dramatist, 245

Wheatley, H. B., 62

Whitacker, Lawrence, 126, 127

White, Thomas, 24

Whitechapel, 18, 164, 195

Whitefriars, 105

Wilcox, T., 24

Wilkenson alias Tooley, 125

Wilkins, George, 139

Wilson, Robert, 9, 36, 37

Thomas, 36

Winchester, Bishop of, 87

Winwood's Memorials, 87, 111

Wit's Treasury, 70, 183

Witt, John de, 62

Witter, John, 104, 115

Wood's Athena Oxonienses, 60

Fasti, 11, 134

Wotton Reliq., 111

Wright's Hist. Histrionica, 136